T0301652

HOLY WAR IN THE BALTIC
AND THE BATTLE
OF LYNDANISE 1219

WAR AND CONFLICT IN PREMODERN SOCIETIES

Further Information and Publications

www.arc-humanities.org/our-series/arc/wcp/

HOLY WAR IN THE BALTIC AND THE BATTLE OF LYNDANISE 1219

by

CARSTEN SELCH JENSEN

British Library Cataloguing in Publication Data

A catalogue record for this book is available from the British Library.

© 2024, Arc Humanities Press, Leeds

The authors assert their moral right to be identified as the authors of their part of this work.

Permission to use brief excerpts from this work in scholarly and educational works is hereby granted provided that the source is acknowledged. Any use of material in this work that is an exception or limitation covered by Article 5 of the European Union's Copyright Directive (2001/29/EC) or would be determined to be "fair use" under Section 107 of the U.S. Copyright Act September 2010 Page 2 or that satisfies the conditions specified in Section 108 of the U.S. Copyright Act (17 USC §108, as revised by P.L. 94-553) does not require the Publisher's permission.

ISBN (hardback): 9781641892858
e-ISBN (PDF): 9781641892858

www.arc-humanities.org

Printed and bound in the UK (by CPI Group [UK] Ltd), USA (by Bookmasters), and elsewhere using print-on-demand technology.

CONTENTS

LIST OF ILLUSTRATIONS

Maps

Figures

ACKNOWLEDGMENTS

THE HISTORY OF the Baltic Crusades in the late twelfth and early thirteenth centuries have, for many years, been a passion of mine—some would probably say an obsession! As Professor of Church History at the Faculty of Theology, University of Copenhagen I have the great privilege of being able to spend quite a bit of my research time on these matters with a special focus on the crusades involving Livonia (roughly coinciding with modern-day Latvia) and Estonia around 1200. In that respect, the medieval holy wars fought in Livonia and Estonia in the forms of Scandinavian and German initiated missionary wars and proper crusades are important historical events in the overall history of the medieval crusades and in the history of the Baltic region in particular. They came to shape the history of the region in profound ways and also became focal points in the national narratives of the involved nations. This is certainly the case with the Danish military conquest of the northern parts of Estonia in the early thirteenth century, which became a powerful narrative in Danish national self-perception as well as in Estonian historiography later on.

I would very much like to thank Dr. Anna Henderson for accepting this manuscript on the Danish-German conquest of Estonia in the early thirteenth century as part of the *War and Conflict in Premodern Societies* series at ARC Humanities Press. I also have to thank Dr. Henderson for her immense patience with me when I more than once had to postpone the completion of the manuscript due to my commitments as dean here at the faculty in Copenhagen.

My thanks go to Dr. Henry Bainton who at an early stage agreed to translate a part of the manuscript into English; My thanks also go to my daughter Astrid Skovgaard, who took care of the index.

I need also to thank my close colleagues in Copenhagen: Vice Dean for Research, Professor Heike Omerzu; Vice Dean for Education, Associate Professor Marlene Ringgaard Lorensen; Faculty Director, Torben Rytter Kristensen; and Head of the Study Administration, Maj-Britt Johannsen, for letting their dean bury himself in the Middle Ages when the modern realities of university administration just became too grey and boring—the university is, after all, a place of teaching and researching.

Sincere thanks are also due to my family, especially my wife, Sonja, who, once again, demonstrated a high degree of endurance and tolerance as I slipped back into another time once more to indulge myself in the histories of the Baltic Crusades.

Odense, December 2023

Introduction

HOLY WAR IN THE BALTIC AND
THE BATTLE OF LYNDANISE 1219

Having collected a very huge army King Valdemar set out for Estonia with one thousand five hundred longships (*longis navibus*), and having fought many battles he eventually converted the entire country to Christianity subjugating it to Denmark as it still is.[1]

SUCH IS THE brief mention in the medieval annalistic chronicle, *Annales Ryenses*, of the military conquest of Estonia in the early thirteenth century by Western (mostly Danish and German) crusaders and one of the pivotal events during the conquest, namely the Battle of Lyndanise 1219. While the chronicle is believed to have been completed sometime around 1300, the actual battle mentioned in the text had taken place in Estonia some eighty years before: on an early summer's day in June a Danish force of crusaders led by the Danish King Valdemar II of Denmark (r. 1202–1241), and supported by the Danish Archbishop of Lund, Anders Sunesen (r. 1202–1224, d. 1228), joined battle with an opposing force of local Estonian warriors led by their elders and war chieftains. As we shall see in this book, the battle was a hard-fought and brutal affair that nearly ended in a total Danish defeat. A series of chance events however completely changed the outcome of the battle and resulted, instead, in what seems to have been a total Estonian defeat—at least according to one (near) contemporary source. It was a defeat that enabled the Danes to firmly establish themselves (politically, militarily, and ecclesiastically) in the northernmost provinces of Estonia for the next almost one hundred fifty years, though they were sincerely challenged by strong ecclesiastical and military powers from German-controlled Livonia as we shall see in this volume.

---

1 *Annales Ryenses*, in *Danmarks middelalderlige annaler*, ed. Erik Kromann (København: Selskabet for udgivelse af kilder til dansk historie, 1980), 149–75. As indicated by its name, the chronicle was compiled in the Cistercian monastery of Rye in the duchy of Schleswig. Parts of this manuscript have previously been published in Danish in the following books: *Da Danskerne fik Dannebrog*, ed. Carsten Selch Jensen, Marika Mägi, Kersti Markus, and Janus Møller Jensen (Tallinn: Argo, 2019). The book was published simultaneously in Estonian: *Taanlaste ristisõda Eestis*, ed. Carsten Selch Jensen, Marika Mägi, Kersti Markus, and Janus Møller Jensen (Tallinn: Argo 2019). See also Carsten Selch Jensen, *Med ord og ikke med slag* (København: Gad 2018). This later book is in the process of being published in English in a slightly shortened form by Brepols (2024) with the title *Through Words, Not Wounds: History and Theology in the Chronicle of Henry of Livonia*. Parts of the original text that will not appear in the English edition have been substantially rewritten and re-edited, and now form part of this book, together with translated and edited sections written by myself in the abovementioned Danish-Estonian books; all to the benefit of a non-Scandinavian speaking (or reading) audience.

From a military perspective and with all due consideration to the tactical and the strategical implications, the conquest of Estonia and the Battle of Lyndanise do not seem overly important in a general medieval setting. The Middle Ages saw countless other battles involving many more fighting men and resulting in outcomes that, in many more profound ways, decided the fate of great lords and entire nations. Not even among the many battles that took place in a distinct crusading setting does the Battle of Lyndanise stand out as something very spectacular or decisive. Most of the other battles clearly exceeded the Battle of Lyndanise with regards to the number of troops involved and the concrete geopolitical consequences. Still, the events that led to the Battle of Lyndanise, the battle itself, and the events that followed immediately after offer an extremely useful insight into the overall history of the Baltic Crusades, with a special focus on the role played by Scandinavian and, in this case Danish, crusaders and missionaries. As such, from a Danish perspective, the Battle of Lyndanise, in many ways, came to mark a pivotal point and temporary high tide in Denmark's involvement in the overall medieval crusading movement that began shortly before 1100 and continued right into the early modern period. It can be viewed as a broadening of the scholarly perspective of the Baltic Crusades that often takes its point of departure from the German involvement in the region around 1200.[2] In the early decades of the thirteenth century, the Danes had been part of the wider European crusading movement with military campaigns going on at different locations such as the Holy Land, Spain, Southern France, Northern Germany, and the Baltic Sea region for little more than a century. One twelfth-century English chronicler even suggests that the Danes were among the first to respond to the papal call for a crusade in 1095 when Pope Urban II (r. 1088–1099) urged kings, princes, magnates, and knights from all over Europe to help their Eastern Christian brethren and sisters and liberate Jerusalem from the infidels. In his chronicle on the history of the English kings, *Gesta regum anglorum* (from about 1120), William of Malmesbury thus states that:

> the Welshman left his hunting; the Scot his fellowship with lice; the Dane his drinking party; the Norwegian his raw fish. Lands were deserted of their husbandmen; houses of their inhabitants; even whole cities migrated. ...God alone was placed before their eyes. ...They hungered and thirsted after Jerusalem alone.[3]

More substantial and less anecdotal sources do, in fact, acknowledge early Scandinavian involvement in the overall European crusading movement and certainly testify to early Danish involvement in the crusades that came to take place in the Baltic Sea region from the early twelfth century onwards.[4]

---

2 The history of the later crusades is discussed in various articles and books, see for example Norman Housley, *The Later Crusades: From Lyon to Alcazar 1274–1580* (Oxford: Oxford University Press, 1992); Janus Møller Jensen, *Denmark and the Crusades 1400–1650* (Leiden: Brill, 2007).

3 *William of Malmesbury's Chronicle of the Kings of England: From the Earliest Period to the Reign of King Stephen*, ed. J. A. Giles (London: Henry G. Bohn, 1847), 379–80.

4 See the general discussion in Ane L. Bysted, Carsten Selch Jensen, Kurt Villads Jensen, and John

From an Estonian perspective, it can also be argued that the Danish military expeditions culminating in the Battle of Lyndanise constituted a decisive period in the long
history of the Estonian people. As we shall see later in this book, a primarily German
mission focused on the subjugation and conversion of the people of medieval Livonia
(corresponding here more or less to modern-day Latvia) which took shape in the later
parts of the twelfth century and eventually turned into proper crusades in the opening
years of the thirteenth century.[5] Soon these crusades also came to involve the Estonians
through land-based attacks from German-controlled territories of Livonia and seafaring
expeditions from Scandinavia, predominately Denmark. Not only did these foreign crusaders come to fight local pagans in an attempt to coerce them into accepting a new religion and foreign lordship, but eventually the crusaders and their followers also ended
up fighting each other—Danes against Germans—in a struggle for hegemony throughout the entire region. Swedes, Norwegians, and the people of medieval Rus' were also
involved in the cause alongside the local peoples.

While the conquest of Estonia in the early part of the thirteenth century essentially
came to mark the high tide of King Valdemar II's political and military influence in the
region, it also became a decisive event in the history of Estonia itself. The Danish military conquest came in reality to signal the beginning of centuries of foreign dominance
with the Danes, the Germans, the Swedes and the Russians each governing the Estonian
people in turn. Only at the end of the twentieth century did Estonia once again become
an independent nation following the collapse of the Soviet Union in 1991, with a brief
intermittently period of national independence from 1918 until the Soviet occupation in
1940, and again in 1945 for a brief period.

From a national perspective, these events around 1200 and especially the Battle
of Lyndanise in 1219, have been firmly embedded in the national narratives of both
Estonia and Denmark. In Denmark, the anniversary of the actual battle is still commemorated as "Valdemar's Day," not so much in honour of King Valdemar himself, but more
in honour of the Danish national flag, called *Dannebrog*. Legend has it that the flag fell
from the sky during the Battle of Lyndanise as a divine sign that the crusaders would
defeat their pagan enemies. At least that has been the national narrative from the early
sixteenth century when Danish historians merged different stories about the appearance of Dannebrog and the Dane's crusading past into one narrative, praising the heroic
deeds of the nation's medieval heroes. While alternative stories seem to suggest that
the (legendary) appearance of Dannebrog originally was believed to have taken place as
early as 1208 at another location in Estonia by the name of Viljandi (German: Fellin), it
was the heroic tale of the Battle of Lyndanise that prevailed in the national narratives in
Denmark and came to shape the imaginations of generations to come.[6]

H. Lind, *Jerusalem in the North: Denmark and the Baltic Crusades, 1100–1522* (Turnhout: Brepols,
2012).

5 Bysted et al., *Jerusalem in the North*, 157–71.

6 Janus Møller Jensen, "Da legenden blev en national fortælling," in Jensen et al., *Da Danskerne fik
Dannebrog*, 192. The possible connection between the legend of Dannebrog and the battles of 1208

From an Estonian perspective, the arrival of the Western crusaders and missionaries during the high medieval period also became a strong part of the national narrative as these events essentially heralded many centuries of foreign domination and outright suppression, with little room for an independent Estonian culture and identity as the centuries went by.[7] A clear symbol of this old history is the nation's own capital, Tallinn.[8] Probably one of the most beautiful cities in modern Europe, Tallinn is, in essence, a dominant symbol in Estonia with regard to the medieval crusades and especially the Danish conquest of the early thirteenth century. Firstly, the old part of the capital is located close to the spot where the army of King Valdemar II disembarked in 1219 and soon after fought the battle that is known to us today as that of Lyndanise since that was then the name of the place. As such the battle is still commemorated in the so-called "Danish King's Garden" on Toompea-Hill in central Tallinn as an important mark in the medieval military conquest of the northernmost provinces of Estonia by the Danish king. Secondly, the name of the capital, Tallinn, literally means "the city of the Danes" or "the castle of the Danes," and the city also has Dannebrog as its civic coat of arms.[9] As such, the Danish military conquest around 1200 and the history of the Battle of Lyndanise are still part of the national narrative. To some extent, the battle is still present in the historical reality of both Denmark and Estonia with some (especially younger) Estonian historians even promoting their medieval forefathers from the times of the crusades, not as the mere victims of foreign aggression, but rather as the first proper Europeans in the long national history of Estonia.[10]

---

and 1219 was also discussed in Paul Johansen, "Lippstadt, Freckenhorst und Fellin in Livland: Werk und Wirkung Bernhards II. Zur Lippe im Ostseeraum," *Veröffentlichungen des Provinzialinstituts für Westfälische Landes- und Volkskunde* 1, no. 17 (1955), 97–160. For a wider perspective on the origin of Dannebrog, see Nils G. Bartholdy, "Die Dannebrog-Legende," in *Denmark and Estonia 1219–2019*, ed. Jens E. Olesen (Greifswald: Druckhaus Panzig, 2019), 57–72.

7 Linda Kaljundi, with the collaboration of Kaspars Klavins, "The Chronicler and the Modern World: Henry of Livonia and the Baltic Crusades in the Enlightenment and National Traditions," in *Crusading and Chronicle Writing on the Medieval Baltic Frontier*, ed. Marek Tamm, Linda Kaljundi, and Carsten Selch Jensen (Farnham: Ashgate, 2011), 449 and 455–56.

8 Relying on several different editions and translations of the *Chronicle of Henry of Livonia*, the use of place names can be a bit confusing. In his excellent English translation of the chronicle from 1961 (reprinted in 2003), Professor James A. Brundage generally refers to the northernmost part of Estonia by the name of "Reval." This is, however, not to be confused with the medieval German name for the city of Tallinn, which is also Reval. I will, therefore, generally use the term "Rävela" when referring to the province, and "Lyndanise" or "Tallinn" when referring to the settlement in the province of Rävela. Similarly, I have chosen to adjust place names in the used translations so that only one form is used throughout this book (for example Daugava River instead of Dvina River, even if the later form is preferred by Brundage in the abovementioned translation of Henry of Livonia's chronicle).

9 Ivar Leimus, "Zur Geschichte der Revaler (Tallinner) Wappen und Siegel," in Olesen, *Denmark and Estonia 1219–2019*, 73–80.

10 Kaljundi and Klavins, "The Chronicler and the Modern World," 449.

The main scope of this book is to present a study of the military conquest of Estonia predominantly by Danish and German military forces around 1200 as a historical lens through which we can study not only how the crusades of the Middle Ages became an integrated part of the history in the Baltic Sea region, but also how they came to influence the primary ways of thinking among all those who took part in these events, whether they were (pagan) Estonians, Livs, Letgallians, Semgallians, Lithuanians, (orthodox) Rus', or (catholic) Germans and Scandinavians who all became embroiled in these wars of expansion, mission, and crusading. Consequently, this study has a primary focus on the contemporary political, religious, and military ideas and concrete practices that came to influence the events in the Baltic Sea region that eventually resulted in the military conquest of Estonia (and Livonia). In this process, the Battle of Lyndanise was one occurrence among many others that will help us to better understand the more general political, religious, and military concurrences in the region at the time. A special focus on the intense rivalry—politically, militarily, and ecclesiastically—between Danish and German prelates and magnates around 1200 also helps.

The first chapter of the book is dedicated to a brief description of the various people who inhabited the Baltic lands when the first missionaries and crusaders came to the region; a continuation of age-old contacts between the East and the West in these parts of the world. The second chapter takes a closer look at the official papal policy of missioning and crusading in the Baltic Sea region during the twelfth and early thirteenth centuries. Here, the theological ideas of holy war and enforced missioning among non-Christian people will also be discussed as important cornerstones in the contemporary developments of the Scandinavian and German missionary activities among the Baltic people, which were strongly supported by military expeditions and genuine crusades in the later part of the twelfth and early parts of the thirteenth centuries.

The third chapter turns to the political and military developments in Denmark as they came to pave the way for the conquest of Estonia during the reign of King Valdemar II. During the better part of the twelfth century, Denmark was marred by long periods of internal unrest and genuine civil wars while, at the same time, it was involved in various external campaigns of expansion and mission. The external campaigns especially were heavily influenced by the papal ideas of holy war and crusading, but were also influenced by general developments of military matters that took place in Western Europe around this time.

Since the German merchants, missionaries, and crusaders came to constitute a strong competitive element to the Danish expansion into the Baltic Sea region, the fourth chapter focuses on the German mission in Livonia and its initial forays into the southernmost parts of Estonia. While discussing the missionary and military strategies of the Germans, the chapter will also discuss how this divine mission (according to contemporary sources) eventually turned into a fierce (and sometimes even violent) rivalry between German and Danish missionaries and crusaders, who truly represented God and the universal church in these lands.

The fifth chapter will study the military tactics and strategies, based on accounts from contemporary sources, employed by Western crusaders and local warriors during the many bloody engagements in both Livonia and Estonia. These accounts not only reveal the brutality of the many military encounters but also demonstrate just how quickly new military technologies and ways of fighting became absorbed into already existing practices both by the local warriors and by the newcomers who had to adapt other's ways of fighting. As we shall see, the crusaders especially had to adjust themselves to an unfamiliar climate and a foreign geography. This chapter will also take a closer look at the local military organizations, the actual recruitment of crusaders for the many expeditions in both Livonia and Estonia and the presumed sizes of the various fighting forces engaged in the military campaigns. Some examples of known campaigns will illustrate the concrete military situation and also help us better understand the conditions that the fighting men had to cope with during the various campaigns, whether these took place in spring, summer or autumn, or during the gruelling months of bitterly, cold winters.

Having presented and discussed the various political, military, religious, and cultural backgrounds of the crusading activities in the Baltic Sea Region around 1200, the sixth chapter examines the Danish attack on Estonia in 1219 as the culmination of the Danish king's effort to expand his power and supremacy into this particular region. It also analyzes the Battle of Lyndanise in-depth, using available sources and what information has been gathered from the previous chapters on the practical and spiritual matters of warfare in the early thirteenth century.

The seventh chapter outlines the immediate aftermath of the Danish attack and the battle and describes how the rivalry between the Germans and the Danes intensified for decades until the Danes gave up their possessions in Estonia entirely in the middle of the fourteenth century.

How Estonia then came to save Denmark in a time of great political crisis and, quite literally, became the last saving penny for the Danes in their kingdom's treasure box is the topic of the last short chapter. This chapter offers a summarizing conclusion that will hopefully help explain why the shared history of the medieval crusades and, more specifically, the Battle of Lyndanise, should not be forgotten as they are important elements in the national narratives of both Denmark and Estonia. More importantly, they provide an important lens that enables us to study a crucial chapter in our common past.

Chapter 1

FOREIGN SHORES—FOREIGN PEOPLE
THE MEDIEVAL BALTIC AND ITS PEOPLE

WHEN NEW WAVES of Western merchants and missionaries and eventually crusaders came to the Baltic lands in the later part of the twelfth and early part of the thirteenth centuries they did not come to a region devoid of people—on the contrary. Already during the early medieval period Scandinavians in particular had visited these lands regularly on their way to the prosperous markets of Kyivan Rus' and the even more prosperous markets of far-away Constantinople and Baghdad.[1] These adventures brought great wealth to the Scandinavian lands and also played a significant role in the founding of several princedoms along the major riverways in modern-day Ukraine and Russia. While some of the Scandinavian merchants and warriors would settle down permanently in these foreign lands, many more simply visited, journeying to and from the local markets and trading posts on an annual basis.[2] On these journeys, travellers also visited the coastal regions of Estonia, Livonia, and Curonia (Latvian: Kurzeme), each having their own important markets and trading hubs as contact points between the East and the West. Such local places also became convenient over winter when travelling became too difficult or outright impossible due to the harsh weather in the eastern parts of the Baltic Sea region.[3] In this way, important bonds were forged between the visitors and the locals.

In the later part of the twelfth century, the local Baltic markets were still important steppingstones in a regional commercial network tying the West to the East and vice versa. Western merchants would do business with Estonians, Livonians, Letgallians, Semgallians, Curonians, Lithuanians, and of course, with people from the Rus' principalities of Novgorod, Pskov, Jersika, and Polotsk bordering the Baltic lands.[4] They met on

---

1 For a general introduction to the Scandinavian involvement in the East, see the following books: Cat Jarman, *River Kings: The Vikings from Scandinavia to the Silk Roads* (London: William Collins, 2021); Valerie Hansen, *The Year 1000: When Explorers Connected the World and Globalization Began* (Dublin: Penguin Books, 2021); Mägi, Marika, *In Austrvegr: The Role of the Eastern Baltic in Viking Age Communication across the Baltic Sea* (Leiden: Brill, 2018). The early histories of Latvia and Estonia are found in Andris Šnē and Heiki Valk, "Vor- und Frühgeschichte," in *Das Baltikum: Geschichte einer europäischen Region*, ed. Karsten Brüggemann, Detlef Henning, Konrad Maier, and Ralph Tuchtenhagen (Stuttgart: Anton Hiersemann, 2018), 77–143 and Anti Selart "Die Eroberung Livlands (12. und 13. Jahrhundert)," in Brüggemann et al., *Das Baltikum*, 159–209. For the original text of this chapter in Danish, see Jensen, *Med ord og ikke med slag*, 84–87.

2 Hansen, *The Year 1000*, 81; Jarman, *River Kings*, 196; Šnē and Valk, "Vor- und Frühgeschichte," 111, 114, and 119–27.

3 Marika Mägi, "Store estiske borge: Handels eller magtcentre?," in *Da Danskerne fik Dannebrog*, ed. Jensen et al., 62 and 65.

4 Šnē and Valk, "Vor- und Frühgeschichte," 127–28.

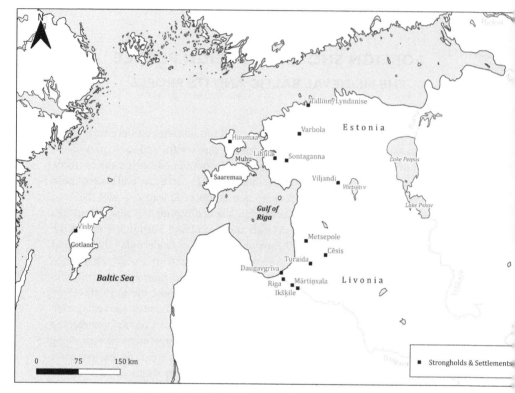

Map 1: The Baltic Sea Region around the time of the Danish conquest of Estonia. Figure by Gregory J. Leighton, 2023.

an annual basis, each having their own cultural and religious traditions through which they turned the entire region into a sort of "middle ground" between an Orthodox East, a Catholic West, and a conglomerate of (mostly still) pagan people in the middle. Throughout the centuries, strong local and regional powers each sought to expand their dominance into this important region. While the Rus' princes seem to have contented themselves with annual tributes, caring less about the actual conversion of the local pagans, conquest and Christianization became the hallmarks of both Scandinavian (especially Danish) and German magnates and ambitious prelates in the later part of the twelfth century and the early part of the thirteenth.[5] The German chronicler, Henry of Livonia, who completed his important *Chronicon Livoniae* in 1227, explicitly states in the opening chapters of his chronicle that German missionaries came to Livonia from Saxony precisely because of the many unbaptized people. These missionaries had an urge (says Henry) to wake the pagans "from the sleep of idolatry and sin" (*ydolatras ab ydoltrie et peccati sompno taliter...excitavit*) and wanted at the same time to establish a new church

---

5 Anti Selart, *Livland und die Rus' im 13. Jahrhundert*, Quelen und Studien zur baltischen Geschichte 21 (Köln: Böhlau, 2007), here especially 18–39. See also Selart, "Die Eroberung Livlands," 166–79.

among these people.[6] As mentioned above, these lands soon became known as Livonia, bordering the lands of the Estonians in the north. As we shall see later in this book, the German missionaries relied heavily on contacts already established between the local people and German merchants who visited the region regularly. Henry of Livonia explains to his readers that a German cleric by the name Meinhard, who would later become the first German bishop in Livonia, arrived together "with a band of merchants simply for the sake of Christ and only to preach."[7] Henry also explains that the "German merchants, bound together through familiarity with the Livonians, were accustomed to go to Livonia, frequently sailing up the Daugava River."[8]

Henry of Livonia presents the most detailed, near-contemporary description of the Christianization and conquest of Livonia and Estonia from the later part of the twelfth century into the early decade of the thirteenth century. However, he focuses more specifically on the German mission and is heavily biased in favour of the Livonian Church (founded by the Germans), often neglecting or downplaying the importance of competing powers like the Danes and their attempts to gain influence in the same region.[9] While we do not have similar detailed and contemporary sources from a specific Danish context, we do know from other sources that the Danes and the Estonians were no strangers to each other around 1200.[10] Even Henry himself mentions Danish merchants being present in Estonia and Livonia around the time when Meinhard became the first bishop of Livonia. Henry explicitly states that Danish merchants, alongside some Germans and Norwegians, had promised to bring an army to support the German mission in Livonia if military force became necessary.[11] While this remark seems to indicate that the German

---

6 Henry of Livonia 1:1 and 3. This study will henceforth refer to Henry of Livonia's chronicle with the abbreviation HCL, together with the book and chapter in question. In cases where there are disagreement in book and chapter numbers between the various editions of the chronicle, the critical editions from 1959 and 1955 have been preferred: Heinrich von Lettland, *Livländische Chronik, Neu übersetzt von Albert Bauer* (Darmstadt: Wissenschaftliche Buchgesellschaft, 1959); *Heinrichi Chronicon Livoniae*, ed. Leonid Arbusow and Albert Bauer, MGH SS rer. Germ. 31 (Hannover: Hahn, 1955). Translations of the chronicle into English are from *The Chronicle of Henry of Livonia*, ed. James A. Brundage (New York: Columbia University Press, 1961 [reprint 2003]). Throughout this book, quotation from contemporary, medieval sources will appear in translation followed by the Latin text either *in extensio* or through the most central of words and phrases. Long quotes—more than one line—will have the Latin text in the footnotes, whereas shorter quotes in both translation and in Latin will appear in the main text.

7 HCL 1:2.

8 HCL 1:2: "Theutonici enim mercatores, Lyvonibus familiaritate coniuncti, Lyvoniam frequenter navigio per Dune flumen adire solebant."

9 For a detailed discussion of Henry of Livonia and his chronicle, see Tamm et al., *Crusading and Chronicle Writing*, and more recently Jensen, *Med ord og ikke med slag*.

10 In this book that deals especially with the Danish crusades in Estonia in the later part of the twelfth and early parts of the thirteenth centuries, we do not go into any detail about the many other markets places found around the Baltic Sea region during this time, like in Pomerania, Prussia, Sambia, Finland, and Russia, for example.

11 See for example HCL 1:11, when the German Bishop Meinhard was in dire straits due to a rebellion among the local Livs against the foreign missionaries and clerics. For the friendly relations

and Scandinavian merchants possessed a certain military capacity, it primarily testifies to the fact that Danish merchants were active in the region, even if their presence is downplayed (if not outright ignored) by Henry in his attempts to promote the German mission as the only legitimate (political and ecclesiastical) power in the region.[12] Other sources—written as well as archaeological—paint a similar picture of the Baltic as a contested and vibrant region, as we shall see a little later in this study.

A Multitude of People

Based on these frequent, and century-long contacts between East and West, it is hardly surprising that modern readers encounter a succession of names concerning various local peoples and tribes in the contemporary sources dealing with the people of the medieval Baltic region. While most modern people seem to think about the people of Estonia, Livonia, and Lithuania (both currently and historically) as "Balts" or "Baltic people," this is not at all accurate from a historical point of view and fails to grasp some very important cultural and linguistic differences between the various people which were of great significance during the crusading period. In reality, we are dealing with two major cultural and linguistic groups, the Baltic Finns and the Baltic People proper. While the first group occupied the territories of modern-day Finland, the western parts of modern-day Russia, Estonia, central parts of modern-day Latvia, and parts of coastal Curonia, the Baltic People proper lived in the southern parts of Latvia, Lithuania, and parts of Poland and Belarus.[13] For obvious reasons, a chronicler like Henry of Livonia did not quite see the ethnic landscape in such a modern way, even if he did notice some important differences between the various people, as we shall see. He was, after all, very actively engaged in concrete missionary work himself and seemingly knew several of

---

between German and Livic merchants, see HCL 1:2. Lübeck later became known as the "door to Livonia." Cf. Wolfgang Bender, "Bernhard II. zur Lippe und die Mission in Livland," in *Lippe und Livland: Mittelalterliche Herrschaftsbildung im Zeichen der Rose*, ed. Jutta Prieur (Gütersloh: Verlag für Regionalgeschichte, 2008), 154. It would become clear later in the thirteenth century when the Danish king blockaded the harbour in order to impose his will over his German opponents in Livonia that access to Lübeck was an instrument of power in the Christianization and colonization of Livonia and Estonia. See Carsten Selch Jensen, "Valdemar Sejr, korstogsbevægelsen og den pavelige reformpolitik i 1200-tallets første halvdel," *Historisk Tidsskrift* 1 (2002), 41–45. See also LUB 1:1.36, where, in a letter dated November 28, 1226, the pope decreed that the crusaders should enjoy his protection for as long as they stayed in Lübeck. Interestingly, the sources also show that Bishop Albert, the Brethren of the Sword, and the citizens of Riga sought peace with Lübeck at a later point—probably in order to secure access to the port's unloading facilities, which were essential for trade. The peace treaty emphasizes, however, that it did not extend to the Danish king. See LUB 1:1.41 (1227).

12 Carsten Selch Jensen, "The Early Church of Livonia, 1186–ca. 1255," in *Die Kirche im mittelalterlichen Livland*, ed. Radoslaw Biskup, Johannes Götz, and Andrzej Radziminski (Torún: Wydawnictwo Naukowe Uniwersytetu Mikolaja Kopernika, 2019), 103; Jensen, *Med ord og ikke med slag*, 246–63.

13 Karsten Brüggemann and Ralph Tuchtenhagen, "Grundzüge," in Brüggemann et al., *Das Baltikum*, 31–37; Šnē and Valk, "Vor- und Frühgeschichte," 96–109 and 115; Marika Mägi, *The Viking Eastern Baltic* (Leeds: Arc Humanities, 2019), 1–2.

the local languages which enabled him to act as an interpreter during various preaching campaigns.[14] Since Henry's point of entry into the region, like most other German missionaries, was the land of the Livs (Latin, *Lyvones*) these are the first of the local people mentioned in his chronicle. The Livs inhabited an area that stretched from the Daugava River in the south, up along the coast of the Gulf of Riga, up to the southernmost part of Estonia. They were a small tribe, but they nevertheless came to give their name to the whole region, as "the Land of the Livs," or Livonia (Latin, *Lyvonia*). They spoke the same language as several other people in the region, most notably the Finns and the Estonians who all belonged to the abovementioned Baltic-Finnic culture.[15] The Finns, for their part, inhabited the coastal areas north of the Gulf of Finland and had already become the target of several Danish and Swedish military expeditions over the twelfth century and probably before.[16]

Especially important to this story are the Estonians (Latin, *Estones*) as a prominent people among the northern Baltic Finns. They were known as a bellicose people, which is reflected in by contemporary chroniclers like Adam of Bremen, Saxo Grammaticus, and Henry of Livonia who, himself, devotes a great part of his chronicle to the actual conquest of the Estonians by German and Danish crusaders. The Estonian tribes inhabited the majority of what is now Estonia, including the islands of Hiiumaa (German, Dagö), Saaremaa (German, Ösel), and the much smaller island of Muhu (German, Moon), which all lie around the entrance to the Gulf of Riga.[17] It would be wrong, however, simply to consider all Estonians alike since even Henry of Livonia made a distinction between the Estonians of the "Maritime Provinces" (*Provincia Maritima*), and those who lived further

---

14 See for example the discussion in Alan V. Murray, "Henry the Interpreter: Language, Orality and Communication in the Thirteenth-century Livonian Mission," in Tamm et al., *Crusading and Chronicle Writing*, 107–34.

15 Šnē and Valk, "Vor- und Frühgeschichte," 127–34; Jensen, *Med ord og ikke med slag*, 84–87.

16 See the very recent discussion in Jens E. Olesen, "Die schwedischen Kreuzzüge nach Finnland aus der Ostsee-Perspektive," in *The Expansion of the Faith: Crusading on the Frontiers of Latin Christendom in the High Middle Ages*, ed. Paul Srodecki and Norbert Kersken, 167–82 (Turnhout: Brepols, 2022).

17 The ethnographical situation in the region is described in detail in a number of important studies, most recently in Jüri Kivimäe, "Henricus the Ethnographer," in *Crusading and Chronicle Writing*, 77–106 and the aforementioned important work Šnē and Valk, "Vor- und Frühgeschichte," 140–43. See also the older, general description in Eric Christiansen, *The Northern Crusades* (London: Penguin, 1997), 40–41; Wolfgang Bender, "Bernhard II. zur Lippe und die Mission in Livland," in *Lippe und Livland*, ed. Prieur, 152–53; Marika Mägi, "Saaremaa and the Danish kingdom: Revisiting Henry's Chronicle and the Archaeological Evidence," in Tamm et al., *Crusading and Chronicle Writing*, 321–22; Murray, "Henry the Interpreter," 107–134. See also Nils Blomkvist, *The Discovery of the Baltic: The Reception of a Catholic World-System in the European North (AD 1075–1225)* (Leiden: Brill, 2005), 505–63, where he deals in detail with the peoples that lived in the areas around the Daugava and their encounters with the German missionaries and crusaders. It should also be noted here that in the Middle Ages the main island of Saaremaa was surrounded by various small islands, which over the coming centuries became joined to the main island. The latter's appearance, therefore, has changed at various important points since the thirteenth century. Cf. Mägi, "Saaremaa and the Danish Kingdom," 321.

inland.[18] Vast, uninhabited stretches of forests and swamps (as wide as 30–40 kilometres in some places) separated these two groups from each other and, in reality, resulted in some very different situations when the Germans and the Danes made their presence felt in earnest in the region around 1200.[19]

The Estonians frequently waged war against their neighbours; and the inhabitants of Saaremaa in particular are famously known for their impressive naval power and raiding skills as well as their habit of attacking enemy ships on open seas—taking much booty and many captives—in attempts to control the prosperous trading routes in and out of the region. The islanders even attacked and plundered the faraway coasts of Skåne and Blekinge—then part of the Danish realm—together with their Curonian cousins to protect trading networks and ward off the encroachment of the Danes who were the only other real threat to their own maritime dominance in the region.[20] To some extent, this is also reflected in the accounts of Saxo Grammaticus. According to him, the relationship between the Danes and the people of Saaremaa (as well as their Couronian allies) was seemingly characterized by an ancient, long-lasting power struggle between two mighty naval powers who constantly raided each other's homelands, testing each other for weak spots and attempting to weaken or intimidate each other into submission. At the same time, however, they also upheld more friendly relations based on the oral or written agreements that enabled prosperous trade throughout the region in between periods of war and raiding. At one point, Saxo Grammaticus even suggests that the people from Skåne raided Estonia out of sheer boredom when things became too quiet at home, thus indicating that warfare with the Estonians was something quite ordinary and almost everyday-like.[21]

Aside from the Livs, the Curonians, and the Estonians, there were also other important and powerful people who inhabited the region, all belonging to the Baltic People

---

18 HCL 21:5. In German the region is often referred to as *"die Gaue der Wiek"* or simply *"Wiek."* See also HCL 26:11: "Wars were then begun afresh in all the regions of Estonia. The people from Saaremaa, the maritime people, and the people of Warbole, together with the people of Jerwan and Wierland, besieged the Danes in Reval for a long time, until the Lord freed them" (*Tunc innovata sunt bella in omnibus finibus Estonie. Nam Osiliani et Maritimi et Warbolenses simul cum Gerwanensibus et Vironensibus obsidione longa Danos in Rävala obsederunt, donec Dominus eos liberavit*). Later national and nationalistic attempts to construct a national unity between these various peoples would have had a hard time finding any such justification in Henry's chronicle. See for example Mägi, "Saaremaa and the Danish Kingdom," 324–25. See also Kivimäe, "Henricus the Ethnographer," 95, where the author clearly shows that the inhabitants of Saaremaa were described as *Osiliensis/Osiliani* in the chronicle, and that Henry never calls them "the Estonians of Saaremaa" or anything similar. In the chronicle, the term *Estones* is reserved for the Estonians of the mainland. See also Šnē and Valk, "Vor- und Frühgeschichte," 128 and 140–43.

19 Mägi, *The Viking Eastern Baltic*, 16–17; Mägi, "Store estiske borge: Handels eller magtcentre?," 61–62.

20 *Jerusalem in the North*, ed. Bysted et al., 195; Mägi, "Saaremaa and the Danish Kingdom," 322.

21 Saxo Grammaticus, *Gesta Danorum: The History of the Danes*, ed. Karsten Friis-Jensen and Peter Fischer (Oxford: Clarendon Press, 2015), 16:4:3. It is worth noting that the term "Curonians" was more or less used around 1200 as a generic term simply referring to (seaborne) pirates, whether they were in fact from Curonia, Saaremaa, coastal Estonia, or from someplace else. Cf. Thomas K.

proper. The sources frequently mention the Lettgallians (Latin, *Lettigali* or *Letti*) having a language that was markedly different from that spoken by the Livs, Finns, and Estonians.[22] The Lettgallians inhabited a large area in the central part of Livonia, which stretched from the Daugava River in the south, up to the southern Estonian provinces. In the west, their land was bordered by the Livic areas around the coast; in the east it was bordered by the Rus' principalities around the upper course of the Daugava, south of Lake Peipus (Estonian: *Peipsi*). The Lettgallians and the Livs were both among the first peoples to become the object of a targeted German mission and military conquest before finally submitting to the Christian religion. Henry of Livonia had a special relationship with the Lettgallians, since he served among them in 1208 and became their priest, a position he retained for many years.[23] Henry also accompanied his Lettgallian parishioners on many of their military campaigns into the Estonian territories, as a missionary set out to persuade the pagan Estonians to accept baptism and submit to the Livonian church, and not to the encroaching Danish church.[24] In this regard, the Livs and the Lettgallians became important partners in the military conquest of Estonia since, as we shall see, both constituted a very large part of the Livonian military host summoned by the German bishops in their attempts to conquer and subdue the inland Estonians especially, in fierce competition with the Danes.[25]

Further to the south—on the south side of Daugava River—lived the Semgallians (Latin, *Semigalli*) and the Selonians (Latin, *Selones*), who belonged to the same overall Baltic people as the Lettgallians. So, too, did the inland Curonians (Latin, *Curones*), though they should not be confused with the coastal Curonians belonging to the Baltic Finnic People.[26] The Lettgallians, Semgallians, Curonians, and Selonians all came to play

---

Heebøll-Holm, "Between Pagan Pirates and Glorious Sea-Warriors: The Portrayal of the Viking Pirate in Danish Twelfth-Century Latin Historiography," *Viking and Medieval Scandinavia* 8 (2012), 143 and 151.

22 Šnē and Valk, "Vor- und Frühgeschichte," 121 and 137–38; Kivimäe, "Henricus the Ethnographer," 90; Christiansen, *Northern Crusades*, 36; Bender, "Bernhard II. zur Lippe," 152–53.

23 Jensen, *Med ord og ikke med slag*, 45–46.

24 See, e.g., HCL 9:7; 18:3. See also Bender, "Bernhard II. zur Lippe," 151–66; Kivimäe, "Henricus the Ethnographer," 90; Jensen, "The Early Church of Livonia," 101–103.

25 Bysted et al., *Jerusalem in the North*, 195–225.

26 Romas Jarockis, "Semigallia 1100–1400: A Review of Archaeological and Historical Sources," in *Culture Clash or Compromise?*, ed. Nils Blomkvist (Visby: Gotland Centre of Baltic Studies, 1998), 45–53; Bender, "Bernhard II. zur Lippe," 152–53; Kivimäe, "Henricus the Ethnographer," 91–93; Christiansen, *Northern Crusades*, 36. The Prussians also belonged to this language group, but do not play a role in the chronicle and are not considered in this overview of the peoples that contributed to the construction of Henry's narrative. Finally, in his descriptions of Curonia, Henry also mentions a "lowly and poor people" that he designates "the Wends," (HCL 10:14): "Wendi autem humiles erant eo tempore et pauperes utpote a Winda repulsi, qui est fluvius Curonie" (the Wends, indeed, were humble and poor at that time, because they had been out from the Windau, a river of Kurland). The Wends who are mentioned in Henry's chronicle should not immediately be identified with the Slavic Wendish people who are often mentioned by Helmold and Saxo as fierce opponents of the Danes. Some scholars have speculated that the Wends in Henry's chronicle were in fact a Slavic people who had migrated from the traditional Slavic areas in the southwestern part of the Baltic

some part in the overall conquest of the region with the Lettgallians and the Livs primarily assisting in the German-led mission along the Daugava River. The coastal Curonians and the Estonians became the common enemy of both the Germans and the Danes.

Besides the Lettgallians, Semgallians, inland Curonians, and Selonians, contemporary sources also often mention one other group, who belonged to the same family of the Baltic People proper and who came to play a very prominent role in overall military history of the region. That is the Lithuanians (Latin, *Lettones*), who lived south of the Semgallians and Selonians. Their lands bordered Poland and the lands of the pagan Prussians in the west that saw some Danish involvement in the early part of the thirteenth century.[27] Towards the northeast, the land of the Lithuanians was bordered by the Rus' principality of Polotsk. The Rus' at times regarded themselves as being very much on the defensive against the warlike Lithuanians, especially after 1230 when the Lithuanian tribes united under Mindaugas (ca. 1203–1263), whom they later chose as their king and the first Grand Duke of Lithuania.[28] Around 1200, the Lithuanians (rather like the Estonians) were engaged in extensive warfare and raiding against the peoples and tribes who lived around them. Henry of Livonia, for example, writes throughout his chronicle how the Lithuanians—either alone or in temporary alliances with Estonians or Rus' forces—conducted attacks deep into Livonia. There, they plundered and burned villages and farms, killed the men, and took the women and children captive, intending to use them as slaves in their own lands. Henry goes as far as to imply that the Lithuanians were simultaneously a tool of the devil and a divine scourge unleashed by God against those who had betrayed his will.[29] Unlike the other peoples in the area, the Lithuanians were neither conquered nor converted to Christianity in the period covered by this study. Neither were they the object of united or targeted missionary efforts from the Germans or the Danes, to any significant degree, at this point in history. That only came later with the many wars between the Lithuanians and the Knights of the Teutonic Order, who would establish themselves first in Prussia in the early decades of the thir-

---

Sea area. See for example Alan V. Murray, "Henry of Livonia and the Wends of the Eastern Baltic: Ethnography and Biography in the Thirteenth-Century Livonian Mission," *Studi Medievali* 54, no. 6 (2013), 814–21. As to the Curonians, the medieval sources seems not to differentiate between the Finnish coastal Curonians, and the Baltic inland Curonians; this is otherwise the norm nowadays amongst contemporary scholars seeing clear differences in culture between these groups of people.

27 Bysted et al., *Jerusalem in the North*, 232–39; Gintautas Zabiela, "Eastern Lithuanian Hill Forts and Origin of the Lithuanian State," in *Strongholds and Power Centers East of the Baltic Sea in the 11th–13th Centuries: A Collection of Articles in Memory of Evald Tõnisson*, ed. Heiki Valk (Tartu: Tartu Ülikooli archeoloogia osakond, 2014), 429–59.

28 Kivimäe, "Henricus the Ethnographer," 102–103; Christiansen, *Northern Crusades*, 139–43.

29 See, e.g., HCL 13:4, where Henry explicitly states that the Lithuanians posed such a threat towards the other peoples that the latter barely dared to stay in their villages out of fear of attack. Instead, they sought shelter in the darkest forests. See also HCL 8:1, where Henry claims that the Lithuanians abhorred the name of Christ. Eva Eihmane, "The Baltic Crusades: A Clash of Two Identities," in *The Clash of Cultures on the Medieval Baltic Frontier*, ed. Alan V. Murray (Farnham: Ashgate, 2009), 44; Kivimäe, "Henricus the Ethnographer," 102.

teenth century and later also in Livonia and Estonia, thereby marginalizing the Danish and German secular powers in the region, to some extent.[30]

The Lithuanians were very much involved in the continual warfare in the region and would ally themselves with whoever offered the best prospects for a rich booty. Sometimes, they would conduct raids on their own, targeting Livonia, Estonia, and the Rus' principalities. At other times, they would join forces with some of the Estonian or Rus' people, for example, to attack either the Danes or the Germans. It is understandable that one should think that contemporary Christian chroniclers actually considered these highly skilled warriors and raiders as tools of the devil and at the same time also a divine scourge.[31]

Finally, the Slavic Rus' (Latin, *Rutheni*), belonging neither to the Baltic Finns or the Baltic People proper, constituted a Slavic people of their own with strong historical ties to Scandinavia.[32] They came to play a central role in the conquest of both Estonia and Livonia. Initially the local Rus' princes seems to have welcomed, or at least accepted, the arrival of the first German missionaries along the lower run of the Daugava River while also entertaining close relations with the ruling families in Denmark. King Valdemar I's mother, Ingeborg Mstislavna (ca. 1100–ca. 1137), was, in fact, the daughter of the grand prince Mstislav of Kyiv (r. 1125–1132) and it is believed that Valdemar spent his early childhood years among his mother's family in Kyiv before he was brought back to Denmark by her.[33]

The open, undecided, and perhaps even friendly, attitude from the side of the Rus' princes towards the newly arrived German missionaries may have been rooted in the abovementioned familiar ties with Scandinavia—and especially Denmark. It did not last very long, however. The expansive Germans soon became a threat to the formal lordship of the Rus' concerning various local people on whom they had levied a tax for years.[34] The Rus' seem not to have cared much for a thorough conversion of the local pagans into orthodox Christianity as long as they paid the annual tributes. Henry of Livonia strongly

---

30 Bysted et al., *Jerusalem in the North*, 269–71.

31 For detailed studies of the Lithuanians' path to Christianity and their associated conflict with the Teutonic Knights, see the following works (which focus partly or wholly on this question): S. C. Rowell, *Lithuania Ascending: A Pagan Empire within East-Central Europe, 1295–1345* (Cambridge: Cambridge University Press, 1994); Rasa Mazeika, "When Crusader and Pagan Agree: Conversion as a Point of Honour in the Baptism of King Mindaugas of Lithuania (c. 1240–63)," in *Crusade and Conversion on the Baltic Frontier 1150–1500*, ed. Alan V. Murray (Aldershot: Ashgate 2001), 197–214; Vladas Zulkus, "Heidentum und Christentum in Litauen im 10.–16. Jahrhundert," in *Rom und Byzanz im Norden: Mission und Glaubenswechsel im Ostseeraum während des 8.–14. Jahrhunderts*, ed. Müller-Wille (Stuttgart: Franz Steiner, 1998), 2:143–62; Housley, *Later Crusades*, 322–75; Christiansen, *Northern Crusades*, 139–76; Darius Baronas and S. C. Rowell, *The Conversion of Lithuania: From Pagan Barbarians to Late Medieval Christians* (Vilnius: Institute of Lithuanian Literature and Folklore, 2015).

32 Selart, *Livland und die Rus'*, 55–68; Jarman, *River Kings*, 195–200.

33 Kurt Villads Jensen, *Korstog ved verdens yderste rand: Danmark og Portugal ca. 1000 til ca. 1250* (Odense: Syddansk Universitetsforlag, 2011), 186–87; Selart, *Livland und die Rus'*, 33–35.

34 Selart, *Livland und die Rus'*, 69–72.

condemns the Rus' people for this and for not taking proper spiritual care of the pagan people in his chronicle. In doing so, he likens the orthodox Rus' Church to a cold and barren mother that cares not for her children.[35] A spiritual and military struggle soon erupted between the Rus' and the Germans in Riga and the foreign crusaders concerning the overall control of the border regions and the upper lands of the Daugava River. The Germans eventually conquered some of the important Rus' border castles and Henry express some regrets about the fact that (Western) Christians were now fighting (Eastern) Christians—even if the latter were considered schismatic by the former.[36] Eventually the conflict evolved into (almost) annual campaigns, with the Rus'ians attacking Livonia—sometimes in alliance with either the Lithuanians or the Estonians—and the Livonians retaliating by sacking Rus' territories.[37] Each of them would destroy the other's farms, villages, and churches, routinely killing all men and taking women and children captive despite the fact that both parties were Christians. As the conflict escalated, Henry describes how Livonia was almost overflowing with Rus' (Christian) slaves at one point.[38] The Rus' also became a powerful enemy to the Danes in northern Estonia despite old family bonds when they actively supported rebellious Estonians or by themselves attacked the Danes in their castles following the Danish conquest of northern Estonia.[39]

As we have seen in this chapter, the Baltic gave room to a multitude of people in the twelfth and thirteenth centuries. Some of these people belonged to the Baltic Finns, while others belonged to the Baltic People proper with the Slavic Rus' living further to the east. They all interacted with each other in times of war as well as in times of peace, with commercial activities taking over from the bellicose ones. Scandinavians and Germans also played their part in this cauldron-mix of different religious, cultural, and political sentiments. Soon, however, the papal idea of fighting a divinely sanctioned, penitential war against the enemies of Christendom became an integrated part of the local Christian ideology. How this came to happen—the introduction of the crusades proper into the Baltic Sea region—will be the topic of the next chapter.

---

35 HCL 28:4.

36 See for example HCL 13:4. See also Jensen, *Med ord og ikke med slag*, 191.

37 Anti Selart, "Orthodox Responses to the Baltic Crusades," in *Christianity and War in Medieval East Central Europe and Scandinavia*, ed. Radoslaw Kotecki, Carsten Selch Jensen, and Stephen Bennett (Amsterdam: Arc Humanities, 2021), 262–78.

38 HCL 25:5. See also Anti Selart, "Slavery in the Eastern Baltic in the 12th–15th Centuries," in *Serfdom and Slavery in the European Economy 11th–18th Centuries*, ed. Simonetta Cavaciocchi (Firenze: Firenze University Press, 2014), 351–55.

39 Selart, *Livland und die Rus'*, 119; Jensen, *Med ord og ikke med slag*, 182–84.

Chapter 2

FIGHTING GOD'S WAR

PAPAL CRUSADING POLITICS IN THE BALTIC
FROM THE EARLY 1100s UNTIL THE EARLY 1200s

CRUSADING BECAME A reality in the Baltic in the context of the wide-scale and papal initiated preaching campaigns that followed in the wake of the fall of Edessa in 1144. But even before that point, some sources suggest that some of the earlier military campaigns in the region, in fact, may have been inspired by the wider crusading movement that had taken root in Europe shortly before 1100 and which eventually came to influence all societies within Western Christendom.[1] The military conquest of Livonia and Estonia, therefore, needs to be viewed within the overall framework of holy war and crusading ideology, taking into account both the general papal crusading politics of the time and the specific papal involvement in the Baltic Sea region during the twelfth and thirteenth centuries.

The particular aim of the preaching campaigns following the fall of Edessa was to recruit crusaders to what would become known as the Second Crusade (1145–1149); the goal being to reconquer what had been lost and to help the hard-pressed Christians in the Holy Land.[2] The loss of Edessa sent shockwaves throughout Europe and led directly to Pope Eugenius III (r. 1145–1153) promulgating the crusading bull *Quantum praedecessores*. The bull exhorted the princes of Christendom to take the cross and come to the aid of their fellow Christians in the Holy Land. Pope Eugenius was wholly dependent on the many preachers who travelled around on his behalf announcing what happened in Edessa, while exhorting their audiences to answer the pope's call to take the cross and go on crusade to the Holy Land.[3] A papal legate also travelled to Denmark

---

1 See the general discussions in Mihai Dragnea, *The Wendish Crusade, 1147: The Development of Crusading Ideology in the Twelfth Century* (London: Routledge, 2019), 5–15 and 30–33; Mihai Dragnea, *Christian Identity Formation Across the Elbe in the Tenth and Eleventh Centuries*, Christianity and Conversion in Scandinavia and the Baltic Region, c. 800–1600, 1 (Frankfurt am Main: Peter Lang, 2021); Norbert Kersken, "The Crusade Ideas in the Areas of the North-Western Slavs around the Time of the Second Crusade," in *The Expansion of the Faith*, ed. Srodecki et al., 113–29; Burnham W. Reynolds, *The Prehistory of the Crusades: Missionary War and the Baltic Crusades* (London: Bloomsbury, 2016), 11–24 and 28–29; Bysted et al., *Jerusalem in the North*, 28 and 45–55. For the original text in Danish, see Jensen, *Med ord og ikke med slag*, 60–84 and 87–105. See also the discussion on mission and the use of violence during the early part of the Baltic Crusades in Marius Ščavinskas, "On the Crusades and Coercive Missions in the Baltic Region in the Mid-12th Century and the Early 13th Century: The Cases of the Wends and Livonians," *Zeitschrift für Ostmitteleuropa-Forschung*, 63, no. 4 (2014), 506–14.

2 See the introduction in Dragnea, *The Wendish Crusade, 1147*, 1–3 and also *Jerusalem in the North*, ed. Bysted et al., 45–46.

3 *Quantum praedecessores* is found in *PL* 180, cols. 1064–66. The bull was released again, with

to persuade the Danes to take part in the planned crusade to reconquer the lost territories.[4]

One of the most prominent of these crusade preachers was the Cistercian abbot Bernard of Clairvaux (1090–1153).[5] Pope Eugenius had appointed him as his special envoy in recognition of his considerable oratorical skills. Bernard's work took him all round France, where he had great success preaching to the king of France and his leading barons at Easter 1146. After that, he went to Germany; at Christmas of the same year, he preached before the king, Conrad III (r. 1138–1152), together with the country's leading magnates.[6] Many of those present immediately answered the pope's call to go on crusade to the Holy Land. However, some of the Saxon princes who were present argued that they should instead fight the pagan Slavic people commonly referred to in Danish and German contemporary sources as "Wends." They lived close to Christian lands, right on the other side of the Elbe River, and had been doing so for centuries as a constant threat—it was argued—against both the Saxons and the Danes.[7]

In reality, these Slavic people made up several different communities with the most important being the western Polabian Slavs, who were subdivided into a number of lesser tribes living along the Elbe River. Another important group was the Rani, most of whom lived on the island of Rügen and who are, therefore, often referred to as Rugian Slavs. According to the Danish medieval chronicler Saxo Grammaticus (ca. 1160-after 1208), the Rugian Slavs were the primary enemies of the Danes while the Germans had their eyes set on the Polabians. To the east, lived then the Slavic Pommeranians who also made up a number of lesser tribes and peoples who had shifting alliances with their neighbours but who also became the target of both Danish and Polish attacks and missionary attempts.[8]

---

small changes, on March 1, 1146. See Iben Fonnesberg-Schmidt, *The Popes and the Baltic Crusades 1147–1254* (Leiden: Brill, 2007), 27. One finds the bull dated in scholarship both to December 1, 1145, and March 1, 1146. For additional historical background, see Dragnea, *The Wendish Crusade, 1147* and Bysted et al., *Jerusalem in the North,* 45–53.

4 Bysted et al., *Jerusalem in the North,* 57.

5 Dragnea, *The Wendish Crusade, 1147,* 5–6.

6 Reynolds, *The Prehistory of the Crusades,* 14.

7 Bysted et al., *Jerusalem in the North,* 45; Friedrich Lotter, "The Crusading Idea and the Conquest of the Region East of the Elbe," in Bartlett and MacKay, *Medieval Frontier Societies,* 287; Janus Møller Jensen, "*Sclavorum expugnator*: Conquest, Crusade, and Danish Royal Ideology in the Twelfth Century," *Crusades* 2 (2003), 55–56. The early mission to the Slavs is discussed in detail in Hans-Dietrich Kahl, "*Compellere intrare*: Die Wendenpolitik Bruns von Querfurt im Lichte hochmittelalterlichen Missions- und Völkerrechts," *Zeitschrift für Ostforschung* 4 (1955), 161–93 and 360–401. The two most important contemporary accounts of the Christianization of the Wends are Helmold von Bosau/*Helmoldi Presbyteri Bozoviensis,* Slawenchronik/*Chronica Slavorum, Neu übertragen und erläutert von Heinz Stoob* (Darmstadt: Wissenschafliche Buchgesellschaft, 1983), and Saxo Grammaticus's *Gesta Danorum,* 1–2, ed. J. Olrik, H. Ræder, and F. Blatt (København: Det Danske Sprog- og Litteraturselskab, 1931): http://www.kb.dk/elib/lit/dan/saxo/lat/or.dsr/, accessed 9 January 2024. For an English translation in parts, see *Saxo Grammaticus: Gesta Danorum, the History of the Danes,* ed. Karsten Friis-Jensen and Peter Fischer (Oxford: Clarendon Press, 2015).

8 See especially Lotter, "The Crusading Idea."

Saxo Grammaticus mentions quite early in his chronicle that the Slavic people were powerful foes who waged constant wars on the Danes on several occasions—the Rani, especially, are referred to as harrying "pirates" (*piratae*).[9] At the same time, the ruling Slavic families also had close dynastic relations to the Danes, upholding strong commercial bonds and frequently making military alliances with the Danish kings.[10] Both the Danes and the Slavs had been exposed to extensive political and military pressure from the Frankish Carolingians and later the Ottonians in the ninth and tenth centuries. Christian missionaries had come to both these peoples about the same time, establishing the very first churches as well as instigating campaigns of conversion and baptism among these pagans. A joint revolt by Danish King Harald Bluetooth (d. ca. 987) and the Abodrite (part of the Polabians) Prince Mstivoj (d. 995) against the Ottonians in the second half of the tenth century, however, resulted in the two peoples taking different paths thereafter. This and other revolts among the Polabians were followed by a major rejection of Christianity, whereas the Danes generally adhered to this religion as a powerful bulwark against the political and military aspirations of the German emperors. Consequently the initial revolts against a common enemy came to place the Danes and the Western Slavic people on opposing sides in the generations to come, introducing strong elements of holy war and wars of mission into the future military conflicts between the two people that eventually turned into proper, papal backed crusades during the first half of the twelfth century.[11]

Bernard of Clairvaux did accept the arguments of the Saxon noblemen who wanted to expand their territories into the lands of the Polabians and Bernard wrote a letter in which he offered his thoughts about the relationship between mission, conversion, and crusade.[12] Among other thing, Bernard characterized the war that the Saxons had waged against the pagans east of the Elbe as a divinely sanctioned fight, through which the enemy should be driven from Christian territory.[13] He also wrote that the devil himself feared that all the pagans would convert to Christianity, and had stirred the pagans up to fight against the Christians. Bernard portrayed the war as one of self-defence, even though in many cases it was the Saxons (and the Danes) who attacked the Slavic people

---

9 Heebøll-Holm, "Between Pagan Pirates and Glorious Sea-Warriors," 143 and 151. See also Mägi, *The Viking Eastern Baltic*, 13.

10 See for example Saxo 2:5.2.

11 Lotter, "The Crusading Idea," 271; Kurt Villads Jensen, "Danske korstog før og under korstogstiden," in *Ett annat 1100-tal: Individ, kollektiv och kulturella mönster i medeltidens Danmark*, ed. Peter Carelli, Lars Hermanson, and Hanne Sanders (Göteborg: Makadam, 2004), 246–83; Manfred Hellmann, "Die Anfänge christlicher Mission in den baltischen Ländern," in *Studien über die Anfänge der Mission in Livland*, Vorträge und Forschungen, Sonderband 37, ed. Manfred Hellmann (Sigmaringen: Jan Thorbecke, 1989), 10–11; Bysted et al., *Jerusalem in the North*, 23–28; Jensen, *"Sclavorum expugnator,"* 70–71; Reynolds, *The Prehistory of the Crusades*, 29.

12 Bernhard of Clairvaux, Letter 457, in *Sancti Bernardi Opera*, ed. J. Leclercq og H. Rochais (Rome: Editiones Cistercienses, 1957–77), 8:433; Bruno Scott James, *The Letters of St. Bernard of Clairvaux* (Stroud, Sutton Publishing, 1998), 466–68 (letter 394).

13 Bernhard of Clairvaux, letter 457, 432–33; Lotter, "The Crusading Idea," 288.

in their homelands.[14] The time had come, Bernard insisted, for the pagans to be defeated once and for all and be converted. He, therefore, encouraged the Saxon magnates and knights to take the cross "and completely destroy or at least convert these [pagan] tribes."[15] Under no circumstances should the Christian knights settle for receiving tribute or gifts of money from the pagans. Instead, pagan customs were to be destroyed with God's help—or else the pagan people themselves should be destroyed.[16] Thus, the Saxon noblemen got what they asked for and, perhaps, even a bit more through the forceful admonitions by Bernard!

Bernard of Clairvaux's preaching campaign of 1146, however, was not the first indication of a crusader ideology taking roots in the Baltic Sea region. Inspired by the recent conquest of Jerusalem in 1099 by the crusaders of the First Crusade, a campaign is believed to have been planned against the Slavic pagans already in 1108.[17] The initiator appears to have been someone close to the archbishop of Magdeburg—perhaps even the archbishop himself, Adalgot of Osterberg (r. 1107–1119). It seems that the archbishop had planned to circulate a letter in which he exhorted the Christians in the surrounding lands to take part in the battle against the pagans, just as their fellow Christians had taken part in the conquest of Jerusalem. The archbishop also promised that those who answered this call to fight against the pagans would save their own souls:

> For so long we have been pressed to the ground by the manifold violence and misdeeds of the pagans, and we cry out for your compassion, that you may come to our aid and lift up with us your mother Church from the dust... . Oh, Saxons, Franks, people from Lorraine, and sons of Flanders, you most illustrious men and lords of the world! Here you can both save your souls (*animas uestras saluificare*) and, if you will, acquire excellent land to live and build on.[18]

In the letter, the archbishop also assures his readers that the Danish King Niels (r. 1104–1134), as well as the German King (and later also Emperor) Heinrich V (king, 1099–1125; emperor, 1111–1125), had already accepted to support the enterprise. It is unclear whether the campaign ever, in fact, came about, or if the archbishop was, in reality, the actual initiator, or if it was the Danish and German kings had made any promises to support the plans, but none of this is important here.[19] What is essential, however, is the fact that the letter was drawn up in the first place, demonstrating even

---

14 Lotter, "The Crusading Idea," 289.

15 "Et ad delendas penitus aut certe convertendas nationes illas."

16 The statement occurs in the following context: "denuntiamus armari christianorum robur adversus illos et ad delendas penitus aut certe convertendas nationes illas signum salutare suscipere...Illud...interdicimus, ne qua ratione ineant foedus cum eis...donec auxiliante Deo aut ritus ipse aut natio deleatur," cited in Lotter, "The Crusading Idea," 289.

17 Reynolds, *The Prehistory of the Crusades*, 151; Mihai Dragnea, *The Wendish Crusade, 1147*, 30–34; Ščavinskas, "On the Crusades and Coercive Missions," 500.

18 DD 1:2.39; see also Bysted et al., *Jerusalem in the North*, 29.

19 Reynolds, *The Prehistory of the Crusades*, 151.

at this early point, there were people in the area who were inspired by the events of the First Crusade and who wanted something similar for their own region. They wished to see their own battles against the pagans as part of a common, holy, and penitential war against the enemies of Christendom, and they interpreted their current battles from that perspective. Subsequently, in the 1120s, a series of missionary campaigns were launched against the pagan Slavic tribes in the areas of eastern Pomerania. In every case, these campaigns had strong military overtones.[20] The same also goes for the Danish campaign launched against the people on Rügen in 1136, in which the Danish King Erik Emune (r. 1134–1137) is said to have forced the inhabitants of Arkona (the island's chief settlement and home to a huge pagan shrine) to convert to Christianity and to pay taxes to the Danish king. The defeated Rani soon went back on the agreements they had made with the Danes, however, reverting to their pagan faith as soon as the Danes left the area. This naturally prompted renewed Danish attacks including the final conquest of Arkona in 1168 by King Valdemar I. (sole regent, 1157–1182) and his close friend and sworn brother, Archbishop Absalon (bishop, 1152–1198, archbishop, 1178–1201), as is described so vividly by Saxo.[21] Despite the destruction of this central pagan sanctuary by the Danes, the fighting between the Slavic people and the Danes did not come to an end, however, until the son of King Valdemar I, King Knud VI (r. 1182–1202) finally forced Duke Bogusław I of Pomerania (r. 1156–1187) to submit to Danish lordship and formally becoming the kings vassal in 1185.[22]

This final subjugation of the Slavic pagans did not in any way bring the involvement of the Danes in the Baltic Crusades to an end—on the contrary. Soon they turned their attention further to the east with concrete expeditions against the pagan Prussians, the people of eastern Finland, and, eventually, the people of Estonia.

Crusade, Missionary Wars, or Wars of Secular Conquest?

Military expeditions, missionary campaigns, holy wars, and proper crusades pretty much went hand-in-hand throughout most of the twelfth century in the Baltic Sea region among both German and Scandinavian magnates and leading prelates. These longstanding associations have raised the question of whether it is possible to distinguish more precisely between the various forms of military endeavours, missionary campaigns, and genuine crusades that were all part of a general trend affecting the whole region only a

---

20 See, e.g., DD 1:2.50–52. See also the discussion in Hans-Dietrich Kahl, "Die ersten Jahrhunderte des missionsgeschichtlichen Mittelalters: Bausteine für eine Phänomenologie bis ca. 1050," in *Kirchengeschichte als Missionsgeschichte*, 1–2, Die Kirche des früheren Mittelalters, erster Halbband, ed. Knut Schäferdiek (München, Chr. Kaiser, 1978), 60–71; Robert Bartlett, "The Conversion of a Pagan Society in the Middle Ages," *History* 70 (1985), 186 and 191; Bysted et al., *Jerusalem in the North*, 32–34.

21 Saxo, 14:1.7. The Danish king's campaign is also mentioned in the *Knytlingesaga*. Cf. Bysted et al., *Jerusalem in the North*, 44. See also Reynolds, *The Prehistory of the Crusades*, 115.

22 Saxo, 16:8.1–10. See also Carsten Selch Jensen, "Religion and War in Saxo Grammaticus's *Gesta Danorum*: The Examples of Bishop Absalon and King Valdemar I," in Kotecki et al., *Christianity and War*, 189–206.

few years after the first crusaders had conquered Jerusalem in 1099 and set an entire European crusading movement in motion. This question is notably prominent in much previous research into the history of the crusades, where one of the key questions has revolved around what constituted a "real" crusade, as opposed to more or less informal military expeditions.[23] Despite the many attempts that have been made to establish clear parameters for the definition of a crusade, however, the main conclusion must be that these modern definitions will always be surrounded by a degree of uncertainty, not least because they often run counter to the ways in which the events were in fact articulated in the past. One historian has pointed out that modern scholarship's demand that each and every type of military expedition be clearly defined has often resulted in definitions that are a long way from the past's own understandings and from its actual practices.[24] Those practices were themselves far from being uniform, especially in the early part of the twelfth century. The early sources, for example, are all highly imprecise in their references to the crusades as a phenomenon. They are imprecise, that is, in terms of their formal framework, their religious substance, and the status of the participants. These are all matters that would otherwise be considered significant in establishing a definition of what might constitute a true crusade, as opposed to being more local and informal military expeditions and missionary campaigns supported by armed force.[25] Recent research has established that papal crusading policy itself was in flux through most of the twelfth century with regards to the Holy Land and the Iberian Peninsula (i.e., the primary areas of crusading). Papal policy, furthermore, diverged fairly significantly from the local initiatives and the crusade policies which various actors attempted to implement in other crusading areas, including the Baltic Sea area.[26] This makes it hard, therefore, to offer clear-cut definitions of the many types of military expeditions, crusades, and missionary campaigns that took place in the period.

Furthermore, the sources strongly suggest that there was an early tradition among local princes, magnates, and ecclesiastic authorities of organizing so-called "missionary wars" (as they would become known in scholarship) in the southwestern parts of the Baltic Sea region. As indicated, the roots of these seems to reach back to Charlemagne's so-called Saxon Wars of the eighth century and the ensuing missionary wars of the Ottonian dynasty from the ninth to the early eleventh centuries.[27] They had also deep roots

23 See especially the discussion of the definitions of a crusade in Norman Housley, *Contesting the Crusades* (Oxford: Blackwell, 2006), 1–23. See also Reynolds, *The Prehistory of the Crusades* with a specific focus on the Baltic Sea Region.

24 Housley, *Contesting the Crusades*, 19–20 and 23.

25 Housley, *Contesting the Crusades*, 8–9.

26 Jessalynn Bird, Edward Peters, and James M. Powell, *Crusade and Christendom: Annotated Documents in Translation from Innocent III to the Fall of Acre, 1187–1291* (Philadelphia: University of Pennsylvania Press, 2013), 18 and 20–21; Fonnesberg-Schmidt, *The Popes and the Baltic Crusades 1147–1254*, 97–8; Christopher Tyerman, "Henry of Livonia and the Ideology of Crusading," in Tamm et al., *Crusading and Chronicle Writing*, 36.

27 Carsten Selch Jensen, "Gud vil det: Om retfærdige og hellige krige i middelalderen," in *Retfærdig krig: Om legitimeringer af krig og voldsudøvelse i historien*, ed. Carsten Selch Jensen (Odense:

back into the early history of the medieval church and the theological debates regarding the legitimacy of the use of force in the conversion of non-Christian people. The important character here is St. Augustine (354–430) and his teachings on the idea of just war, and how this type of war came to be used in the spreading of Christendom during the early and high medieval periods. For Augustine, the basic rationale for a just war was that any war should be a war of self-defence like the one Bernard came to promulgate more than seven centuries later. Augustine also emphasized that war was an unavoidable feature of the created world: war was simultaneously a consequence of worldly sin and a penance to be undertaken in order to atone for sin.[28] According to Augustine, war was thus both a necessity—which could protect Christians and the church alike against any conceivable attack—and an instrument of punishment, which God could use to chastise the faithful should they break his laws or act against his will.[29] The question here, however, is what role Augustine authorized for warfare as a tool for the expansion of Christendom. His viewpoint in this respect was clear: he maintained that nobody should be forced to accept Christianity without their explicit consent. Any conversion to Christianity, therefore, was always to be voluntary.[30] Nevertheless, Augustine also argued that compulsion had its place—it was necessary, for example, in the case of heretics and apostates who had once belonged to the true church but for one reason or another had abandoned it or adopted a heretical belief. According to Augustine, it was more or less a duty for the authorities to use coercion in these cases. He referred to the story of the banquet in Luke 14 of the New Testament by way of an example. In this story, the servants (i.e., the servants of the church) had to go out into the streets of the city and compel people to come to a banquet so that God's house would be filled. Augustine placed special emphasis on the verb "to compel" (*compellere*) which, in this particular biblical context had clear overtones of duress—especially in relation to heretics and apostates.[31]

For Augustine, this special focus on heretics and apostates did not mean that war had no place in Christian missionary work in general and he found New Testament arguments to support this view. For example, he referred to the apostle Peter, who defended Christ with his sword when the temple guards attacked him shortly before the crucifixion. Christians were likewise allowed to defend the church, its priests, and its missionaries against any conceivable attack by the pagans. The rationale here was that the use

---

Syddansk Universitetsforlag, 2006), 91–92. See also Reynolds, *The Prehistory of the Crusades*, 62 and 116; Mihai Dragnea, *The Wendish Crusade, 1147*, 2–3.

28 Carsten Selch Jensen, "Gå ud til vejene og langs gærderne og nød dem til at komme, så mit hus kan blive fyldt" Pavernes holdning til tvangsomvendelser og mission i Baltikum omkring år 1200," in *Reformationer: Universitet, Kirkehistorie, Luther: Festskrift til Steffen Kjeldgaard-Pedersen, 28 April 2006*, ed. Tine Reeh and Anna Vind (København: C. A. Reitzels, 2006), 187–8; Jensen, "God's War," 134; Reynolds, *The Prehistory of the Crusades*, 83, 104, and 107. See also the recent discussion of the idea of holy war in the early and high medieval period in Boris Gübele, *Deus vult, Deus vult: Der christliche heilige Krieg im Früh- und Hochmittelalter* (Ostfildern: Thorbecke, 2018).

29 Jensen, "Gå ud til vejene og langs gærderne," 188.

30 Jensen, "God's War," 134.

3 1 Jensen, "Gå ud til vejene og langs gærderne," 188.

of force did not have as its aim the specific conversion of the pagans. It rather ensured simply that Christian evangelization might take place freely. According to Augustine, therefore, missionary war was more a war of self-defence than a war for (enforced) conversion.[32]

In many ways, Augustine's theology of just war came to establish the framework for the church's theology in this area for the coming centuries. This can be seen in canon law, for example in Gratian's *Causa 23*, where the just war is discussed in-depth.[33] Here Gratian reemphasized Augustine's central argument, namely that war has an important role in punishing sin and injustice in the world. Gratian thus drew the conclusion that a just war would not bring guilt upon the soldiers involved provided they fought with the right motives and under lawful authority.[34] Gratian also underlined that the just war was a defensive war which led later canonists to conclude that he had, in fact, sanctioned forcible conversion, because it was the last line of defence against pagans who threatened Christendom.[35] It is more likely, however, that Gratian did in fact maintain the Augustinian tradition of prohibiting the use of compulsion in the conversion of non-Christians. It is undeniable, though, that there existed other understandings of this difficult question. As an example some scholars have suggested that leading prelates in the earlier Carolingian and Ottonian periods—some centuries before Gratian—generally accepted the role of compulsion as a direct tool in the missionary wars of those periods. This is especially clear with regards to Charlemagne's Saxon wars.[36] The question, therefore, is how Bernard's bombastic statements in his address to the Saxon magnates in 1146 about the pagans' choice between baptism or death should in fact be understood. Did they actually belong to the tradition of Augustinian thought? Or did they belong to a parallel tradition which had developed in northeast Europe from the early Middle Ages onwards among the theologians of the Carolingian or Ottonian churches? Either way,

---

32 Dragnea, *The Wendish Crusade, 1147*, 25.

33 Gratian, *Causa 23, Decretum*, in *Corpus iuris canonici*, ed. E. Friedberg (Leipzig: Tauchnitz, 1879; repr. 1959), 1:889–965.

34 Frederick H. Russell, *The Just War in the Middle Ages* (Cambridge: Cambridge University Press, 1975), 60, 69, and 73.

35 Ernst-Dieter Hehl, *Kirche und Krieg im 1. Jahrhundert: Studien zu kanonischem Recht und politischer Wirklichkeit* (Stuttgart: Anton Hiersemann, 1980), 69, 71–72, and 85; Russell, *The Just War in the Middle Ages*, 75. Another important point that Gratian dealt with exhaustively was the prohibition on clerics taking part in bloodshed, which included warfare. Gratian's view did not go unchallenged, however, and it is clear from contemporary texts that clerics in the lowest orders up to the highest-ranking prelates in fact took a very active and direct part in the warfare connected with various military campaigns, apparently without unleashing any moral condemnation on the part of their contemporaries. The same is also true for the way in which some medieval chroniclers like Henry of Livonia, Saxo Grammaticus, and many more talk very positively about the clerics who took an active part in military activities: they do not blame these clerics for taking part; if anything, the opposite is true. See also Sini Kangas, "The Image of 'Warrior-Bishops' in the Northern Tradition of the Crusades," in Kotecki et al., *Christianity and War*, 60–63.

36 Benjamin Z. Kedar, *Crusade and Mission: European Approaches toward the Muslims* (Princeton: University of Princeton Press, 1984), 68; Kahl, "Die ersten Jahrhunderte des missionsgeschichtlichen Mittelalters," 43. For a further discussion of this topic, see also Jensen, "Gud vil det," 91–94;

there is certainly no doubt that these thoughts came to play a central role in the later missionary crusades in the Baltic Sea region.[37]

As such, the ideas also came to influence the various missionary chronicles of the region in their portrayal of war and mission among the pagan people. A very concrete example is the aforementioned Henry of Livonia who, in very specific terms, describes the wars in Livonia and Estonia as a scourge of God and, at the same time, implies that the pagans were confronted with a choice between baptism and destruction, very similar to the viewpoints ascribed to Bernard of Clairvaux a couple of generations earlier. Scholarly debate has thus turned on the question of whether Bernard actually encouraged forcible conversion of the pagans in his letter—i.e., whether he expressed the clear opinion that the pagans should be compelled to accept Christianity in exchange for letting them live. That position, of course, would have run directly counter to canon law and to the tradition among most (it seems) theologians and canon lawyers of the time with strong roots back to Augustine.[38] Scholars have also discussed the extent to which Bernard's argument depended on the notion that the west Slavic people had once been Christians, but had since abandoned the faith, which meant that they should be considered apostates, which, on Augustinian grounds, would in fact have legitimized compulsion as an explicit goal.[39] The Western Slavs were indeed viewed as apostates in some contexts which may therefore explain why Bernard thought that they should be faced with the direct choice of baptism or death.[40] This would also place him within the same tradition as some of the ideas expressed by for example Henry of Livonia about the question of baptism and apostasy, which seems also to have had their own roots in an Augustinian theology of just war.[41] Other scholars have, however, suggested that Bernard's appeal to the Saxon knights was actually calling for the Christian warriors

---

37 See for example Reynolds, *The Prehistory of the Crusades*, 69–96.

38 See the discussions in Jensen, "God's War," 133–34; Russell, *The Just War*, 23–25; F. H. Russell, "Love and Hate in Medieval Warfare: The Contribution of Saint Augustine," *Nottingham Medieval Studies* 31 (1987), 115–16; Kahl, *Compellere intrare*, 178–87; Volker Mertens, "Religious Identity in Middle High German Crusader Epics," *History of European Ideas* 20 (1995), 852. See also the reflections in Reynolds, *The Prehistory of the Crusades*, 73.

39 Jensen, "God's War," 134; Kahl, "Die ersten Jahrhunderte des missionsgeschichtlichen Mittelalters," 52–56; Kahl, *"Compellere intrare,"* 366; Kurt Villads Jensen, "Martyrs, Total War, and Heavenly Horses: Scandinavia as Centre and Periphery in the Expansion of Medieval Christendom," in *Medieval Christianity in the North: New Studies*, ed. Kirsi Salonen, Kurt Villads Jensen, and Torstein Jørgensen, (Turnhout: Brepols, 2013), 101.

40 Such an opinion can be found, for example, in Saxo Grammaticus, where he says the following about the Wends' worship of an effigy of Saint Vitus: "Charlemagne had at one time taken Rügen by assault and commanded its inhabitants to pay tribute to St. Vitus of Corvey, who had died an illustrious martyr's death. The islanders, anxious to claim back freedom after their vanquisher's decease, exchanged thraldom for superstition and erected within their community an effigy which they proposed to call St Vitus." (Saxo, 14:39.13). See also the discussions in Kahl, *"Compellere intrare,"* 186–87; Lotter, "The Crusading Idea," 291.

41 Jensen, "God's War," 139–46. It is worth noting that Bernard does not directly say that the Western Slavs were apostates. One might have expected him to have done so if that is what he indeed meant. Cf. Bysted et al., *Jerusalem in the North*, 49–52.

and crusaders to crush the pagans as a (pagan) people rather than simply putting the choices of baptism or death before them. Bernard describes the pagans in his letter as a *natio*. This is a term frequently used in the Vulgate to denote pagan tribes against which God's people had fought.[42] This would suggest, therefore, that Bernard thought that the Saxon knights should defeat the pagans' armies, destroy their political structures, and annihilate pagan cultic practices rather than simply kill them as individuals—because, taken together, all these things stood in the way of the Slavs' conversion (or reconversion) to Christianity as the one true faith. According to Bernard, this would make it possible to begin a genuine missionary work undertaken by priests and missionaries, which would lead to the pagans' eventual, actual conversion, their lands subsumbed into the Christian world.[43]

This interpretation has much in common with similar ideas expressed in various contemporary texts like, for example, the chronicle of aforementioned Henry of Livonia and, to some extent, Saxo Grammaticus. They were themselves witness to the fact that such ideas had won acceptance in the region during the twelfth century. At the same time, this notion also fits perfectly within the theology of legitimate missionary warfare that had evolved since Augustine's day. That theology suggested, that Christians could legitimately defend themselves against pagans when and if they attacked any clerics and missionaries. It also suggested that the Christians should destroy the pagans' armies— together with their societies—in order to ensure that the gospel could be preached freely. This would explain, in the first place, how Bernard's viewpoint might have been closely aligned with traditional thinking within the church. It would also explain why the same thinking came to be applied to the colonization and Christianization of Livonia and Estonia some decades later by German and Danish magnates, crusaders, and ecclesiastical leaders. At the same time, such an approach to war against the church's enemies offered an implicit acceptance of the notion that one could wage war in order to force pagans to convert, provided that the compulsion was indirect, rather than direct. This would explain the parallel development that seems to have evolved in the whole Baltic Sea region, which de facto resulted in a general acceptance of forcible conversion by the primary initiators.[44]

The initiators of the wars of conquest and mission in the Baltic Sea area were mostly local magnates, who undertook expeditions in an attempt to subjugate and Christian-

---

42 Bysted et al., *Jerusalem in the North*, 51–52. See also Villads Jensen, *Korstog ved verdens yderste rand*, 173.

43 Friedrich Lotter in particular has argued for this interpretation of Bernard's words. Cf. Lotter, "The Crusading Idea." The argument is also supported in Bysted et al., *Jerusalem in the North*, 50–53. Some scholars have detected an especially Cistercian strain of thought in the reflections about forcible conversion and forced baptism; See, e.g., Tyerman, "Henry of Livonia and the Ideology of Crusading," 39–41. The Cistercian elements were indeed a marked feature of the picture in Livonia; they can easily be imagined having influenced Henry's representation of the wars there as holy and just missionary wars, whose main goal was the conversion of the pagans. See also Dragnea, *The Wendish Crusade, 1147*, 9–10.

44 Dragnea, *The Wendish Crusade, 1147*, 25; Reynolds, *The Prehistory of the Crusades*, 72–73.

ize the Slavic tribes who lived along the borders of the existing Christian lands.[45] The papacy, on the other hand, was not significantly involved in the early expeditions of the first half of the twelfth century; in fact, the papacy in general seems not to have shown much interest in increasing its influence over the missionary activities and conquests that were taking place across the border regions east of the Elbe River at this point.[46] All the same, local powers continued to view their own expeditions as a part of a wider struggle against the enemies of the church and of Christendom; a fight that was being fought on many fronts. This was a view that was already in evidence in the early plans for the abovementioned campaign of 1108, which seems to have been entrenched region-ally and had not involved the papacy. The view certainly made itself felt in the course of Bernard of Clairvaux's preaching campaign among the German magnates in 1146 and the simultaneous visit by a papal legate in Denmark. Both their tasks were made easier, no doubt, by the fact that, as an idea, the crusades fitted in well with the familiar (and proven) tradition of missionary wars that had long been practised in the region.[47] These campaigns were understood by their local participants to be on a par with the papal-sanctioned expeditions directed towards the more central crusading regions. The crucial thing here is that the local participants in the expeditions understood—and, above all, represented—local expeditions as being consistent with papal policy regarding crusad-ing; they did so even in periods where the policy was not so fixed that its substance and overall priorities could not change. The relatively loose formal structure of the crusades had its advantages, however. It undoubtedly meant that it was easier to fit the old tradi-tions of missionary wars against non-Christian enemies into the concept of crusading, which itself gained more and more ground in the region as time went on.[48] This view has been developed even further, suggesting that the crusades in Livonia and Estonia were, in reality, the first genuinely successful examples of a symbiotic convergence of mission, crusade, and conquest, playing a definitive role in the history of the Baltic Sea region. It came to influence the development of crusading in other regions too: the idea of con-verting the Muslims, for example, gained more and more prominence in the rhetoric surrounding contemporary expeditions in the Holy Land and on the Spanish Peninsular in the early thirteenth century.[49]

It is also interesting to note that the sources for the first crusades usually talk about the crusades as armed pilgrimages. This was especially true for the First Crusade. The participants (i.e., the crusaders) were understood to be pilgrims (*peregrini*) on the road to the holy places in and around Jerusalem who shared certain spiritual privileges. The important thing about these pilgrims was that they were armed, and that—for them—

45 Lotter, "The Crusading Idea," 285–94; Kahl, *"Compellere intrare,"* 161–93 and 360–401; Kahl, "Die ersten Jahrhunderte des missionsgeschichtlichen Mittelalters"; Jensen, "Danske korstog"; Jensen, *"Sclavorum expugnator."*

46 See for example Fonnesberg-Schmidt, *The Popes and the Baltic Crusades 1147–1254*, 43–52.

47 See esp. Jensen, "Danske korstog," 256–63; Reynolds, *The Prehistory of the Crusades*, 81.

48 Jensen, "Danske korstog," 261–63.

49 Marek Tamm, "How to justify a crusade? The conquest of Livonia and new crusade rhetoric in the early thirteenth century," *Journal of Medieval History*, 39, no. 4 (2013), 442.

warfare was not simply a necessary precondition of travelling through areas beset with enemies. Warfare was, rather, essential to the purpose of the journey itself, which was to fight against the enemies of God and Christ. These armed pilgrims were thus bound to warfare through their crusading vows, which in turn made them *crucesignati*, i.e., "those signed with the cross."[50] There were other pilgrims in the Holy Land, of course, who were bound only by traditional pilgrimage vows, not having taken the same vows as the crusaders, in which a commitment to warfare was implicit. But they did have one thing in common, namely that both armed and unarmed pilgrimages were understood as being penitential acts connected to a spiritual reward that took the form of an indulgence, i.e., a whole or partial absolution for specific penances that had been imposed by the church on an individual penitent.

This is important to emphasize, because the notion of warfare as a penance was not something that only belonged to the context of crusading. As an example, Pope John VIII's (r. 872–882) promises of indulgence for those who died in defence of God's church—and salvation for them who died in the fight against pagans and unbelievers—have often been emphasized.[51] Throughout the majority of the twelfth century, the extent of the indulgence for the crusaders, and their precise liturgical formulations, remained unclear however, which, in itself, makes it hard to precisely determine when an expedition was formally regarded as an actual crusade with papal sanction and promises of indulgence, in contract to (just) being local expeditions as would have been the case so many times across the Baltic Sea region. The latter often continued older traditions of penitential warfare, to which various forms of spiritual reward were attached, for example through a fundamental understanding of these wars as God's war, i.e., *bellum Domini*.[52]

---

50 Housley, *Contesting the Crusades*, 50. Housely, however, is careful to point out that not everyone who fought in the Holy Land was necessarily signed with the cross, i.e., *crucesignati*.

51 Russell, *The Just War in the Middle Ages*, 33; Gübele, *Deus vult*, 193–96. In the period before the First Crusade, participation in warfare usually enjoined a form of penance on individual soldiers because of the bloodshed in which they had taken part. The penance enjoined on the archers after the Battle of Hastings in 1066 is an especially well-known example of this; see. H. E. J. Cowdrey, "Bishop Ermenfrid of Sion and the Penitential Ordinance following the Battle of Hastings," *Journal of Ecclesiastical History*, 20, no. 2 (1969), 233–36; the penance for the archers is discussed at page 234, point E. This situation changed significantly in the period after the First Crusade. See the comprehensive account of early penitential warfare in Carl Erdmann, *Die Entstehung des Kreuzzugsgedankens* (Stuttgart: W. Kohlhammer, 1935/1974). See also Kahl, "*Compellere intrare*," 170–72.

52 The notion of "God's war" rested on the notion of a divinely sanctioned war, which was not however embraced by the prevalent legal notion of the just war. "God's war" was a based on the biblical notion of God's holy war. This distinction between a just and a holy war will be discussed in chapter five below, because it has a special significance for Henry's view of warfare as God's war. See also Housley, *Contesting the Crusades*, 17, together with the detailed discussion in John Gilchrist, "The Lord's War as the Proving Ground of Faith: Pope Innocent III and the Propagation of Violence (1198–1216)," in *Crusaders and Muslims in Twelfth-Century Syria*, ed. Maya Shatzmiller (Leiden: Brill, 1993), 65–83; John Gilchrist, "The Papacy and the War against the 'Saracens'," 795–1216," *International History Review*, 10 (1988), 174–97.

Given the continuation of these traditions, it is hardly surprising that the excursions undertaken by crusaders (i.e., pilgrims) often came to be described in sources in terms such as a "journey" (*iter*) or "expedition" (*expeditio*), both of which encompassed broad and general semantic associations with travelling.[53] All the same, these words came to be used in a narrower sense and in connection with military operations in general, and they thus do not have an exclusively crusading significance.[54] It is, then, hard to decide whether a source is dealing with one sort of expedition or the other. The context and the wider narrative thus determine how a specific expedition should be interpreted in each particular instance and how it was interpreted by those who actually took part in the events.

It has been suggested that it was only around 1200 during the pontificate of Innocent III (r. 1198–1216), that the crusading movement was afforded a more formal framework that drew on theology and canon law, and thus had an effect on status of participants.[55] A certain emphasis, however, must also be put on Pope Gregory VIII's (r. October 1187–December 1187) crusading bull, *Audita tremendi*, issued on October 29, 1187, which, as has been suggested, seems to have been fundamental to the development of Innocent III's own crusading policy some ten years later.[56] A recent edition of the bull describes it as "the most impassioned plea for a crusade ever issued by a pope until then," pointing towards a deeper formalization of papal crusading policy after 1200.[57]

As far as the Baltic Sea region is concerned, papal engagement has been characterized by some scholars as being more reactive than active. This marks papal involvement here as significantly different to that in the Holy Land and, to a certain extent, that in Spain.[58] With special reference to the papacy of Eugenius III, it has also been noted that "the papacy was forced to take a reactive, rather than an initiating and intervening, position," ascribing this partly to a distinctive hesitancy on the part of the papacy to involve itself in such local and regional missionary campaigns. Furthermore, a specific weakness of the papacy's position in this period also may have limited its ability to play an active and offensive role in the Baltic and elsewhere.[59]

---

53 Dragnea, *The Wendish Crusade, 1147*, 34.

54 See, e.g., Jensen, *Korstog ved verdens yderste rand*, 336.

55 See for example Tyerman's argument in, Christopher Tyerman, *The Invention of the Crusades* (Toronto: Palgrave, 1989), alongside the discussion in Housley, *Contesting the Crusades*, 50.

56 Bird, *Crusade and Christendom*, 4.

57 Bird, *Crusade and Christendom*, 3–5.

58 Iben Fonnesberg-Schmidt, "Pope Honorius III and Mission and Crusades in the Baltic Region," in Murray, *The Clash of Cultures*, 103–22. See also the more comprehensive analysis in Fonnesberg-Schmidt, *The Popes and the Baltic Crusades 1147–1254*, 39.

59 Fonnesberg-Schmidt, *The Popes and the Baltic Crusades 1147–1254*, 39.

Papal Missionary and Crusading Policy
in the Baltic between 1146 and 1168

Turning again to specific developments in the Baltic Sea area, the widespread and persistent resistance of the Western Slavic peoples to adopting Christianity up to the second half of the twelfth century took on a particular significance when it came to the
outcome of Bernard of Clairvaux's meeting with the Saxon magnates at Christmas of
1146.[60] First of all, it led to the first concrete and direct papal involvement in these wars
of conquest and mission in the Baltic Sea area and, as such, also came to influence the
continued Danish involvement in the crusading movement. As mentioned previously, in
response to Bernard's powerful sermons, some of the Saxon magnates maintained that
it was better for them to fight against the pagans who lived close to their own borders
than to travel all the way to the Holy Land. The Saxon knights also gained Eugenius's
direct support, because in his letter *Divini dispensatione*, which was written at Bernard's
request, he equated the crusades against the Western Slavs with the crusades to the
Holy Land and the Iberian Peninsula. More specifically, the pope promised the participants that they would enjoy the same protection and the same full (*plenar*) indulgence
as the other crusaders. He emphasized, moreover, that the primary goal of the fight
against the pagans was to convert them to Christianity.[61] Eugenius also made clear that
the promise of indulgences was dependent on the Saxon knights and magnates not taking money from pagans seeking to pay their way out of having to receive the Christian
faith.[62]

The papal bull and Bernard's letter to the Saxon noblemen emphasized a new equivalence between the various crusading areas that also came to include the Danish expeditions against the Slavic people on Rügen or in Pommerania. They made clear that the
conversion of the pagans should be the main aim of the campaigns. This latter point,
in particular, has led scholars to conclude that, when Eugenius III officially sanctioned
the crusade against the Western Slavs in 1147, he introduced a new type of crusade,
which could be called a "missionary crusade," whose primary goal was the conversion of
the pagans.[63] There was, moreover, an understanding among the participants that these
wars also offered a form of spiritual reward in the afterlife for the Christians who participated in them.[64] Thus, the thing that was actually new in 1147 was not the desire to
undertake mission and convert the pagans through war and military campaigns in the
Baltic Sea area. It was rather the formal connection made between crusade *and* mission,

---

60 Dragnea, *The Wendish Crusade, 1147*, 13–15 and 22–23.

61 *Divini dispensatione*: PL, vol. 180, cols. 1203–04; Fonnesberg-Schmidt, *The Popes and the Baltic
Crusades 1147–1254*, 31 and 64–65; Fonnesberg-Schmidt, "Pope Honorius III and Mission and
Crusades in the Baltic Region," 103.

62 This important point is also made in Lotter, "The Crusading Idea," 288; Bysted et al., *Jerusalem
in the North*, 49.

63 See especially the discussion in Ščavinskas, "On the Crusades and Coercive Missions," 505–14.

64 With regards to an early notion of spiritual rewards connected to (missionary) warfare that
predates the crusades proper, see Adam of Bremen, III.21. See also Kahl, "*Compellere intrare*," esp.
170–72.

as mentioned earlier in this chapter. This manifested itself in the middle of the twelfth century and culminated in the crusades in Livonia and Estonia around 1200.[65]

While conversion did not initially play a significant role in the Holy Land or Spain, the conversion of pagan peoples was a key motive behind the crusades in the Baltic Sea area from the very beginning, just as it had been a fundamental element in the legitimization of many of the military campaigns that had happened prior to the first official crusades in the region. The renewed Danish campaigns against the Rani on Rügen, which led to the conquest of the key pagan shrine in Arkona in 1168, are especially important in this respect. Saxo Grammaticus described the battles and the destruction of the idol of Svantevit, the supreme pagan god of the Slavs, especially vividly and the incident, in reality, came to pave the way for the first Danish attacks on Estonia only a few years later.[66] Saxo mentions that the military conquest was followed by the missionary work of Danish clerics and the construction of churches among the still pagan but soon to become (nominally), Christian people on Rügen.[67]

From a curial perspective, papal involvement with the missionary wars in the Baltic Sea area seems at this point in time to have been broadly determined by whether or not regional or local powers requested papal support for a given objective. The Saxon and Danish magnates' desire that their fight against the Western Slavs be regarded as a fully-fledged expression of the broader crusading movement was one such possible objective. On the other hand, the popes themselves did not take the initiative in such missionary campaigns.[68] This was true both in the case of Eugenius III and in that of his immediate successors, Anastasius IV (r. 1153–1154) and Adrian IV (r. 1154–1159).[69] Under Alexander III (r. 1159–1181), however, the area around the Baltic certainly came to the pope's attention, even if that attention was focused not on the Western Slavic territories, but rather further to the east. In September 1171 or 1172, the pope issued the bull *Non parum animus*, which was addressed to the kings, princes, and all the faithful in the kingdoms of the Danes, Norwegians, and Swedes. The bull exhorted them to take up arms against the pagan Estonians who were threatening the church and Christians alike. In the letter, the pope promises that everyone who took part in the fight would receive:

---

65 Tamm, "How to Justify a Crusade," 442; Bysted et al., *Jerusalem in the North*, 48. See also Kahl, *Compellere intrare*," 178–79; Lotter, "The Crusading Idea"; Jensen, *Korstog ved verdens yderste rand*, 408. See also the discussions about the older roots of crusading thought in Jensen, "Danske korstog"; Jensen, "Martyrs, Total War, and Heavenly Horses," 91–120.

66 Saxo, 14:39.1–49. Saxo's description is very detailed; see, e.g., the almost iconic account of the destruction of the idol of Svantevits, v. 31–33. See also Bysted et al., *Jerusalem in the North*, 59–76; Fonnesberg-Schmidt, *The Popes and the Baltic Crusades 1147–1254*, 43–52.

67 Saxo 14:39:45 and 47. With regards to the transformation of pagan lands into Christian places and the rise of new holy landscapes, see the recent discussion in Gregory Leighton, *Ideology and Holy Landscape in the Baltic Crusades* (Amsterdam: Arc Humanities, 2022).

68 Fonnesberg-Schmidt, *The Popes and the Baltic Crusades*, 27–37; Fonnesberg-Schmidt, "Pope Honorius III and Mission and Crusades in the Baltic Region," 103.

69 Fonnesberg-Schmidt, *The Popes and the Baltic Crusades*, 39 and 63; Dragnea, *The Wendish Crusade, 1147*, 40.

one year's remission of the sins for which they have made confession and received a penance as we are accustomed to grant those who go to the Lord's Sepulchre. To those who die in this fight we grant remission of all their sins, if they have received a penance.[70]

Like Bernard of Clairvaux had done with regards to the Western Slavs, Alexander III emphasized that this was a defensive war: the Estonians threatened Christians and threatened the church. In doing so, Alexander also sanctioned his predecessors' acknowledgment that forcible conversion of the pagans might be necessary cases where they were actively fighting against Christians and were, thus, a threat to the church and the faithful. The letter also promised an indulgence that put those who took part in the fighting on equal footing with those who had visited the tomb of Jesus. Alexander III was referring here to the pilgrims who had travelled to the Church of the Holy Sepulchre in Jerusalem, earning themselves a year's indulgence in the process.[71]

The rhetoric of pilgrimage is clear enough, but the reduction of the length of the indulgence to just a year is also a notable change to Eugenius III's earlier promise of full (*plenar*) indulgence. It also seems that Alexander limited the other privileges which had been granted to the crusaders in the Baltic Sea area earlier on. These privileges included a special papal protection for the crusaders and their property while they were away on crusade. The reason behind the reduction in the scope of these privileges can be found in Alexander's concern that these military campaigns would lead to a reduction in the resources that could otherwise have been diverted towards the Holy Land. Relief provided by crusaders continued to be sorely needed there in this period. It seems that Alexander also scaled down the level of the indulgence promised to those who fought in Spain for the same reason.[72] Perhaps even more interesting in this context is a letter that Alexander III sent a few days later to all the Danes "who wish to live piously in Christ" (*qui pie volunt in Christo vivere*). The letter is dated September 17, and it includes an exhortation to help "our Brother Fulco, the Bishop of the Estonians" (*frater noster Fulco Estonum episcopus*).[73]

This is the first time that we hear about a bishop in Estonia, although it is not the first time that the sources mention a (semi) missionary campaign in that part of the Baltic. As previously mentioned, there had been commercial connections across the Bal-

---

70 DD 1:3.27: "De peccatis suis, de quibus confessi fuerint et poenitentiam acceperint, remissionem unius anni...sicut his qui sepulcrum dominicum uisitant concedere consueuimus. Illis autem, qui in conflictu illo decesserint, omnium suorum, si poenitentiam acceperint, remissionem indulgemus peccatorum." Translated in Fonnesberg-Schmidt, *The Popes and the Baltic Crusades 1147–1254*, 60; Hellmann, "Die Anfänge christlicher Mission in den baltischen Ländern," 12–13; Bysted et al., *Jerusalem in the North*, 139–43; Dragnea, *The Wendish Crusade, 1147*, 43.

71 Fonnesberg-Schmidt, *The Popes and the Baltic Crusades 1147–1254*, 60–61.

72 Fonnesberg-Schmidt, *The Popes and the Baltic Crusades 1147–1254*, 62–65, esp. 65.

73 DD 1:3.28. See also the discussion in Peep Peter Rebane, "From Fulco to Theoderic: The Changing Face of the Livonian Mission," in *Muinasaja loojangust omariikluse läveni: Pühendusteos Sulev Vahtre 75. sünnipäevaks*, ed. Andres Andressen (Tartu: Kleio, 2001), 37–68; Selart, "Die Eroberung Livlands," 169; Dragnea, *The Wendish Crusade, 1147*, 42–43.

tic Sea region for centuries and in his *Historia Hammaburgensis Ecclesiae* Adam of Bremen states that a Danish king—probably Svend Estridsen (r. 1047–1076)—had already
ordered a church to be built in Curonia.[74] Adam also tells us that the church was, in fact,
built by an energetic and adventurous Danish merchant who had been persuaded by
the king to settle in Curonia on what appears to have been a permanent basis. In return
for his efforts, the king offered the merchant gifts because of his willingness to commit
himself to such a new daunting enterprise. Nothing seems to indicate, however, that the
construction of this particular church was in any way part of an overall plan to initiate a systematic and thorough missionary enterprise among the local pagan people in
Curonia.[75] Adam of Bremen does, however, also mention that in the 1060s—before the
abovementioned Danish settlement in Curonia—the archbishopric of Hamburg-Bremen
had appointed a missionary bishop whose task it was to Christianize the "islands in the
Baltic Sea" (*insulas Baltici maris destinatus est*).[76] At first, this bishop took residence
(or simply overwintered) at the important market place in Birka in Sweden, halfway
between the Danish lands and "the land of the Rus" (*Ruzziam*).[77] "Ruzziam" is in all likelihood used by Adam as a collective term covering both Livonia, Estonia, Curonia as well
as the lands of the Rus' proper. These territories all seem to have been pretty much the
same to Adam, and some hundred years later, the popes continued to refer to Livonia as
essential a part of *Ruthenia*.[78] It has been suggested that the planned target area of the
German mission in the eleventh century could either have been the important Estonian
island of Saaremaa in the north or Curonia further to the south. We do not know exactly
what came of this planned mission, but the aforementioned bishop seems not to have
been alone. Adam actually mentions other missionary bishops from Hamburg-Bremen
who had all been sent to do the Lord's work among those pagans who were living along
the periphery of the Christian lands.

   Not all of these bishops, however, were spiritually suited to the job according to
Adam. He states in his chronicle that some of them remained outside of the Lord's vineyard, seeking "only their own, and not what belonged to Jesus Christ" (*sua querentes,
non quae Iesu Christi*).[79] They simply did not have the courage to commit themselves
to the hard and dangerous work as missionaries among the "wild" pagan peoples.

---

74 Adam of Bremen, IV.16–17. See also Edgar Anderson, "Early Danish Missionaries in the
Baltic Countries," in *Gli inizi del cristianesimo in Livonia-Lettonia, atti del Colloquio internazionale
di storia ecclesiastica in occasione dell'VIII centenario della Chiesa in Livonia (1186–1986)*, ed.
Michele Maccarrone (Città della Vaticana: Libreria Editrice Vaticana, 1989), 252 and 265. See
also the discussion in the following: Ilmar Arens, "Zur Frage der ältesten Berührungen mit
dem Christentum," *Papers of the Estonian Theological Society in Exile* 15 (1965), 25–43; Evalds
Mugurevics, "Die Verbreitung des Christentums in Lettland vom 11 Jahrhundert bis zum Anfang
des 13 Jahrhunderts," in *Rom und Byzanz im* Norden, 1–2, ed. Michael Müller-Wille (Stuttgart:
Franz-Steiner, 1989), 2:81–96.

75 Adam of Bremen, IV.16.

76 Adam of Bremen, III.77 (addition 94).

77 Adam of Bremen, IV.20 (addition 126).

78 Marika Mägi, "Deres største styrke er skibe," in ed. Jensen et al., *Da Danskerne fik Dannebrog*, 71.

79 Adam of Bremen, III.77.

In this way, says Adam, they failed utterly in their Christian duties but at the same time he clearly suggests that a mission among the Baltic people may have been on the mind of the northern churches already in the eleventh century, some hundred years before Pope Alexander III formally appointed Brother Fulco to the post as bishop of the Estonians.

While it has been suggested that there was also an early Swedish presence in the northern parts of Estonia that could have brought a certain degree of Christian influence in its wake, there is no definite proof to such an early Swedish missionary efforts among the northernmost Estonians at this early point.[80] Furthermore, resent archaeological investigations in modern-day Latvia also suggest an early Danish presence in the region which is otherwise unknown from contemporary sources. The archaeological research coupled with close readings of the available written source material have been focused especially on the island of Mārtiņsala (referred to in the chronicle of Henry of Livonia as *Holme*) located in the Daugava River some 10–15 kilometres upstream from present-day Riga. A (tower) castle on the island is mentioned several times in the chronicle of Henry of Livonia, who refers to the place as *Castrum Holme*. In his chronicle, Henry claims that the castle was built as a refuge for the local people with the direct support of the first German missionaries who went there in the 1180s to establish a permanent mission among the local pagan Livic and Lettgallian people. In return for a fortified refuge, the locals had promised to accept Christianity and become baptized.[81] As we shall see later, a similar castle was build a little further upstream in the Livic village of Ikšķile with the help of stonemasons from Gotland. This castle is also said to have been constructed in return for the local's conversion into Christendom.[82] The castle in Ikšķile, however, also came to serve as the German bishop's first, fortified residence in Livonia on his appointment as bishop in 1186.[83] In both cases, the locals lapsed back into paganism as soon as the castles had been erected and Henry subsequently refers to Mārtiņsala as the seed bed for an especially strong (pagan) opposition to the Christian mission around Ikšķile. The locals threatened to kill the German bishops and instigated violent uprisings on several occasions during the early phase of the German based mission in Livonia.[84]

Archaeological surveys seem to indicate that the two strongholds of Mārtiņsala and Ikšķile respectively had two distinctly different layouts. This suggests different master builders and probably different times of construction, with the one on Mārtiņsala being older and pointing towards Scandinavia. This particular castle on Mārtiņsala also seems to have been a strictly military installation whereas the castle at Ikšķile served

---

80 The thesis was originally presented by Paul Johansen, *Nordische Mission: Revals Gründung und die Schwedensiedlung in Estland* (Stockholm: Wahlström och Widstrand, 1951), 132. See also the discussion in Hellmann, "Die Anfänge christlicher Mission," 11; Bernhart Jähnig, "Die Anfänge der Sakraltopographie von Riga," in *Studien zu den Anfängen der Mission in Livland*, ed. Manfred Hellmann (Sigmaringen: Thorbecke, 1989), 124–25. For a general analysis of the region's history as regards colonization and Christianization, see Blomkvist, *The Discovery of the Baltic*.

81 HCL 1:7.

82 HCL 1:6.

83 HCL 1:5–6.

84 See for example HCL 2:2.

not only military purposes but also functioned as an episcopal residence, as a refuge for the locals, and perhaps even as a safe storage place for German merchants.[85] The name *Castrum Holme* has also been interpreted as having a distinct Scandinavian-Danish origin through the term "Holm," referring in the Danish language to a small island or islet, that was a common feature in Denmark at the time. Taken together, this could indicate an early Danish presence in Livonia at the lower run of the Daugava River that outdates the arrival of the Germans by decades.[86] This is something that Henry of Livonia is completely silent about, since his primary interest was to assert the full and unchallenged legitimacy of the Livonian Church against any foreign claim for supremacy, such as from the Danish kings and archbishops.[87] Furthermore, sources outside Henry of Livonia refer to the neighbouring island of Dole (lying next to Mārtiņsala) as "the Kings Island" (*Insula Regis*). This has been interpreted as a reference to a Danish king, which could either have been the aforementioned Svend Estridsen, or perhaps more likely, one of his sons, King Knud IV (r. 1080–1086) or King Erik I Ejegod (r. 1095–1103), who were both heavily involved in various activities in the Baltic Sea region during their periods of reign.[88] A final argument supporting the assumption of an early Danish (or at least a Scandinavian) presence along the lower runs of the Daugava River is the local peoples fierce opposition towards the German mission as described by Henry of Livonia. This exceptionally strong opposition may not only have been rooted solely in pagan opposition to a Christian mission, but could also be related to the fact that the German missionaries represented new masters in the region thereby threatening the more or less autonomous status of the (possible) Scandinavian merchant outpost in Livonia.[89] The alleged leader of the rebellious Livs was a man by the name Ako. He was eventually killed during a final uprising in 1206 and his head taken to the German Bishop Albert (1199–1229) to prove that the rebellion had been crushed once and for all so that the missionary work could commence. Incidentally, the suppression of this particular rebellion in Livonia happened at a point in time when the Danes were very active in the region, although further to the north, challenging the alleged supremacy of the German Church in Livonia. A presumed hostile enclave with ties towards the Danes located at the very heart of the German controlled territories in Livonia may simply not have been acceptable to Bishop Albert.

Even if these clues and proposed interpretations are at best circumstantial, they could point towards a quite early Scandinavian (probably Danish) presence at the lower run of the Daugava River suggesting some early (Christian) influence from Scandinavia

---

85 Kersti Markus, *Visual Culture and Politics in the Baltic Sea Region, 1100–1250* (Leiden: Brill, 2020), 243–45; Kersti Markus, "Danskernes støttepunkter og handelsruter," in Jensen et al., *Da Danskerne fik Dannebrog*, 118–29.

86 Markus, *Visual Culture*, 252–55; Markus, "Danskernes støttepunkter og handelsruter," 120.

87 Markus, *Visual Culture*, 255.

88 Markus, *Visual Culture*, 251; Markus, "Danskernes støttepunkter og handelsruter," 120–22.

89 See HCL 10:8 and 25:2. A further argument about the Scandinavian or perhaps even Danish routings of the people of Mārtiņsala has been put forward by Kersti Markus. She suggests that Ako could be of Scandinavian/Danish origin since it was a very common name in Denmark at the time; see Markus, "Danskernes støttepunkter og handelsruter," 124; Markus, *Visual Culture*, 255.

towards the local Letgallian and Livic people that predates the more permanent German mission of the 1180s. That may also help explain Pope Alexander's sudden interest in a permanent mission among the Estonians in the 1170s when initiated by the Danish archbishop. Livonia and Estonia were not, after all, totally *terra incognita* to the popes in the later part of the twelfth century.[90]

Returning to the Cistercian monk and to-be-missionary, Fulco, it has been assumed that he may have been consecrated as a missionary bishop by the Danish Archbishop Eskil (r. 1137–1181) at some point while the archbishop himself was absent from Denmark.[91] In another letter, this time dated to September of the same year, either 1171 or 1172, the pope requests that the archbishop of Trondheim and the bishop of Stavanger help Bishop Fulco in his forthcoming missionary work. He asks that they ensure that one Nicholas, a monk "who comes from this people" (*de gente illo...est oriundus*), be allowed to accompany him.[92] As such, Nicholas seems to have come from Estonia and, at some point, became a Christian, ending up in Norway where he became a monk in the Augustinian priory at Stavanger. Apart from this reference to Nicholas in the specific letter, we know nothing about him or his fate. Some scholars have suggested that he might have come from Estonia along with Norwegian seafarers, who could have named him after their patron saint, St. Nicholas of Myra.[93] The baptism of local boys and their subsequent schooling in the Christian faith to become priests and missionaries among their own people is certainly a well-attested phenomenon in missionary history.[94] As an example, Henry of Livonia describes this same practice among Livonian and Estonian boys, who were sent to monasteries in Germany (mostly Saxony) so that they could later work as missionaries amongst their own people.[95] There are good grounds, then, for thinking that Nicholas from Stavanger may well have been an early example of a practice that had broad currency in the eastern part of the Baltic.

Fulco received support from the pope and presumably also from the local ecclesiastical authorities in Denmark and Norway. However, we know little about his journey to Estonia, or whether he even ever got there. One of the papal letters mentions that he was prevented from travelling at one point because of great floods, but we do not know where they occurred. There is also no clear evidence that he ever made it to Estonia,

90 Dragnea, *The Wendish Crusade, 1147*, 43.

91 DD 1:3.34. See also Bysted et al., *Jerusalem in the North*, 140; Hellmann, "Die Anfänge christlicher Mission in den baltischen Ländern," 12; Johansen, *Nordische Mission*, 90ff; Selart, "Die Eroberung Livlands," 169.

92 DD 1:3.26. See also Hellmann, "Die Anfänge christlicher Mission in den baltischen Ländern," 12; Dragnea, *The Wendish Crusade, 1147*, 42.

93 Hellmann, "Die Anfänge christlicher Mission in den baltischen Ländern," 12–13.

94 Lutz E. von Padberg, *Die Inszenierung religiöser Konfrontationen: Theorie und Praxis der Missionspredigt im frühen Mittelalter* (Stuttgart: Hierseman, 2003), 49; Olav Tveito, *Ad fines orbis terrae: Like til jordens ender. En studie i primær trosformidling i nordisk kristningskontekst* (Oslo: Unipub, 2005), 240.

95 See, e.g., HCL 10: 7, where Henry mentions a local convert called Johannes who was ordained a priest.

although some scholars have assumed that he lived among the Estonians for five years before returning to Denmark and from there continued to France in 1180. No actual documentation for this assumption is found in the sources, however.[96]

As suggested above, Alexander III did consider the war against the Estonians to be a defensive war and thereby also a just war. Other sources indicate that, in the summer of 1170, raiders from Estonia and Curonia had attacked the coastal regions of Blekinge and Öland, where they unexpectedly ran into a Danish fleet under the leadership of the Danish Duke Christoffer and Bishop Absalon.[97] This and similar pagan raids against Christian lands intensified Swedish missionary activities in Finland at that same time and might have resulted in the issue of the papal bulls by the pope. But these did not change the papal view of the missionary work in the Baltic region, which continued for some time to be organized and carried out on the initiative of local and regional powers.[98]

Looking more closely at the sources, it becomes clear there are, in fact, many other witnesses to Scandinavian involvement in the eastern part of the Baltic that more or less coincide with the time of the early German missionary endeavours in Livonia. Various sources relate, for example, that Danes went to Estonia in 1184, and again in 1196 or 1197. Danish campaigns in Finland in 1191 and 1202 are also mentioned; the latter probably took place under the leadership of Archbishop Anders Sunesen.[99] We also know that Swedish campaigns had taken place in Finland as far back as the 1120s, as well as in 1155 or 1157, which had a more lasting impact on the region. Unlike the Danish campaigns, these Swedish campaigns can be best characterized as individual episodes within a long-term Swedish involvement in the region.[100] The sources also mention that the Norwegians undertook a campaign in Estonia in 1185 (or 1188) with a modest fleet

---

96 Hellmann, "Die Anfänge christlicher Mission," 13; Dragnea, *The Wendish Crusade, 1147*, 42. Fulco's journey home is mentioned in DD 1:3.88. For further discussions, see Bysted et al., *Jerusalem in the North*, 140–41; Fonnesberg-Schmidt, *The Popes and the Baltic Crusades 1147–1254*, 53–55. A number of letters referring to Fulco can be found in the *Diplomatarium Danicae*, but none of them offers any secure indications of whether any possible missionary work was carried out in Estonia. In addition to the document already mentioned, see also DD 1:3.21, 1:3.22, 1:3.26, 1:3.28, 1:3.29, 1:3.34, 1:3.81, 1:3.88, and 1:3.91. The last letter is dated 1180 and the flooding is mentioned in DD 1:3.29.

97 Saxo, 14:40.3–11. The events are also described in the *Knytlinga Saga* (chapter 123). For an edition in English, see *Knytlinga Saga: The History of the Kings of Denmark*, ed. Hermann Pálsson and Paul Edwards (Odense: Odense University Press, 1986). See also Anderson, "Early Danish Missionaries in the Baltic Countries," 265.

98 Bysted et al., *Jerusalem in the North*, 140–41; Fonnesberg-Schmidt, *The Popes and the Baltic Crusades 1147–1254*, 56–57.

99 Saxo writes about the early campaign of 1184 (16:4.3), and the *Annales Ryenses* mentions the campaign of 1196. The *Older Chronicle of Sjælland* mentions the campaign in Finland in 1191. Details of the campaign in 1202 are only found in a younger translation of the *Annales Ryenses* in Danish. See Kromann, *Danmarks middelalderlige annaler*, 199. For these chronicles, see in general the editions mentioned above. A Danish expedition (*expeditio*) in 1210 to Prussia and Sambia is also mentioned in the *Annales Ryenses*.

100 Bysted et al., *Jerusalem in the North*, 141–42 and 145–55, here especially 147; Hellmann, "Die Anfänge christlicher Mission," 11; Dragnea, *The Wendish Crusade, 1147*, 44.

of five ships, one of which was under the command of a priest named Osur.[101] Taken together, the papal bulls and the concrete expeditions towards Estonia seem to suggest a special interest for this part of the Baltic among Scandinavian magnates in the later part of the twelfth century, paving the way for the Danish conquest proper of Estonia in the early decades of the thirteenth century.

Papal Involvement in the Livonian and Estonian Mission after 1200

We saw in the introduction to this chapter how, through most of the twelfth century, the papacy was largely reluctant to respond to calls for support from local participants in the Christianization of the Baltic areas. The same was also true in the pontificate of Innocent III, who received frequent appeals for support for expeditions and missionary campaigns on the part of both Danish and German actors in the Baltic Sea area.[102] There are several surviving papal letters from the early thirteenth century that deal with the Danish mission in Estonia and the German involvement in Livonia.[103] Analysis of these letters has demonstrated a certain interest on Innocent's part in supporting the conversion of the pagans through the dissemination of the Christian faith, as well as in preventing new converts from apostatizing.[104] Although Innocent III draws a certain equivalence between the Holy Land and the campaigns in Livonia and Estonia in some of his letters, he did not promise the same full (*plenar*) indulgences in these letters that he promised in his letters focused on the Holy Land.[105] This practice marks him out from some of his predecessors, and certainly from his successor Honorius III (r. 1216–1227), who stated the equivalence between the various crusading areas more clearly. Innocent

---

101 Bysted et al., *Jerusalem in the North*, 141. On a more legendary level one of the hagiographical accounts of the deeds of the Norwegian Saint Olaf Haraldsson (r. 1015–1128, died 1030), the Oxford-version of the *Passio et Miracula Beati Olau* from around 1180 mentions two young Estonian boys who had had recently (in the 1180s) converted and visiting St. Olaf's church in Nidaros; Kersti Markus, "From Rus' Trade to Crusade: St. Olaf's Churches in the Eastern Baltic Sea Region," *Acta Historica Tallinnensia* 23 (2017), 3–25.

102 The pontificate of Innocent III is handled in detail in Fonnesberg-Schmidt, *The Popes and the Baltic Crusades*, 79–131, here 83). See also Fonnesberg-Schmidt, "Pope Honorius III and Mission and Crusades in the Baltic Region," 104. See also the older account in Helmut Roscher, *Papst Innocenz III und die Kreuzzüge* (Göttingen: Vandenhoeck, 1969), 179–81; Benno Abers, "Zur päpstlichen Missionspolitik in Lettland und Estland zur Zeit Innocenz' III," *Commentationes Balticae*, 4–5 (1958), 3–18. The latter is especially preoccupied with the relations between Bishop Albert and the later Estonian bishop, Theoderic, and with their respective relationships with the papacy under Innocent III. See also Christian Krötzl, "Finnen, Liven, Russen: Zur päpstlichen Politik im nördlichen Ostseeraum im 12. und 13. Jahrhundert," in *Ab Aquilone: Nordic Studies in Honor and Memory of Leonard E. Boyle, O. P.*, ed. Marie-Louise Rodén (Stockholm: Swedish National Archives, 1999), 44–56; Dragnea, *The Wendish Crusade, 1147*, 46.

103 See, e.g., DD 1:3.254 (1199); 1:4.162–64 and 173 (1209–1210); 1:4.109 and 1:5.13, 1:5.61 (1215). See also Fonnesberg-Schmidt, *The Popes and the Baltic Crusades 1147–1254*, 85–86.

104 Fonnesberg-Schmidt, *The Popes and the Baltic Crusades 1147–1254*, 91; Dragnea, *The Wendish Crusade, 1147*, 46–47.

105 Fonnesberg-Schmidt, *The Popes and the Baltic Crusades 1147–1254*, 97.

III offered a more limited form of indulgence when it came to the campaigns in the Baltic Sea area. This has led many scholars to assume that the campaigns in the Baltic had a lower priority for the pope than other crusades current at the time.[106] It is important, however, to emphasize the fact that Innocent III primarily directed his attention at two subjects: the defence of the Holy Land and the fight against the heretic Cathars in southern France. It is clear, therefore, that he shared some of his predecessors' worries about letting areas such as Livonia and Estonia leach away valuable resources from the areas that he considered to be more important in the immediate term. Papal support can certainly appear to have been rather sporadic. But this is entirely understandable from the perspective of the strategy of the papal church's policy at the time, which suggests something other—or perhaps something more—than a simple neglect or lack of interest in what happening in the eastern part of the Baltic Sea area. It is clear that the pope entrusted the planning and implementation of the crusades in the Baltic to local magnates and churchmen. This has led historians to characterize these campaigns as "papally authorized royal warfare in the service of the Church."[107] This idea continued to have currency in Innocent III's time.[108] Several studies have shown, furthermore, that Innocent III—like his predecessors—was not himself particularly interested in launching a widespread or systematic missionary campaign among the non-Christians who lived beyond the borders of Christendom. This could also have influenced his view of the Baltic Crusades, since time and again he emphasized that individual expeditions should aim to protect the church in the first instance, its missionaries, and the newly converted against continual attack from the pagans.[109]

Honorius III, however, decisively changed the curia's view of the missionary work being undertaken in Livonia and Estonia. It was Honorius, for example, who acceded to the Livonian Bishop Albert's wish to have a papal legate sent to the area some seven years after the important Danish attack on Estonia in 1219. We know a fair amount about the legate's visit in 1226–1227 from Henry's chronicle describing the legate as a prelate who went to great lengths to visit the congregations in the area, whom he first admonished and then encouraged to live a god-fearing and Christian life.[110] The legate's name was William of Modena (ca. 1185–1251), and he also sat as a papal judge delegate over the conflicts between the Sword Brethren, Bishop Albert, and the Danes in Estonia, which revolved around their claims to the contested Estonian provinces. Furthermore

---

106 Fonnesberg-Schmidt, *The Popes and the Baltic Crusades 1147–1254*, 98.

107 Fonnesberg-Schmidt, *The Popes and the Baltic Crusades 1147–1254*, 102–105.

108 Lotter, "The Crusading Idea," 291–92; Jensen, "God's War," 139. See also the discussion in Alan V. Murray, "'Adding to the Multitude of Fish: Pope Innocent III, Bishop Albert of Riga and the Conversion of the Indigenous Peoples of Livonia," in *The Fourth Lateran Council and the Crusade Movement*, ed. J. L. Bird and D. J. Smith (Turnhout: Brepols, 2018), 153–70.

109 Kedar, "Crusade and Mission," 131, note 122; Fonnesberg-Schmidt, *The Popes and the Baltic Crusades 1147–1254*, 92–3 and 119–22.

110 Dragnea, *The Wendish Crusade, 1147*, 54–56.

he held an important church council in Riga to signal that the Christianization of the area had been brought to a (temporary) conclusion.[111]

The legate's visit should probably be viewed as evidence that the papacy's view on its active involvement in missionary work and crusading in the area had fundamentally shifted. It appears from Honorius III's letters that he had instructed William to preach to the faithful during his visit to Livonia and Estonia.[112] This was entirely consistent with the higher priority that Honorius placed on the mission to non-Christians, which he had set in motion some years before William's journey north. Honorius spoke in detail of the lands beyond "the Lord's vineyard" (*vinea Domini*), which needed expert evangelists to preach to the pagans and unbelievers, and convert them to Christianity.[113] Like his predecessors, Honorius III understood the use of force to be a natural and necessary part of missionary work, which was used partly in order to protect the missionaries, and partly to lessen the opportunity for any potential opponents to resist the Christian mission.[114] However, Honorius broke, to some extent, with his predecessors in regard to the spiritual rewards traditionally associated with the crusading vow. In 1217, he promised the same full indulgence to those who were campaigning in Prussia that was offered to those fighting in the Holy Land. He also promised an indulgence to those who did not them-

---

111 There are various sources for the legate's deeds in Livonia and Estonia. See, e.g., LEC 1:1.86–87 (concerning the relationship between the bishop and Riga); 1:1.89, 95–96, and 1:3.93–98 (concerning the conflict between the bishop and the Sword Brothers); and 1:1.90–91 (concerning the conflicts between the bishop, the town and the Dünamünde Abbey). See also Fonnesberg-Schmidt, *The Popes and the Baltic Crusades 1147–1254*, 135; Tamm, "How to Justify a Crusade," 436.

112 William undertook a total of three official trips to the area: in 1225–1226, he visited Livonia and Estonia; in 1228–1230, he visited Prussia; and in 1234–1242 he travelled through most of the Baltic Sea region. Fonnesberg-Schmidt, *The Popes and the Baltic Crusades 1147–1254*, 175. Authorization for a possible elevation of the see of Riga to an archdiocese was given by the pope on November 19, 1225. See "Regesten Wilhelm's von Modena," SRP II, 120.

113 See, e.g., DD 1:6.29 and 1:5.192, which refer respectively to William's legatine authority and the pope's favoured metaphor for the ongoing missionary work, *vinea Domini*. See also Fonnesberg-Schmidt, "Pope Honorius III and Mission and Crusades in the Baltic Region," 105–06 and 110; Fonnesberg-Schmidt, *The Popes and the Baltic Crusades 1147–1254*, 162–68. For a more detailed discussion of the use of the motif of the vineyard in papal crusading and missionary rhetoric, see Beverly Mayne Kienzle, *Cistercians, Heresy and Crusade in Occitania, 1145–1229* (York: Boydell, 2001), 150–55.

114 Fonnesberg-Schmidt, *The Popes and the Baltic Crusades 1147–1254*, 137. Fonnesberg-Schmidt's analysis of Honorius's letter leads her to consider the extent to which the wording of the papal letters actually authorized the use of force in the conversion of the pagans. I am of the opinion that this is an anachronistic reading of the texts in question, which does not take account of Honorius III's (or his contemporaries') way of thinking. As noted above, the ideas expressed in the papal letters were wholly consistent with Augustine's views on the question. They were also consistent with Bernard of Clairvaux's later views regarding the necessity of destroying the pagans' ability to hinder missionary work. The latter would be explicitly formulated under Honorius IV (r. 1285–1287), who clearly stated the view that force could be used to impose Christian preaching upon the pagans. See Jensen, "God's War," 133–39. See also the account of forcible conversion vs. peaceful mission in Kahl, "Die ersten Jahrhunderte des missionsgeschichtlichen Mittelalters," 42–45 and 60–71.

selves have the opportunity to go on crusade but who sent someone else on their behalf. The crusades in the Baltic Sea area thus were put on an equal footing with the crusades in the Holy Land. This could only benefit the expeditions to Livonia and Estonia.[115]

Honorius III's use of biblical references are also interesting in the context of his prioritizing of the missionary work and the care of the newly converted. The comparison between the vital work of the missionaries with that of the labourers in the vineyard (Matthew 20.1–16) was one of Honorius's favourites; similarly, he also often compared the missionaries' work with the gospels invocation of harvest labourers (John 4.35–38): that the "harvest is great, but the laborers are few" was a worry that Honorius often expressed in his letters, using some well-known biblical formulas (Matthew 9.36–38; Luke 10.2).[116] This was wholly in line with the pope's thinking: he had repeatedly upbraided priests and monks for having neglected their duties regarding the non-Christians, and had made it clear that those missionaries who obediently and willingly went out to evangelize and convert pagans and nonbelievers should be seen as the new apostles.[117] This is not a unique or even exceptional use of biblical imagery in a missionary context, but it is nevertheless striking how explicit the pope was in his figurative language.

The later decades of the twelfth century and the early decade of the thirteenth century were an extremely important period with regards to the overall military conquest of Livonia and Estonia, demonstrating, among other things, the deep involvement of the Danes in fierce competition with German missionaries and soon-to-be crusaders in Livonia. During these decades, papal support also shifted from a rather reactive stand to a more active involvement in the political and ecclesiastical matters that went on in the region so far from Rome but that were still considered to be part of the Lord's vineyard. In the next chapter, we will have a closer look at Denmark as a society organized for war and military expansion around 1200, while we also return to German involvement in Livonia and their first forays into Estonia in the chapter after that.

I15 PrUB 1:1.15. See also Fonnesberg-Schmidt, *The Popes and the Baltic Crusades 1147–1254*, 139–40 and 143–44; Fonnesberg-Schmidt, "Pope Honorius III and Mission and Crusades in the Baltic Region," 121.

I16 DD 1:6.29. Dragnea, *The Wendish Crusade, 1147*, 54–55; Fonnesberg-Schmidt, "Pope Honorius III and Mission and Crusades in the Baltic Region," 109–10.

I17 Honorius III was clearly disappointed with some of the older orders' unwillingness to engage in missionary work, and he persistently tried to make the Dominicans and the Franciscans take an active role in the mission to the non-Christians; see Fonnesberg-Schmidt, "Pope Honorius III and Mission and Crusades in the Baltic Region," 112 and 114; Fonnesberg-Schmidt, *The Popes and the Baltic Crusades 1147–1254*, 168–70 and 174–75. In this context, it is worth considering whether Bishop Albert might have been worried by the prospect of welcoming two new orders to Livonia, both of which were exempt from episcopal control. This could be an alternative explanation for why Henry placed such emphasis on the zeal and piety with which the older orders' representatives carried out their missionary work in the area. A few years after Albert's death, the first mendicants came to Livonia and settled in Riga; they also became involved in other places in the Baltic Sea area. See Jähnig, "Die Anfänge der Sakraltopographie von Riga," 158; Bysted et al., *Jerusalem in the North*, 260–64.

Chapter 3

A SOCIETY ORGANIZED FOR WAR

DENMARK AT THE BEGINNING
OF THE THIRTEENTH CENTURY

THE SUCCESSFUL SUBJUGATION of the Western Slavic people between the Elbe River and Eastern Pomerania in the later part of the twelfth century made the Danes turn their attention towards the troublesome (according to Saxo Grammaticus) people of Estonia. They had continually raided the easternmost provinces of Denmark, Skåne, and Blekinge in modern-day Sweden, while also attacking ships in open waters in their quest for booty and captives, says Saxo. A similar view is found in the chronicle of Henry of Livonia, who, at one point, indignantly records the consequences of these attacks where endless numbers of enslaved young Christian (Scandinavian) women were forced into marrying pagan men because of the slave-raiding marauders.[1] As we have already seen, the Estonians were indeed frequently engaged in various forms of warfare and raiding activities as an integrated part of their societal structures.[2] The islanders of Saaremaa were, in that respect, especially renowned for their superior naval power equalled only by the Danes. Quite often, the people from Saaremaa operated in close alliance with their Curonian cousins during such raids while, at the same time, eagerly protecting their own dominant position in the eastern parts of the Baltic Sea region. Consequently, they would do anything in their power to ward off the encroachment of any foreign people venturing too deep into their spheres of interest, like the Danes or the Germans for exmple, who looked more and more like a serious threat to the Estonians. The term "Curonians" actually seems to have been used as a generic term to simply refer to seaborne pirates, whether they were in fact from Curonia, from Saaremaa, from coastal Estonia, or from someplace else.[3]

The relationship between the Danes and the people of Saaremaa and their Curonian allies did have very long historical roots with intermingling periods of trading and raiding. As is already mentioned, Saxo suggested that sheer boredom enticed the Danes to attack Estonia when things became too quiet at home for them![4] Both parties—the Danes and the Estonians—possessed very powerful naval forces that were frequently brought into action during various military expeditions. Both parties were

---

1 HCL 30:1. For the original text in Danish, see Jensen, *Med ord og ikke med slag*, 105–12.

2 With regards to the topic of exploiting the enemy through raiding, see especially Kristjan Kaljusaar, "Exploiting the Conquerors: Socio-political Strategies of Estonian Elites During the Crusades and Christianization, 1200–1300," in *Baltic Crusades and Societal Innovation in Medieval Livonia, 1200–1350*, ed. Anti Selart (Leiden: Brill 2022), 59.

3 See discussions in Heebøll-Holm, "Between Pagan Pirates and Glorious Sea-Warriors," and Mägi, *The Viking Eastern Baltic*, 10–14.

4 Saxo 16:4.3.

also helped by different forms of treaties and written agreements that allowed them to sail freely through waters and use certain "neutral" harbours as stop-overs or meeting points. Henry of Livonia has a specific reference to such non-attack-agreements between the people on Saaremaa and the merchants in Visby on Gotland, and also mentions a neutral harbour on Saaremaa itself that was used by ships from Riga sailing for Visby despite the (mostly) extremely warlike relationship between the pagan islanders and the Germans in Riga.[5] A similar arrangement may also have been behind a particular incident referred to by Saxo who describes the clash in 1170 between a Danish naval force and some Estonian and Curonian pirates harrying the waters around the island of Öland. It seems from the chronicle that the Estonians and Curonians were operating out of a nearby harbour—probably on Öland itself. Despite warnings, the Danes were lured into a reckless, unprepared attack on the enemy ships that had been beached and pulled out of the water while the Estonians and Curonians hid in a prepared ambush not far from them. Saxo says that when a smaller part of the Danish fleet reached the beach and disembarked in an unorderly fashion, and in no coherent battle order, they were immediately attacked by the enemy warriors. The Danes were killed almost to the man while the Estonians and Curonians hacked huge holes in the Danish ships and quickly prepared a provisional fortification on the beach for the expected counter attacks by the remainder of the Danish forces.[6] Having reconsidered their tactics, the Danes made landfall a short distance from the actual harbour area, while leaving a few ships on guard should the pagans try to escape. This time the Danes prepared themselves properly and Saxo explains how the warriors who had the best armour were placed in the front ranks while the lesser well-armed stood in the rear ranks. A very brutal encounter then ensued, ending in a total Danish victory which saw all of the pagans killed. Saxo states that the common men among the Danes who had been killed during the fighting were buried on the spot while the bodies of the more prominent men were preserved in salt and taken home for a proper burial.[7]

This example seems very typical of the constant, low-intensity type of warfare that existed between the Danes and the Estonians with the occasional involvement of German, Swedish, Norwegian, and Curonian forces; each trying to protect their local and regional trading networks while at the same time hunting for slaves and rich booty.[8]

---

5 HCL 19:5–6, 7:2 and 14:3. Carsten Selch Jensen, "Fighting in the Wilderness: Military Campaigning in 13th Century Livonia with a Special Focus on Coastal and Riverine Warfare Summer and Winter," to be published in *The Material Culture of Medieval Warfare*, ed. Alan V. Murray and James Titterton (Leiden: Brill 2023), aprox. twenty pages; Mägi, "Deres største styrke er skibe," 74–76 with an image of the reconstructed harbour facilities on Saaremaa. See also Marika Mägi, "Saaremaa and the Danish Kingdom: Revisiting Henry's Chronicle and the Archaeological Evidence," in Tamm et al., *Crusading and Chronicle Writing*, 317–41.

6 Saxo 14:40.3–4.

7 Saxo 14:40.10–11.

8 For a general discussion on this type of low-intensity type of warfare—the *petite guerre*—in the high medieval period, see John France, "Medieval Irregular Warfare, c. 1000–1300," *Journal of Medieval Military History* 14 (2017), 123–32. With regards to developments in naval warfare in the Baltic Sea region during the twelfth and thirteenth centuries, see also Beñat Elortza Larrea, "The

Obviously, the Danish counterattacks (and occasional victories) did not deter the Estonians from renewing attacks in any decisive way. On the contrary, they raided Danish lands in the years to come, taking much booty and many people as slaves whenever possible.

Henry of Livonia mentions one particular incident in the year 1203 when a small fleet of German crusaders came upon a fleet from Saaremaa. The crusaders were travelling in the company of Bishop Albert on their way to Visby and, from there, onwards to Riga. The fleet from Saaremaa counted sixteen ships and probably around four hundred fifty fighting men.[9] The Estonians were on their way back home from a raiding expedition fully laden with booty taken from the Danish province of Blekinge (the peninsular of Listerland) in present-day Sweden. Churches had been burned, their bells and other belongings taken from them, says Henry, and many people killed while others were taken as slaves.[10]

In the first instance, the people from Saaremaa actually managed to convince the crusaders that they had a peace agreement with the people of Riga and, therefore, should not be attacked by the German crusaders. Shortly thereafter, however, the crusaders arrived at Visby and witnessed the very same islanders freely entering the same harbour laden with the aforementioned booty and many Christian slaves. The crusaders realized that the pagan Estonians also had a peace agreement with the citizens of Visby, allowing them to safely use the harbour on their way home to Saaremaa even while carrying Christian slaves and booty stolen from the Danes. This deeply offended the crusaders, though it is not clear from the text why they accepted the Saarema people's initial claim that they had a peace agreement with the people of Riga, but then found it unacceptable that a similar agreement existed between the people of Saaremaa and the people of Visby. Important, however, is the fact that such agreements were seemingly quite common at the time, enabling these various populations to travel freely even if they were technically on opposing sides in a divinely sanctioned war between Christians and pagans. The pragmatic reality clearly mingled with theological (and political) ideals!

Following a heated debate amongst the German crusaders, they persuaded Bishop Albert to let them attack the fleet from Saaremaa "for the remission of their sins" (*in remissionem eis peccatorum*).[11] A vicious naval battle ensued in which the German crusaders managed to conqueror two enemy ships, killing sixty enemy warriors (suggesting an average of about thirty men on a ship from Saaremaa) before bringing "the ships, loaded with bells, sacerdotal vestments, and captive Christians, to the city of Visby" (*indumentis sacerdotalibus et captivis christianis onerate ad civitatem Wysbu*

Transformation of Naval Warfare in Scandinavia during the Twelfth Century," *Journal of Medieval Military History* 18 (2020), 81–98.

9 An average of thirty men per ship seems to have been the norm among the people from Saaremaa as we shall see shortly from Henry of Livonia's own descriptions in his chronicle. See also Larrea, "The Transformation of Naval Warfare in Scandinavia," 94, with regards to the varying sizes of the local ship types in both Scandinavia and the Baltic.

10 HCL 7:1.

11 HCL 7:2.

Figure 1: King Valdemar II as he is
depicted on a contemporary royal seal.
From Niels Bache, *Nordens Historie*
(1881–1887). Public domain.

deducuntur).[12] Bishop Albert immediately shipped the freed Christians back to the Danish Archbishop Anders Sunesen, along with all the booty that had been retaken from the islanders.[13]

It seems plausible that these types of continued raids against the coastal regions of Eastern Denmark may have prompted King Valdemar to take more direct action against these troublesome marauders from Curonia, Saaremaa, and mainland Estonia. Following a number of lesser military expeditions in the later part of the twelfth century, the Danes began planning a major attack on the island of Saaremaa that was to take place in 1206.[14] A few years earlier, in 1202 King Valdemar II had succeeded his older brother, King Knud VI, to the throne, intent on continuing the expansive politic of his father and older brother.

On Valdemar's accession, Denmark was a dominating political and military power in the Baltic Sea region. While the king controlled the Danish heartlands of Jylland, Fyn, Sjælland, and Skåne, he also controlled sizeable territories in Northern Germany and the recently conquered Slavic territories from the Elbe River in the west to Pomerania in the east.[15] Furthermore, the king was a prominent player in the complicated inner-political games that were simultaneously being played out in the northernmost parts of the German empire. At the same time Danish ships ventured deep into the eastern part of the Baltic Sea in close competition with German, Swedish, and Norwegian merchants, missionaries, raiders, and (soon to be) crusaders coming toe-to-toe with the various locals. While alliances were forged between the newcomers and some of the

---

12 HCL 7:2.

13 HCL 7:4.

14 HCL 10:13.

15 Beñat Elortza Larrea, *Polity Consolidation and Military Transformation in Medieval Scandinavia: A European Perspective, c. 1035–1320*, The Northern World Series 94 (Leiden: Brill, 2023), 93–94.

local people as we have already seen, not everybody accepted the intrusion of foreigners into their lands and fiercely opposed any attempt to dominate or conquer their homelands. This was the case with the German conquest of Livonia, as we shall see in the next chapter, but certainly was also the case in Estonia—especially among the islanders from Saaremaa and the people living in the coastal regions: they fought hard to uphold their freedom and influential position in the region.

From a Danish perspective, King Valdemar II wanted to contain the military power of both the Curonians and the Estonians, focusing especially on Saaremaa while, at the same time, demonstrating his own military power.[16] As such, the attack in 1206 should be viewed as an important prequel to the conquest of Estonia proper in 1219 and the Battle of Lyndanise. According to Henry of Livonia, King Valdemar had been preparing himself for the attack on Saaremaa for nearly three years, collecting a huge army (*exercitu magno*) intent on taking vengeance on the pagans while subjecting them to Christianity. Apart from King Valdemar himself, Archbishop Anders Sunesen and Bishop Nicholas of Schleswig (r. 1209–1233) also took part in the expedition. We are also told that the archbishop signed a great many men with the cross, promising them indulgences in return for their military service, thus suggesting that the expedition was, in fact, considered to be a proper crusade by those who took part.[17]

Upon the arrival on Saaremaa, King Valdemar immediately ordered the construction of a stronghold (*castrum*), probably mostly out of wood since we are told a little later that it was easily burned down when the Danes left the island. Henry then continues his narrative of the Danish expedition by ridiculing the (lack of) bravery among the Danish crusaders. He states that none of the Danes dared to stay behind to garrison the stronghold when King Valdemar asked for volunteers and, at the same time, announced that he would return home with the rest of the fleet. Consequently, says Henry, the king ordered the stronghold to be burned down and immediately thereafter left Saaremaa with the entire army.

This story about timid and fearsome Danish warriors may not, however, be the most obvious interpretation of the strategical outcome of the Danish attack on Saaremaa in 1206. It seems more likely that Henry of Livonia simply chose this not so flattering description of the Danes and their lack of bravery to downplay the actual power of the Danish king who, in reality, threatened the supremacy of the Livonian Church through his obvious military capabilities and the close alliance with the primus of the Danish church, Archbishop Anders Sunesen.[18] The Danish expedition should instead be viewed as a well-planned and skilfully executed display of Danish military strength, intended to intimidate and humiliate the people of Saaremaa rather than actually establish a permanent (Danish) military presence on the island or even conquer Saaremaa. It was, in

---

16 Mägi, "Saaremaa and the Danish Kingdom," 333. This (expanded) analysis and discussion on the Danish attack on Saaremaa in 1206 is also found in the article Jensen, "Fighting in the Wilderness," forthcoming. See also Carsten Selch Jensen, "The Lord's Vineyard. Henry of Livonia and the Danish conquest of Estonia," in *Denmark and Estonia 1219–2019*, ed. Olesen, 43–46.

17 HCL 10:13; Selart, "Die Eroberung Livlands," 177–78.

18 Jensen, "The Early Church of Livonia," 101.

itself, an impressive show of organizational skills and military power to launch such a (seemingly) huge naval attack, disembark on a hostile coast, and quickly erect a stronghold while keeping any local attackers at bay, only to withdraw again a short while later extracting the entire force in good order.[19] We should, therefore, view the attack on Saaremaa in 1206 not as a failed attempt to conquer the island, but rather as a very successful demonstration of the military power of King Valdemar II shortly after his accession to the throne. It was clear to everybody that King Valdemar was indeed a skilful military commander capable of attacking his most powerful enemies at the very heart of their lands and far from the Danish lands. In this respect, the king probably had no intention of leaving a garrison behind on Saaremaa, but simply wanted to demonstrate his military power and strategic reach, and prepare an intended attack on mainland Estonia with the intention of establishing a real foothold there comparable to the German settlement in Riga.

This interpretation is supported by the fact that the attack on Saaremaa is echoed in some of the Danish medieval yearbooks, adding more information to the overall plans. According to the *Annales Ryenses*, Archbishop Anders Sunesen namely took an army into the Estonian province of Rävala while Valdemar attacked Saaremaa.[20] If true, the attack on Saaremaa may even be viewed as an even stronger show of power, in a sense, since the Danes had the capacity to launch not just one, but two simultaneous attacks against the Estonians.[21] Henry of Livonia makes no mention of Anders Sunesen leading a separate attack in Rävala, but it has recently been argued that the Danes hardly would have come to Lyndanise had it not been a place of some importance to them in the first place.[22] The natural harbour at Lyndanise in the bottom of the Gulf of Tallinn was probably the best anchorage place in all of northern Estonia, well protected by the outlying peninsulas, and easy to spot due to the impressive and grandiose Toompea Hill.[23] In this

---

19 On the offensive use of castles and strongholds, see Larrea, *Polity Consolidation and Military Transformation*, 115.

20 *Annales Ryenses* (year 1206). The information is repeated in *Chronica Sialandie* (same year). These remarks in some of the Danish medieval yearbooks have led to some speculations whether or not the actual foundation of the Danish castle and settlement in Tallinn rather should be dated to 1206 than 1219. For a discussion of this, see Markus, *Visual Culture*, 261–63 and 328; Kersti Markus, "Blev der grundlagt en by i Tallinn i 1206 eller 1219?," in Jensen et al., *Da Danskerne fik Dannebrog*, 141–53. Here Professor Kersti Markus suggest that the Danish castle was probably founded in 1219 but an early—if failed—attempt was made in 1206 by Archbishop Andrew Sunesen. Henry ignores this altogether, and only informs his readers that the Danish archbishop came to Riga. Cf. HCL 10:13. Reflecting on this, Henry dryly remarks, that "quite properly theological doctrine followed the wars" (*et merito post bella doctrina sequitur thelogica*).

21 Kristjan Kaljusaar has recently suggested that there may have been some sort of military network between the people from Rävala and the people from Saaremaa making it even more important for the Danes to militarily subdue both regions. See Kaljusaar, "Exploiting the Conquerors," 60.

22 Markus, *Visual Culture*, 261; Markus, "Blev der grundlagt en by i Tallinn i 1206 eller 1219?," 141.

23 Marika Mägi, "Fra fortidens havneplads til middelalderens bosættelse," in Jensen et al., *Da Danskerne fik Dannebrog*, 131.

respect, the brief reference in *Annales Ryenses* may offer a clue to why the Danes had their eyes set on this particular place in northern Estonia.

A well-known papal letter from 1206 actually allowed Archbishop Anders Sunesen to appoint a bishop *in civitate*, literally meaning "in the town."[24] Traditionally, the letter has been interpreted as a general papal permission to appoint new bishops in the pagan lands that were to be conquered.[25] The actual wording, however, suggests something slightly different in as much as the archbishop was allowed to appoint *a bishop* in *a particular town* if Anders Sunesen managed to convert the people of this particular town into Christianity.[26] This has made some scholars consider if Anders Sunesen's expedition in 1206 actually happened with the specific purpose of establishing a new settlement at Lyndanise alongside an already existing Estonian village that could serve as the bridgehead for a planned Danish conquest of northern Estonia comparably to Riga in the south. As such, the location was perfect, with direct access to the sea enabling the Danes to control the important trading routes between Scandinavia and Novgorod while, at the same time, contain the islanders on Saaremaa, and prevent (or at least discourage) them from continual attacks on the Danish territories.[27]

Taken together, it seems plausible that the Danish expedition, or rather expeditions, in 1206 were the first steps in a general plan probably conceived in conjunction by King Valdemar and Archbishop Anders Sunesen to gain a secure foothold in northern Estonia. If so, we may wonder why there were no immediate follow-ups. Some late sources from the sixteenth century mention a Danish expedition into the central parts of Estonia already in 1208, which around 1500 became connected with an early version of the legendary appearance of Dannebrog during a battle between Danish crusaders and pagan Estonians.[28] As we have already seen, the legend was later ascribed to the Battle of Lyndanise in 1219 and became a fundamental part of a Danish national narrative about the nations (former) glory. In a contemporary aspect, and ignoring such later legendary national narratives, it does still seem plausible that there may actually have been Danish crusaders in Estonia in 1208, in a joint campaign with the Germans from Riga as such a campaign is mentioned by Henry, though without mentioning the Danes.[29] We also know that one of King Valdemars strong supporters, Count Albrecht II of Orlamünde (1182–1245), went to Livonia as a crusader more than once in the years between 1206 and 1219, campaigning alongside the Germans from Riga. It is nevertheless strange that the sources don't have any references to (larger) Danish military expeditions directed towards Estonia in this period. It has been suggested that some of the Danish-lead cam-

---

24 DD 1:4.109.

25 Iben Fonnesberg-Schmidt, *The Popes and the Baltic Crusades, 1147–1254*. The Northern World 26 (Leiden: Brill 2007), 85–86; Markus, *Visual Culture*, 261; Markus, "Blev der grundlagt en by i Tallinn i 1206 eller 1219?," 141–43.

26 DD 1:4.109. See also Markus, "Blev der grundlagt en by i Tallinn i 1206 eller 1219?," 141–43.

27 Markus, *Visual Culture*, 263; Markus, "Blev der grundlagt en by i Tallinn i 1206 eller 1219?" 143.

28 Jensen, "Da legenden blev en national fortælling," 192; John H. Lind, "Dannebrog and the Danish Crusades to Estonia," in *Denmark and Estonia 1219–2019*, ed. Olesen, 24.

29 Lind, "Dannebrog and the Danish Crusades to Estonia," 23–24.

paigns are actually mentioned by Henry of Livonia in his chronicle but disguised as pure German ventures that did not involve the Danes. This would comply with Henry's general tendency to downplay any actors in the region other than the Germans and the Rigan Church.[30]

Apart from the fact that not all (Danish) military expeditions against Estonia may have found their way into contemporary sources, another reason for a somewhat reduced involvement in Estonia between 1206 (or 1208) and 1219 from the side of the Danes may also be found in the fact that they were heavily involved in the internal conflicts in Sweden between various royal pretenders, at this time. In 1208, an important battle was fought at Lena in Sweden in which the ruling Swedish King Sverker (r. 1196–1208, d. 1210) was supported by a strong Danish force, while his opponent, Erik Knutsson (d. 1216) was supported by strong contingents of Swedes and Norwegians. Erik Knutsson won the battle and became new king of Sweden, but a large number of prominent Danish knights and magnates perished in the fights. The loss of so many prominent men from the leading families in Denmark, and other internal matters, may simply have thwarted any serious attempts by King Valdemar to follow up on his plans to establish himself in northern Estonia until the early summer of 1219.[31] On top of this, during the same period King Valdemar was also heavily involved in the political struggles in Northern Germany, with several military campaigns being carried out between 1207 and 1216 and leading, for example, to the conquest of the important towns of Hamburg and Stade. All in all, to some extent, these matters may simply have diverted Valdemar's attention (and his military resources) away from Estonia and towards other more pressing (and local) matters between 1206 and 1219.[32]

Henry of Livonia completely ignores a (possible) Danish expedition against Lyndanise in 1206, nor does he mention a presumed Danish expedition in 1208. Instead, we are told that the Danish archbishop, together with Bishop Nicholas of Schleswig, took two ships fully laden with supplies and sailed to Riga together with their entire retinue (*omnis familia ipsorum*) when King Valdemar sailed back to Denmark following the attack on Saaremaa in 1206.[33] Henry explains how the Danish archbishop gave a series of theological and devotional lectures to the clergy of the Livonian Church, urging them to keep up the fight against the pagans.[34] Coincidentally, this visit by the Danish archbishop (Anders stayed in Riga the entire winter) happened at a time when Bishop Albert was not present and was thus spared the apparent humiliation of being admonished by the Danish archbishop. Apart from the obvious statement in the Danish archbishop's visit to Riga as an ecclesiastical sovereign visiting a (presumed) subordinate church—probably much to the dismay of Bishop Albert—, the Danes also demonstrated their

---

30 Lind, "Dannebrog and the Danish Crusades to Estonia," 20. See also Markus, "Blev der grundlagt en by i Tallinn i 1206 eller 1219?" 143.

31 Markus, *Visual Culture*, 313; Markus, "Blev der grundlagt en by i Tallinn i 1206 eller 1219?" 143–44.

32 Larrea, *Polity Consolidation and Military Transformation*, 141.

33 HCL 10:13.

34 HCL 10:13.

superior resources by bringing an abundance of supplies to the allegedly starving people of Riga. Consequently, the Danish attack on Saaremaa, the presumed expedition to Lyndanise in 1206, and Anders Sunesen's visit in Riga, above anything else, demonstrate the supreme military capabilities of King Valdemar II backed by a an equally powerful archbishop. Together, they had proven that they were capable of attacking their most powerful enemies in their very own homelands whilst dominating the Germans in Riga at the same time. A relevant question would be, therefore, what kind of military power did King Valdemar and his archbishop have at their disposal when they turned their attention towards the Estonian lands in earnest

Lessons Learnt and New Ideas:
The Reorganization of the Danish Military During the Twelfth Century

Both King Valdemar I and his son, King Knud VI, were gifted politicians and skilled military commanders who had successfully subjugated both internal and external enemies during the second part of the twelfth century—strongly supported by Archbishop Absalon.[35] The archbishop was personally very active in these wars against the pagans even if canon law technically prohibited clerics from taking part in the shedding of blood. At one point, the archbishop expressed the belief (says Saxo) that the actual fight against the pagans was as much a divine service as the celebration of mass in his church.[36]

As noted in a previous chapter, the Danes had quickly become involved in the emerging ideas of crusading while, at the same time, suffering from internal, prolonged conflicts and outright civil wars between various fractions of the royal family; each sup-

---

35 As very recent discussion on the military developments in Scandinavia during the twelfth century is Larrea, *Polity Consolidation and Military Transformation*, 89–118; see also the aforementioned Larrea, "The Transformation of Naval Warfare in Scandinavia," 83–87.

36 Carsten Selch Jensen, "Bishops and Abbots at War: Some Aspects of Clerical Involvement in Warfare in Twelfth and early Thirteenth Century Livonia and Estonia," in *Between Sword and Prayer: Warfare and Medieval Clergy in Cultural Perspective, Explorations in Medieval Culture*, ed. Radosław Kotecki, Jacek Maciejewski, and John S. Ott (Leiden: Brill 2018) 404–34; Lawrence G. Duggan, "The Evolution of Latin Canon Law on the Clergy and Armsbearing to the Thirteenth Century," in Kotecki et al., *Christianity and War*, 498–516; David S. Bachrach, *Religion and the Conduct of War c. 300–c. 1215* (Woodbridge: Boydell 2003); Gübele, *Deaus vult*, 335–37; David S. Bachrach, "The Medieval Military Chaplain and his Duties," in *The Sword of the Lord: Military Chaplains from the First to the Twenty-First Century*, ed. Doris L. Bergen (Indiana: University of Notre Dame Press, 2004), 69–88; James A. Brundage, "Crusades, Clerics and Violence: Reflections on a Canonical Theme," in *The Experience of Crusading, Vol. 1: Western Approaches*, ed. Marcus Bull and Norman Housley (Cambridge, Cambridge University Press, 2003), 148–50; James A. Brundage, "Holy War and the Medieval Lawyers," in *Holy War*, ed. T. P. Murphy (Ohio: Ohio State University Press, 1976), 99–140; James A. Brundage, "The Hierarchy of Violence in the Twelfth- and Thirteenth-Century Canonists," *International History Review* 17 (1995), 670–92; Carsten Selch Selch, "Clerics and War in Denmark and the Baltic: Ideals and Realities around 1200," in *Fighting for the Faith*, ed. Kurt Villads Jensen, Janus Møller Jensen, and Carsten Selch Jensen (Stockholm: Runica et Mediaevalia, 2018) 187–218; Carsten Selch Jensen, "Religion and War in Saxo Grammaticus's *Gesta Danorum*: The Examples of Bishop Absalon and King Valdemar I," in Kotecki et al., *Christianity and War*, 189–206.

ported by various magnates until finally King Valdemar I in 1157 became sole regent in Denmark. The adoption of the new ideas of holy and penitential war into the Baltic Sea region alongside prolonged internal civil wars evoked a series of reorganizations and reforms of the main military systems in Denmark during the better part of the twelfth century. Throughout this century and well into the thirteenth century, the Danish kings relied on changing forms of the old military organization of the *ledung* or *lething* (Latin, *expeditio*) when defending the realm.[37] The ledung has often been associated with the many wars fought by various Scandinavian Viking lords in the early medieval period right through to the eleventh century. In Demark, the basic structure of the ledung remained pretty much the same throughout the centuries and was essentially based on the subdivision of Skåne, Sjælland, Fyn, and Jylland into a number of lesser administrative districts each referred to as a *herred*. There seems to have been roughly two hundred such districts, each responsible for upholding and operating a total of four ships for military purposes. In times of war, the ledung would be summoned by the king or his appointed (local) officials.[38] The ledung is described in various sources throughout medieval Scandinavia, most detailed, however, in the provincial laws of Jylland, Sjælland, and Skåne written down in the early part of the thirteenth century during the reign of King Valdemar II.[39] Within each herred, a number of so-called *skipæn* (literally meaning "a ship") and *hafnæ* (literally meaning "a harbour") was responsible for maintaining and crewing each of the four ships. According to contemporary sources, each of these ships is said to have been crewed by forty to forty-two men.[40] The men were individually referred to as a *hafne bonde* (literarily meaning "a harbour peasant"), and in its earliest form, the ledung was essentially based on a peasant levy who would take turns manning the ships in times of war—some would crew the ship and some would stay home in a (more or less) fixed rotation.[41] The provincial laws of Jylland specifically state that only those of proper age were required to serve: those who were either too young (under fifteen) or too old (more than sixty) were exempted from the ledung and deemed unfit for military service, as were women and clerics.[42] Each of the ships would be commanded by a *styresmand* ("the man who steers the ship"). The styresmand had a special responsibility towards maintaining the ship and preparing it for war and seems most often to have been from one of the local landowning families of which some eventually evolved into a proper knightly class of titled families in Denmark. According to the provincial

---

37 See the lengthy discussion on the *ledung* in Denmark from the early middle ages into the high medieval period in Larrea, *Polity Consolidation and Military Transformation*, 69–151.

38 Larrea, *Polity Consolidation and Military Transformation*, 105.

39 For an English translation of these laws, see Ditlev Tamm and Helle Vogt, *The Danish Medieval Laws: The laws of Scania, Zealand and Jutland* (London: Routledge, 2016). See also Larrea, *Polity Consolidation and Military Transformation*, 104.

40 Rikke Malmros, *Bønder og Leding i Valdemartidens Danmark* (Aarhus: Aarhus Universitetsforlag, 2019), 26; Larrea, "The Transformation of Naval Warfare in Scandinavia," 81–98.

41 Larrea, "The Transformation of Naval Warfare in Scandinavia," 83.

42 Malmros, *Bønder og Leding*, 71.

Figure 2: An important element in the conquest of Northern Estonia was King Valdemar II's powerful naval force, which enabled him to attack not only the Estonian mainland but also the important island of Saaremaa while at the same time defending his own realm against any marauding enemies. This nineteenth-century illustration gives an impression of how the Danish ledung may have looked around 1200. "Absalon's Victory over Bugislav," Alfred Jacobsen, 1892–1898. Copenhagen, Danish Royal Library, Historical Chronological Collection. Public domain.

law of Jylland, the styresmand was also the only one aboard the ship that initially was required to bring a horse when the ledung was called upon by the king.[43]

The provincial laws in their written form dates back to the early part of the thirteenth century. Therefore, they may not entirely reflect the situation of the early twelfth century and it is still debated whether or not the ledung was purely (or at least primarily) a defensive military organization or rather a generically defensive or offensive one, as required by the circumstances. Some contemporary sources actually do refer to the ledung (*expeditio*) when referring to rather offensive campaigns directed towards Frisland (1153), Pomerania (1184), the Slavic lands (1189), Finland (1191), Estonia (1194), Norway (1204), Saaremaa (1206), and Prussia and Sambia (1210), while at the same time also referring more generically to "armies" (*exercitum*) when writing about battles

---

43 Malmros, *Bønder og Leding*, 19, 28, and 39–40; Larrea, *Polity Consolidation and Military Transformation*, 107–08.

fought outside Denmark and local battles fought inside Denmark.[44] This seems to suggest that the ledung could, in fact, be used either as defensive or offensive as required. This is probably especially the case following a major military reform of 1168, as we shall see shortly. Around this time, the older form of the ledung as a traditional peasants levy gave way to a smaller, more professionalized military organization with a strong focus on the combined arms of well-trained foot soldiers and mounted knights as was the norm in most contemporary European armies.[45] This reorganized ledung proved much more suited to the offensive campaigns into the easternmost parts of the Baltic that became important during the reign of King Valdemar II, operating in close concord with the retinues of the various magnates and lords supporting the king during these expeditions.

With regards to the growing importance of the mounted knights in Denmark, King Erik Emune is said to have been the first to actually bring horses onboard his ships in an oversea attack against Arkona on Rügen. The expedition took place in 1136 and Saxo mentions that the king had decided that there should be four horses on each ship, with a total of eleven hundred ships. The chronicler also states that this practice of having horses onboard the ships of the ledung was carefully upheld right until Saxo's own time early in the thirteenth century.[46] It seems very plausibly that King Erik Emune may in fact have been especially aware of the importance of the heavy (knightly) cavalry as a battle-winning weapon in the 1130s. During the battle of Fodevig in 1134—one of the decisive battles of the early civil wars in Denmark—Erik Emune had defeated the royal army of his rival, King Niels (r. 1104–1134), winning the throne for himself when he deployed a substantial number of mounted men-at-arms that completely uprooted the enemy force.[47] We should, therefore, regard this added inclusion of (more) mounted men in the ledung as an important step towards an overall reorganization of the Danish military system in course of the twelfth century.

While most scholars seem to accept this rising awareness in Denmark of the importance of mounted cavalry during times of war already during the 1130s, there is, however, also some doubt about the actual numbers of mounted warriors in the ledung at this early point. Recent studies suggest that the ledung probably did not exceeded a total of eight hundred ships throughout the twelfth century (the aforementioned four ships per *herred*) deeming it less likely that Erik Emune should have had, in fact, thousand

---

44 See especially *Annales Ryenses* in the relevant years.

45 Larrea, "The Transformation of Naval Warfare in Scandinavia," 85. See also Beñat Elortza Larrea, "Kinsmen, Friends or Mercenaries? Problematising the Preference of International Forces in Scandinavia Between the Twelfth and the Fourteenth Centuries," *Scandia. Journal of Medieval Norse Studies* 4 (2021), 252; Larrea, *Polity Consolidation and Military Transformation*, 105–6.

46 Saxo 14:1.6.

47 According to contemporary sources King Niels lost his son Magnus in the battle as well as a high number of the leading magnates alongside no less than six bishops and sixty lesser clerics. See *Annales Ryenses* (year 1134). See also the discussion on the use of foreign soldiers and mercenaries in Scandinavia in Larrea, "Kinsmen, Frieds or Mercenaries," 230–61; Larrea, *Polity Consolidation and Military Transformation*, 94, 97, and 116–17.

ships at his disposal in 1136.[48] The high number is probably thus an exaggeration by Saxo. As previously mentioned, the provincial law of Jylland speaks of only one horse per ship which seems to suggest that Erik Emune may have been, in fact, the first Danish king to include horses in the ledung, while the quadrupling of the number of horses on each ship only came later, during the reign of King Valdemar I, as we shall see. Following the many battles of the civil wars and the constant conflicts with the Slavs, an increased importance of the heavy cavalry and the wish for a more professionalized military force probably obliged King Valdemar I to reorganize the ledung once more, right after the conquest of Arkona in 1168.[49] Saxo claims that from then on it was decided that only one quarter of the ledung was required to serve, leaving the rest at home:

> after the capture of Rügen every corner of the Baltic was still polluted with the blemish of piracy and so the Danes prepared a clever scheme whereby, when the numbers of their fleet had been surveyed, every fourth ship was to keep watch for those sea robbers, as long as the seasons and conditions would allow it; in this way the continued vigilance of certain crews would relieve them of universal hardship. Our nation saw as great an advantage in the constant service performed by a few as in the divided employment of the entire navy. For this duty they decided to choose young bachelors in particular, so that nostalgia for the marriage bed should not dull men's zest for warfare.[50]

The reorganized ledung was immediately employed in offensive actions against the remaining Slavic strongholds and marauding Estonian and Curonian pirates, as we have already seen.[51] Scholars have concluded that it probably was not before this reform of the ledung in 1168 that it actually became the norm to have four horses on each ship. While only one quarter of the ledung's ship were supposed to be on active service at any given time, it seems plausible that King Valdemar may have decided to uphold the total number of mounted men even with a reduced number of ships. That would leave around two hundred ships in constant service with roughly forty to forty-two men per ship, four of whom would be mounted men-at-arms/knights. The rest would then have been semi-professional foot soldiers armed with swords, spears, and missile weapons like bows and crossbows. The year 1168 probably saw the (final) transformation of the ledung from a one-time, predominately seasonal peasant levy into a (more or less semi-) professional force composed of de-facto trained foot soldiers and mounted knights who

---

48 Malmros, *Bønder og Leding*, 85; Larrea, *Polity Consolidation and Military Transformation*, 108.

49 Larrea, "The Transformation of Naval Warfare in Scandinavia," 85; Larrea, *Polity Consolidation and Military Transformation*, 99.

50 Saxo 14:39.49: "Capta Rugia, cum adhuc pyratice labes cunctos maris nostri secessus foedaret, sollerti Danorum instituto prouisum est, ut eorum classe recensita quarta quaeque nauis aduersum maritimos predones, quoad temporum habitus sineret, excubandi officio fungeretur, sicque quorundam assiduitas uniuersorum laborem absolueret. Tantum enim commodi gens nostra in paucitatis continua quantum in multitudinis intercisa militia reponebat. In quod munus potissimum iuuenes coniugiorum expertes legi placuit, ne militie studium thori charitate torpesceret."

51 Saxo 14:39.49.

were used to work together and to support each other in battle. The king also decided that the men who did not serve as an active part of the ledung should instead pay an annual tax in support of the professionalized ledung, while also boosting the transformation of the wealthy, landowning families into a proper class of magnates and noblemen (*hærre mæn* according to the contemporary sources), serving their king on the battlefields mainly as mounted knights and perhaps even with their own retinues.[52]

Of course, one has to be very careful about making too specific an assumption about the exact size of the ledung during the reign of the kings Valdemar I, Knud VI, and Valdemar II. The current research suggests a fleet of roughly two hundred ships, perhaps a little less if we leave room for missing ships and crews due to shipwrecks, loss in battle, or general maintenance and training. Four horses and some forty men onboard each ship, therefore, suggests an average force of roughly six hundred to eight hundred mounted men-at-arms, with some additional five-and-a-half thousand to seven-and-a-half thousand men serving on foot in support of the cavalry whenever the ledung would be activated. This certainly constituted a sizeable, powerful military force enabling King Valdemar II to pursue his political and military goals along the coasts of the Baltic Sea.[53] In addition to that, the king would augment this force through the summoning of additional forces from among the retinues of his Danish magnates and German and Slavic vassals as we shall see shortly.

Even in its reorganized form, the ledung essentially was a naval-based military institution, primarily reflecting the historical and geographical nature of the Scandinavian countries from the early medieval times well into the high medieval period. This suggests that the members of the ledung predominately fought on foot during the early

---

52 Malmros, *Bønder og Leding*, 122, and 125; Larrea, "The Transformation of Naval Warfare in Scandinavia," 85. While some Danish scholars have argued against this transformation of the ledung from a peasant levy and into a more professionalized fighting force already in the twelfth century—see especially Niels Lund, *Lid, leding og landeværn* (Roskilde: Vikingeskibshallen, 1996)—, Malmros et al. have in my opinion argued very convincingly for the early transformation based on the available (written) sources. In this discussion, Larrea seems to represent a cautious "middle-position" acknowledging the transformation of the twelfth century but leaving some time for the fully matured, professionalized, and offensive ledung to emerge in the early thirteenth century when the overall transformation of the military service became what is referred to as predominately "aristocratic endeavours" like in Europe in general. See as examples the lengthy discussion in Larrea, *Polity Consolidation and Military Transformation*, 103, 116 (the quote), 135, and 138.

53 Larrea and Jensen tentatively suggest larger armies based on the total number of available men as ships in the ledung (around one thousand ships and thirty to forty thousand men including one thousand mounted on horses); Larrea, *Polity Consolidation and Military Transformation*, 110 and Kurt Villads Jensen, "Large Castles and Large War Machines in Denmark and the Baltic around 1200: An Early Military Revolution?," *Revista de História das Ideias* 30 (2009), 193. Both scholars admit, however, that the ledung would hardly ever have been mobilized in its entirety. For an outer regional, yet contemporary comparison, see the discussions on the sizes of the various crusader armies during the siege of Damietta, 1218–1219, in James M. Powell, *Anatomy of a Crusade 1213–1221* (Philadelphia: University of Pennsylvania Press, 1986). These comparative examples seem to point towards the lower numbers based on the reorganized ledung post 1168.

period, either onboard the ships in naval combat or when fighting close to the beaches, or on land when making forays into enemy territory or defending the homelands. Only later did the cavalry become more prominent, as we have seen, changing to some degree, also, the standard equipment of the fighting men.[54] It was, of course, the king who had the right to summon the entire ledung, whereas the magnates, bishops, and abbots were only allowed to call upon those men who lived within their specific lands.[55] Apart from actual military expeditions and battles, the able-bodied men were also required to take part in such activities as guarding the local coasts, constructing and manning castles and strongholds close to their homes, and serving in the local militias.[56] Similar activities, moreover, like guard-duty, construction, and manning of fortifications, roads and bridges also befell regular crusaders while on campaign as we saw, for example, with regards to the attack by the Danes on Saaremaa in 1206: not only did the Danish crusaders have to hastily construct a wooden fortress as a defensive measure against the islanders, they also immediately burned it down again upon leaving the island.

The type of ships used in the ledung during the twelfth and early thirteenth centuries seems for the most part to have been the type of ship most commonly referred to in the sources as (plur.) *snekker* (latin, *sneccis*). It had been in widespread use in Scandinavia from the early medieval period onwards as an extremely versatile type of ship. It could be rowed by its crew, but also operated by sail and was particular suited to the waters around Denmark and the inner waters of the Baltic Sea. It was also a type of ship that could be manhandled fairly easily by its crew when they were required to take the ships overland or navigate smaller rivers and streams during inland attacks.[57] An average crew could be as low as a few handfuls of men, but, as we have seen, contemporary sources seem to suggest around forty men in one ship when they formed part of the ledung.[58]

The snekke seems to have stayed in use well into the late medieval period.[59] In the later part of the period, another type of ship began to appear in the sources however, namely the cog.[60] Soon it became the most common ship in the Baltic Sea region and the workhorse of the merchant's guilds throughout the region with room for several tones of goods. With its raised fore and aft-castles and room for more cargo, this particular type of ship was extremely well-suited as a mean of transporting large quan-

---

54 Larrea, *Polity Consolidation and Military Transformation*, 106–08.

55 Larrea, *Polity Consolidation and Military Transformation*, 124–25.

56 Malmros, *Bønder og Leding*, 101–2.

57 Jan Bill, Bjørn Poulsen, Flemming Rieck, and Ole Ventegodt, *Dansk søfarts historie, I, Indtil 1588: Fra Stammebåd til Skib* (København: Gyldendal, 1997), 74. See for example *Annales Ryenses* describing how the ledung, during the battles of the civil wars, was required to haul the ships overland from Schleswig to Hollingsted in 1153 in an attempt to conquer the newly erected stronghold Mildeborg. For the later types of ships, see Larrea, "The Transformation of Naval Warfare in Scandinavia," 87–93.

58 Larrea, "The Transformation of Naval Warfare in Scandinavia," 94.

59 Bill et al., *Dansk søfarts historie*, 208–09.

60 Larrea, "The Transformation of Naval Warfare in Scandinavia," 87–93.

tum of men, horses and supplies.[61] In shallow waters, however, the cog was not easy to navigate and could be outmanoeuvred by the smaller and more nimble ship-types used by the pagan people, which were closer in construction to the aforementioned snekke.[62]

One of the first references to the use of the cog in Denmark is found in a document from 1224 discussing the release of king Valdemar II and his son (they had been taken prisoner by one of the king's German vassals in 1223). The document stipulates that on his release from captivity the king should embark on a crusade to the Holy Land with a fleet of no less than hundred "cogs and snekker" (*naves cockonibus et sneccis*).[63] During the next decades, these particular ship-types became increasingly more common in Danish waters, until eventually in 1304, King Erik Menved (r. 1286–1319) proclaimed that the ledung, henceforth, should use only cogs when called upon. While the snekke stayed in use, it seems to have lost its military function by then.[64]

With regards to the arming of the average Danish warriors during the twelfth and early thirteenth centuries, there is also information to be found in the provincial laws dealing with the ledung. In the law of Jylland it is said that each member of a ship's crew was required to carry a shield, a sword, a spear, and a kettle hat as his personal armoury whenever the ledung was summoned for war. These basic arms are normally referred to in contemporary sources as *folkvapn* ("weapons of war"). It was these types of weapons that were supposed to be used in times of war and not merely as tools for hunting or farming. The *styresmand*—apart from the abovementioned horse and his personal weapons—was also required to carry a mail shirt, pointing towards his increased importance as a (more) heavily armoured, mounted man-at-arms.[65] It is also stated that the styresmand should bring a crossbow and some bolts. At one point in his chronicle Saxo Grammaticus mentions how the sons of prominent magnates in Denmark did learn to shoot the crossbow as part of their general military training, even if it tends to have been the arms of the common soldiers in the European armies at the time.[66] Perhaps, echoing these general trends, the provincial law of Jylland also states that if the styresmand did not know how to fire a crossbow, he should instead bring a man who had the acquired skills and therefore act as a designated crossbow-man onboard the ship while

---

61 Bill et al., *Dansk søfarts historie*, 138–54.

62 Larrea, "The Transformation of Naval Warfare in Scandinavia," 88.

63 DD 1:6.16. See also Malmros, *Bønder og Leding*, 41–42; Kirsi Salonen and Kurt Villads Jensen, *Scandinavia in the Middle Ages, 900–1550: Between Two Oceans* (London: Routledge, 2023), here esp. 121–22.

64 DD. 2:5.310; Malmros, *Bønder og Leding*, 43. Bill et al., *Dansk søfarts historie*, 208–09; Larrea, "The Transformation of Naval Warfare in Scandinavia," 96; Larrea, *Polity Consolidation and Military Transformation*, 108–10 and 146.

65 Malmros, *Bønder og Leding*, 19. See also the discussion in Larrea, *Polity Consolidation and Military Transformation*, 149.

66 Malmros, *Bønder og Leding*, 20.

on campaign.[67] Some contemporary Norwegian provincial laws states that the common warriors (mostly peasants) should carry bows and arrows when summoned for war. This could very well have been the case in Denmark also before the crossbow became more widespread during the middle of the twelfth century and we actually do have references to bows used by the Danes during military engagements in the second part of the twelfth century.[68]

Especially interesting in the law of Jylland is the fact that the costs for shields seems to have be considered a shared expense that should be evenly divided among all the members of the individual hafnæ and skipæn, and not something paid for solely by those who did the fighting.[69] Something similar also seems to have been the case in the provincial laws of Skåne, while at the same time indicating that spears, too, were considered a common responsibility that did not rest solely on the individual warrior.[70] The particular references to shields (and to some extent also the spears) as part of a common responsibility could for one point towards the fact that shields (and spears) often would not last an entire campaign due to heavy man-to-man fighting. This required a fairly large quantity of spare shields to be brought along as replacements whenever they were needed during a campaign, if the fighting men should keep up their efficiency in battle. Had it relied solely on the individual men to bring along spare shields for an entire campaign, it may simply have been a too heavy burden for them, making them less efficient in battle during prolonged expeditions. The common supply of shields could also point toward a rising practice of letting particular warriors—perhaps an entire ship's crew or the retinue of a local magnate—use the same colours and/or symbols on their shields along with the banners so often mentioned in contemporary chronicles.

Taken together the average Danish warrior in the early thirteenth century, on the brink of the renewed expeditions to Estonia, would have been armed with sword, spear, kettle hat, shield, and perhaps crossbows. Some of the men would probably also have had lighter types of body armour, like, for example, woollens, quilted gamesons as is known from contemporary Europe.[71] The magnates and the sons of the ruling manorial families would have owned additional armoury, such as mail coats, helmets suited to mounted warfare, and, of course, horses, swords, shields, and lances.[72] These knights had learned their trade during the civil wars and in the many wars against the pagan Slaves while also upholding their skills as maritime warriors. This made the German chronicler, Arnold of Lübeck (d. ca. 1211), note that "the Danes had imitated the customs

---

67 Malmros, *Bønder og Leding*, 19–20.

68 Malmros, *Bønder og Leding*, 20. See, for example, how Danish archers at one point reused enemy arrows, Saxo 14:43.4.

69 Malmros, *Bønder og Leding*, 20.

70 Malmros, *Bønder og Leding*, 98.

71 For a general discussion of textile armour and terminology during the high middle ages, see Stephen Bennett, "Under and Over (or Both)?: Textile Armour and the Warrior in the High Middle Ages," *Arms and Armour* (2023), 4–5 and 12.

72 Larrea, *Polity Consolidation and Military Transformation*, 149.

of the Germans" and since they had such rich pastures they had a wealth of horses and were indeed "expert in cavalry tactics and…glory in battles both on horseback and at sea."[73] As it turned out, this also proved to be the ideal tactical combination with regards to the ensuing conquest of Estonia that would require both the skills of the heavily armed knights and the ability of a well-trained naval force to strike hard and unexpected against enemy key locations.

Chapter 4

COMPETING POWERS

THE GERMAN MISSION IN LIVONIA
AND THE INITIAL QUEST FOR ESTONIA

THE MAJOR RIVAL to the Danes and their expansion into Estonia was the German mission in Livonia. This mission had taken roots in the mid-1180s not long after the first attempts had been made to establish a formal (Danish) mission in Estonia through the consecration of Bishop Fulco.[1] While we do not know if anything actually came of this early attempt to convert the Estonians, German clerics managed to establish themselves in Livonia along the lower runs of the Daugava River, connecting the market places of western Livonia with the rich markets of the Rus' lands further to the east.

The early history of the Livonian Church is described in great detail, although with a strong supportive bias towards the Germans by the aforementioned chronicler, Henry of Livonia. In his chronicle, German priests and missionaries (who also included Henry himself), and the Livonian Church headed, in turn, by the bishops Meinhard (r. 1186–1196), Bertold (r. 1196–1198), and Albert are portrayed essentially as God's only true representatives among the local (pagan) people. Any encroachment by foreign (ecclesiastical) powers was fiercely opposed by the Livonian Church as well as by Henry himself. Primary among these foreign powers were, of course, the Danes and to a lesser extent, the Swedes and the Norwegians.

The *Chronica Livoniae* is, in essence, the foundational narrative of the German mission in Livonia and Estonia and, therefore, a very important source with regards to the various aspects of the conquests of these lands. In the chronicle, Henry explains, how Meinhard came to Livonia in the early 1180s together with some German merchants who had sailed there in order to trade at the local market in Ikšķile.[2] This village lay near an important crossing over Daugava River and was an key centre in the region's travel networks. It was a well-chosen starting point for the intended mission.[3] The sources indicate that Meinhard had been sent to Livonia by the archbishop of Hamburg-Bremen as part of a well-planned attempt to establish a permanent mission among the predominately pagan Livs who inhabited these lands.[4] Apart from the overall ambitions

---

1 Selart, "Die Eroberung Livlands," 170–71; Dragnea, *The Wendish Crusade, 1147,* 47.

2 Meinhard's endeavours are described in some detail in HCL 1:1–14. For the original text in Danish, see Jensen, *Med ord og ikke med slag,* 80–84 and 87–94.

3 Jähnig, "Die Anfänge der Sakraltopographie von Riga," 126; Selart, "Die Eroberung Livlands," 171. As we shall see below, the site also had some tactical disadvantages from the point of view of warfare and siege, which later led to the ecclesiastical centre being moved to the newly established town of Riga.

4 This argument is supported, for example, by the writings of Arnold of Lübeck, who explicitly stated that the missionary work took place with the support of the archbishop of Hamburg-Bremen:

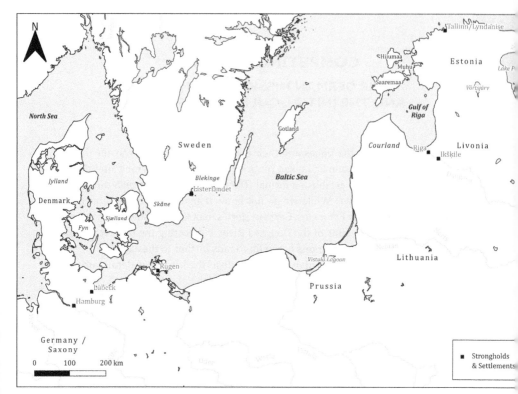

Map 2: Livonia and Estonia with main strongholds and settlements around 1200. Figure by Gregory J. Leighton, 2023.

of the church to convert more people into Christendom, it seems likely that Archbishop Hartwig II of Hamburg-Bremen (r. 1185–1190 and again r. 1192–1207) wanted to secure a foothold in a highly contested region while knowing about the Danish Church's attempts to convert the Estonians only a few years earlier. The support of the German merchants was essential: Henry mentions both the close relationship between these merchants and the local people and the various measures that were taken to secure the merchants' continued and active support for the missionary work. As such, it would have been impossible for Meinhard to uphold his work had it not been for the merchants' ships ensuring a continued flow of supplies and people to the mouth of the Daugava River and further upstream to Ikšķile.[5] Already in 1159, the foundation of the town of

---

Arnold, 5:30. Arnold von Lübeck, *Arnoldi Chronica Slavorum*, J. M. Lappenberg (Hrsg.), MGH SS 14 (Hannover: Hahn 1868). For an excellent English translation, see Graham A. Loud, *The Chronicle of Arnold of Lübeck*, Crusade Texts in Translation (London: Routledge, 2019). See also Hellmann, "Die Anfänge christlicher Mission," 19ff. and 27; Bysted et al., *Jerusalem in the North*, 157–61; Selart, "Die Eroberung Livlands," 173.

5 See, e.g., HCL 4:2–3 and 7. See also Carsten Selch Jensen, "Byer og borgere i 1200-tallets baltiske korstog," *Den Jyske Historiker* 89 (2000), 74–75; Carsten Selch Jensen, "Urban Life and the Crusades

Lübeck in northern Germany had created an important foothold at the Baltic Sea for German merchants who wanted to expand further into the region.

As we saw earlier with the Danish merchants who settled in Curonia in the middle of the eleventh century, the construction of churches at such places was not unheard of and may also have been part of the overall plan in Livonia around Ikšķile.[6] Meinhard, himself, came from the Augustinian priory of Segeberg, and was probably a member of a lesser noble family (*ministerialis*) in the archbishopric of Hamburg-Bremen.[7] On his arrival, he received permission from the Rus' prince in Polotsk to preach and baptize the local Livs, since they were considered among the prince's tributes.[8] Meinhard was accompanied by other priests and they soon managed to baptize some of the local pagan Livs and erect a church.[9] Repeated attacks on the village from Lithuanian raiders, however, forced Meinhard to fortify—quite literally—his mission when initiating the construction of a stone castle and a fortified church in the village. This probably took place in 1185. Henry of Livonia claims in his chronicle, that shortly thereafter, another church and a fortress were built on the nearby island of Mārtiņsala, which also housed a village. This happened despite some reservations from the side of the locals.[10] As argued in an earlier chapter, this may very well have been only partly true since there seems already to have been a fortress tower at Mārtiņsala on the arrival of the Germans, pointing towards an early Danish settlement. This is completely ignored by Henry, who exclusively refers to the German mission and the stubbornness of the people at Mārtiņsala with regards to accepting Christianity and/or German lordship. Without going into any detail, Henry also suggests that Meinhard had at his disposal armed men who could be used to defend the newly built castle in Ikšķile against pagan attacks.[11]

---

in Northern Germany and the Baltic Lands in the early Thirteenth Century," Morray, *Crusade and Conversion*, 77–88; Mark R. Munzinger, "The Profits of the Cross: Merchant Involvement in the Baltic Crusade (c. 1180–1230)," *Journal of Medieval History* 32 (2006), 166; Bernd Ulrich Hucker, "Der Zisterzienserabt Bertold, Bischof von Livland, und der erste Livlandkreuzzug," in *Studien über die Anfänge der Mission in Livland*, Vorträge und Forschungen, Sonderband 37, ed. Manfred Hellmann (Sigmaringen: Jan Thorbecke, 1989), 46; Selart, "Die Eroberung Livlands," 170.

6 Hellmann, "Die Anfänge christlicher Mission," 20; Jähnig, "Die Anfänge der Sakraltopographie von Riga," 125; Hucker, "Der Zisterzienserabt Bertold," 56–57.

7 For the cleric's northern German background see Kaspar Elm, "Der Anteil niederdeutscher, vornehmlich westfälischer Laien, Kleriker und Ordensleute an der Christianisierung des Baltikums," in *Transit Brügge: Nowgorod, 3.500 Kilometer Geschichte*, ed. Krzysztof Rumiński (n.p., 1998), 205.

8 HCL 1: 3. Selart, *Livland und die Rus'*, 75; Hellmann, "Die Anfänge christlicher Mission," 21–23; Jähnig, "Die Anfänge der Sakraltopographie von Riga," 126; Barbara Bombi, "Celestine III and the Conversion of the Heathen on the Baltic Frontier," in *Pope Celestine III (1191–1198): Diplomat and Pastor*," ed. John Doran and Damian J. Smith (Aldershot: Ashgate, 2008), 147; John H. Lind, "Collaboration and Confrontation between East and West on the Baltic Rim as a result of the Baltic Crusades," in *Der Ostseeraum und Kontinentaleuropa 1100–1600: Einflussnahme, Rezeption, Wandel, Culture Clash or Compromise 7*, ed. Detlef Kattinger, Jens E. Olesen, and Horst Wernicke (Schwerin: T. Helms, 2004), 124–25.

9 HCL 1:33–4. Hellmann, "Die Anfänge christlicher Mission," 21–23.

10 HCL 1:6–7.

11 Regarding the conflict at Mārtiņsala, see HCL 1:88. As to the armed men in the service of Bishop

In 1186, Meinhard was consecrated bishop of Livonia by Archbishop Hartwig II. Pope Clement III (r. 1187–1191) confirmed the election in 1188 and also approved the subjugation of the new bishopric to Hamburg-Bremen. However, there seems to have been some uncertainty in Rome about the exact location of this new bishopric. In his confirmation of Meinhard's election, Clement III refers to the bishopric of Ikšķile (*episcopatus Ixcolanensis*), while also stating that it lay in *Ruthenia*, i.e., the lands of the Rus'.[12] This could of course have been down to simple (geographical) ignorance on the part of the curia, but also seems to be in accordance with the older traditions of seeing the region as part of a greater territory commonly referred to as "Rus,'" as we saw with Adam of Bremen a while back. Livonia lay, after all, in a border region on the very periphery of Latin Christendom.

There is no doubt that both Archbishop Hartwig and Bishop Meinhard tried very hard to keep the pope informed about the mission's progress through various letters that sought his approval and continual support at a point when the Danes obviously had plans of their own for a permanent mission foray into the eastern parts of the Baltic. We know, for example, that in 1191 Meinhard requested permission from Clement III for him and the other priests in Ikšķile to eat the food they received from the pagans. Meinhard also received permission to recruit more clerics for his missionary work and to found a small cathedral chapter in Ikšķile that would follow the rule of the Augustinian canons.[13] Celestine III seems to have followed the missionary work in Livonia with some interest. He granted Meinhard further privileges and encouraged him to keep going with his work. Celestine also confirmed, among other things, the sanction that his predecessors had granted Meinhard to recruit more people for missionary efforts. He even went so far as to allow Meinhard to recruit whomever he found suitable for the work at hand, without first seeking permission from superiors. Furthermore, he permitted the new missionaries to preach freely in the cause of the pagans' conversion.[14] In 1193, the pope also granted missionaries in Livonia dispensation from the various religious order's rules about clothing and eating. At this point, many missionaries belonged to different orders: aside from the Augustinians and Cistercians, there were probably also Premonstratensians and Benedictines missionaries and priests.[15] We do not know many of these clerics by name, but the Cistercian monk

---

Meinhard, see HCL 1:6. Marius Ščavinskas has argued against this thesis about the military support of the early bishops in Livonia without, however, convincingly explaining the obvious military support at hand during the reign of Meinhard. See Ščavinskas, "On the Crusades and Coercive Missions," 514–21.

12 LEC 1:1.9; Fonnesberg-Schmidt, *The Popes and the Baltic Crusades 1147–1254*, 66; Hellmann, "Die Anfänge christlicher Mission in den baltischen Ländern," 28–29.

13 The question surrounding food presumably stemmed from a worry about accidentally eating meat from sacrifices offered to idols: LEC 1:3.11a. See also Fonnesberg-Schmidt, *The Popes and the Baltic Crusades*, 66–67; Hellmann, "Die Anfänge christlicher Mission," 30–31; Jähnig, "Die Anfänge der Sakraltopographie von Riga," 130. See also Selart, "Die Eroberung Livlands," 171.

14 Hellmann, "Die Anfänge christlicher Mission," 31; Bombi, "Celestine III and the Conversion of the Heathen on the Baltic Frontier," 147 and 155.

15 LEC 1:1.12. See also Fonnesberg-Schmidt, *The Popes and the Baltic Crusades 1147–1254*, 67;

Theoderic seems to have been an important character among the first German monks and missionaries. He was especially active in an area a little further north in the locality of Turadia (German: *Treiden*), where an important Christian missionary centre later came into being. Theoderic became a key player in the Danish involvement in Estonia and was present at the important Battle of Lyndanise as we shall see in a later chapter.[16] Another Cistercian monk, the future Bishop Bertold, came early to Livonia in order to participate in the missionary work.[17]

It appears from Henry's account that Meinhard's missionary efforts were an arduous business; he apparently came close to giving up several times. Celestine III's exhortations, which refer to the Livs' recalcitrance and resistance in accepting Christianity, gives the same impression, albeit less directly. Henry's chronicle, moreover, mentions that there were several rebellions aimed directly at the German priests and that these threatened to destroy the mission. There was even talk of summoning an army to come and relieve the bishop, underscoring the fact that military solutions were far from alien to Meinhard. It is especially interesting to note that Henry of Livonia specifically mentions Danish and Norwegian merchants as some of those who had promised Meinhard that they would bring an army if he needed military support.[18] That seems to indicate that Danes (and other Scandinavians) were in fact present and active in the region, perhaps even visiting the old market at Mārtiņsala. This likelihood is, however, almost totally ignored by Henry, apart from little hints, as he clearly wished to dismiss any Danish presence in the region that may have challenged the supremacy of the Livonian Church. The chronicle also mentions that Theoderic was sent to Rome to ask for the pope's support in protecting the young church in Livonia. Henry claims that the pope proclaimed a crusade against the rebellious and partially apostate Livs. No such bull, however, survives, and it is possible that Henry mistakenly attributed a later papal letter to Celestine, or else that he simply predated the first formal crusades in Livonia by some years.[19] Whatever the case, the ageing bishop Meinhard died shortly afterwards, in August 1196. He was buried in the church at Ikšķile, before the papal aid he had requested materialized.[20]

Bernd Ulrich Hucker, "'Fürst aller Christen Livlands': Bernhard II und sein Sohn Hermann zur Lippe," in *Lippe und Livland*, ed. Prieur, 176; Jähnig, "Die Anfänge der Sakraltopographie von Riga," 143.

16 HCL 1: 10. Henry offers an account here of Theoderic's early missionary efforts among the pagans in Turadia, along with some associated miracle accounts. For these see Jähnig, "Die Anfänge der Sakraltopographie von Riga," 131.

17 Hucker, "Der Zisterzienserabt Bertold," 43; Jähnig, "Die Anfänge der Sakraltopographie von Riga," 131; Selart, "Die Eroberung Livlands," 173.

18 HCL 1:11.

19 Bombi, "Celestine III and the Conversion of the Heathens," 153–54.

20 HCL 1:14. Hellmann, "Die Anfänge christlicher Mission," 33; Bysted et al., *Jerusalem in the North*, 164.

The Appointment of Bishop Bertold and
the First Proper Crusades in Livonia

Meinhard's successor was Bertold, who had likely been an active participant in the mission for some years.[21] Bertold had been abbot of the Cistercian monastery of Loccum, but it seems that he came into conflict with his order following the orders General Chapter's prohibition of its members preaching outside the confines of the monastery. This has to be compared with the fact that Celestine had allowed missionaries to be recruited freely for work in Livonia, thereby bypassing the leadership of the various different orders involved. Bertold, therefore, was probably forced to give up his abbacy and seems to have been removed from the monastery's list of abbots when he conclusively decided to dedicate himself to the mission to the pagans in Livonia.[22]

Bertold was consecrated as bishop in 1196 by the archbishop of Hamburg-Bremen; the archdiocese also provided him with financial support.[23] We learn from the chronicle that Bertold first visited Livonia alone in his capacity as bishop in 1197.[24] The Livs did not extend him a friendly welcome; in fact, they drove him away again, threatening to kill him.[25] The people of Mārtiņsala seems to have been especially hostile towards the new bishop, disinclined as they were in supporting a German bishop in nearby Ikšķile.[26] Henry ignores a possible Danish/Scandinavian presence in Livonia, ascribing the hostility of the people in Mārtiņsala solely to their apostasy and pagan beliefs. The unwelcoming reception in Livonia made Bertold appeal to Pope Celestine III. Henry says that the pope was attentive to the troubles of the Livonian Church, granting an indulgence to anyone who took the cross in order to quell the rebellious Livs and to protect the newly converted.[27] The following year, Bertold returned to Livonia, accompanied by an army of crusaders, which is the first time that we have a specific mentioning of crusaders in this part of the Baltic. Bertold was prepared to fight in order to take up his episcopal seat. Negotiations began with the Livic elders. However, in July of 1198, serious fighting broke out between the crusaders and the assembled Livic warriors. A battle seems to have taken place in the area where Riga would later be founded—a place that probably also housed a pagan holy place.[28] The battle led to victory for the Christian crusaders, whose better and heavier armour was no match for the lightly armed Livs and they were put

---

21 Arnold, 5:30; Hucker, "Der Zisterzienserabt Bertold," 43; Selart, "Die Eroberung Livlands," 173.

22 Hucker, "Der Zisterzienserabt Bertold," 42–43; Bombi, "Celestine III and the Conversion of the Heathen," 153. The chronicle describes Bertold's short episcopacy at HCL 2:1–6. Chapters 7–10, which conclude the second book of the chronicle, describe the time immediately after the bishop's death.

23 Arnold, 5:30. See also Hucker, "Der Zisterzienserabt Bertold," 45–46.

24 Probably not alone in a literal sense, but rather without military support, as we shall see.

25 HCL 2:2–3.

26 Markus, *Visual Culture*, 255; Markus, "Danskernes støttepunkter og handelsruter," 118–20.

27 HCL 2:3. Fonnesberg-Schmidt, *The Popes and the Baltic Crusades 1147–1254*, 68–69.

28 Mägi, "Fra fortidens havneplads til middelalderens bosættelse," 137.

Figure 3: Bishop Albert of Riga as he is depicted today on the façade of Riga Cathedral. The statue was made by sculptor Kārlis Bernevics (1858–1934). Photograph by Artifex, Wikimedia Commons. Public domain.

to flight. In the heat of the battle, however, Bertold was captured by some of the Livic warriors and killed on the spot.[29]

Consolidation and the Initial Incursion into the Southernmost Estonian Provinces

The third bishop in Livonia was Albert of Riga (also commonly known as Albert of Buxhödven), who was a canon of the cathedral of Hamburg when he was appointed. Like his predecessors, his origins lay in the local lower aristocracy. He was also related to Archbishop Hartwig II, which probably explains why he was appointed bishop of Livonia at a point in his life where he had not yet had the opportunity to make much of a name for himself through his clerical career. On the other hand, his family connections must have meant that he had a relatively close knowledge of the mission taking place in Livonia.[30]

Bishop Albert enjoyed a long episcopacy that lasted from 1199 to 1229 and was thus still bishop when Henry of Livonia completed his chronicle in 1227. Furthermore, Albert became closely involved in the debacle with the Danes concerning the conquest, overall supremacy—politically as well as ecclesiastically—, and Christianization of Estonia in the region, and is, thus, an important character in the narrative of the military conquest of Estonia.

Aware of the violent fate of his predecessors, Albert did not attempt to establish himself in Livonia before he ensured the enjoyment of the widespread support of the local powers in the area, both clerical and secular. Henry reports in the third book of his

---

29 HCL 2:6. Hucker, "Der Zisterzienserabt Bertold," 49–51.

30 The foundational account of Bishop Albert's life and career remains Gisela Gnegel-Waitschies, *Bishof Albert von Riga: Ein Bremer Domherr als Kirchenfürst im Osten* (Hamburg: Velmede, 1958). See also Jähnig, "Die Anfänge der Sakraltopographie von Riga," 131; Selart, "Die Eroberung Livlands," 173.

chronicle that, before the bishop's first visit to Livonia, he recruited a large party of crusaders who would accompany him there. He also petitioned King Knud VI of Denmark, his brother, Duke (and later King) Valdemar, and Archbishop Absalon for their support in his work around the Daugava River. According to the chronicle, he then met with the German King Philip (r. 1198–1208), assuring him of the pope's full support for the coming crusade.[31] It was only in the following year (1200) that Albert made it to Livonia, where he immediately made for the episcopal seat in Ikšķile. His army of crusaders presumably had to fight fiercely with the Livs in order to reach the bishop's castle while, at the same time, experiencing some difficulties in navigating the Daugava River so far upstream from the coast due to a number of lesser rapids and torrents.[32] The large cogs that transported most of the crusaders over the Baltic Sea to the mouth of the Daugava had to be anchored further downriver, more or less where Riga would later be founded. The passengers then either had to disembark into smaller boats or travel overland to Ikšķile. This is presumably one of the important reasons why Bishop Albert soon began building a new mercantile and ecclesiastical centre at Riga shortly after his arrival.[33] At the same time, the pope was persuaded to excommunicate (*anathemata*) any (German) merchants who continued to visit the "the port of Semgallia" (*portu Semigallie*). This may be a reference to a major marketplace once located close to the entrance of the Daugava River where the Leilupa River meet Daugava. The river was then an important route into Semgallia and would eventually be used for river-borne military expeditions against some of the major Semgallian fortresses.[34] Another possibility is that the ban was meant to weaken the central Livic fortress of Daugmale, an equally important political and commercial centre located on the southernmost river bank of Daugava between Ikšķile and Mārtiņsala.[35] In either case, it must have been essential to Bishop Albert to subdue any locality that could become a political, commercial, or even military threat to his new city. In a slightly naïve narrative, Henry claims that the merchants were happy with the papal decree, deciding to place an embargo of their own on the very same market (*sub interdicto ponunt*). At the same time, they stressed that anyone who violated these decrees would lose both their goods and their lives.[36] When the merchants discovered two years later that some others had ignored both the papal ban and their own embargo and continued to trade at the said place, reprisals were indeed harsh; the offenders were attacked by some of the merchants ships and the captains and pilots of the rouge ships put "to a cruel death" (*crudely morte peremptis*). The rest of the crew were forced back

31 HCL 3:2.

32 HCL 4:2–3.

33 Carsten Selch Jensen, "Byer og borgere i 1200-tallets baltiske korstog," *Den Jyske Historiker* 89 (2000), 74; Selart, "Die Eroberung Livlands," 173 and 175; Bysted et al., *Jerusalem in the North*, 169.

34 See HCL 23:3–4.

35 Andris Šnē, "Daugmale: Eine frühe Stadt am Flusslauf der Daugava," in Brüggemann et al., *Das Baltikum*, 129–31.

36 HCL 4:7, 38.

Figure 4: The seal of the Order of the Sword Brethren, reading +S•MAGISTRI•ETFRM•MILICIE CRI•DE•LIVONIA, which can be translated as *Masters and Knightly Brethren of Christ in Livonia*. From Constantine Mettig, *Geschichte der Stadt Riga* (1897). London, British Library Digital Store 10292.h.24. Image from the British Library's Mechanical Curator collection on Flickr. Courtesy of the British Library.

to Riga.[37] From a merchants perspective, the elimination of competing markets and entrepreneurial rivals was no bad thing. We probably have here a subtle reference to a deal struck between Bishop Albert and some of the ambitious German merchants who saw an opportunity with this new foundation at Riga: they would provide the bishop with a steady and reliable (maritime) lifeline between the important ports of Lübeck and Visby and the new mission in Livonia. In return, the bishop offered these merchants favourable commercial treaties, making sure that unwanted competition was thwarted through such means as papal excommunication and civil embargo.

Riga was founded in 1201 at the site where German merchants, over the course of the decades, had made their anchorage when they arrived from the west to trade with the local people.[38] It was also the same place that Bishop Bertold had been killed in the battle between the crusaders and a local army, ascribing to the location, a certain air of sanctity as a martyrs place.[39] Bishop Albert worked hard to persuade German merchants to establish themselves in his new founded city on a more permanent basis and thus laid the foundations for a new urban mercantile corporation, with all the rights and privileges associated with it.[40]

37 HCL 4:7, 38.

38 Mägi, "Deres største styrke er skibe," 78–79; Jensen, "Byer og borgere i 1200-tallets baltiske korstog," 74; Robert Bartlett, *The Making of Europe: Conquest, Colonization and Cultural Change 950–1350* (London: Penguin, 1994), 194; Bysted et al., *Jerusalem in the North*, 168–70; Marek Tamm, "Mission and Mobility: The Travels and Networking of Biskop Albert of Riga (c. 1165–1229)," in *Making Livonia: Actors and Networks in the Medieval and Early Modern Baltic Sea Region*, ed. Anu Mänd and Marek Tamm (London: Routledge, 2020), 18–19. For a wider perspective, see Evgeniya L. Nazarova, "Riga as the Participant of the Trade Blockades in the Baltic Region (13th Century)," in *Riga und der Ostseeraum: Von der Gründung 1201 bis in die frühe Neuzeit*, ed. Ilgvars Misans and Horst Wernicke (Marburg: Herder-Institut, 2005), 108–15.

39 Selart, "Die Eroberung Livlands," 173. See also Kaljusaar, "Martyrdom on the Field of Battle in Livonia During Thirteenth-Century Holy Wars and Christianization: Popular Belief and the Image of a Catholic Frontier," in Kotecki et al., *Christianity and War*, 246–49 and 261.

40 HCL 6:4. Benninghoven, *Der Orden der Schwertbrüder*, 62; Ekdahl, "Die Rolle der Ritterorden,"

The foundation of the military order of the Sword Brethren in 1202 reflected a desire on the bishop's part to secure the presence of a permanent military force that could protect the Christians and ensure the safety of the ongoing missionary work by fighting and subduing the pagans militarily. This new order, however, had serious difficulties in doing so, and was eventually marginalized and taken over by the much larger Teutonic Order, which, over time, became a central power broker in both Prussia and the Baltic Lands, as we shall see later.[41]

Although the chronicle of Henry of Livonia suggests that it was Theoderic who was the main figure behind the foundation of the Sword Brethren, it seems more likely that the main initiator and founding figure was in fact Bishop Albert himself.[42] Henry, however, choses to describe things a little differently in his chronicle, probably because a tense relationship quickly developed between the bishop and the knights of the Order: the knights demanded independence from the bishop. Furthermore, they demanded the right to rule more or less unhindered over the parts of Livonia and Estonia that they themselves conquered, and which they came to control through a network of castles. It was more convenient for Henry, therefore, to shift responsibility for the Order's foundation—and its later slightly recalcitrant behaviour—onto someone other than the leader of the Church of Livonia. Henry was happy enough to tell the story as if Bishop Albert's authorization for the Order took place *after* the foundation itself. The disagreements between successive bishops and the Sword Brethren continued until the Order suffered a decisive military defeat in 1236, after which the surviving knights of the Order were absorbed into the Teutonic Order. The papacy had directed both the Sword Brethren and the bishop a number of times before this not to impose too harsh a burden on the newly converted, lest they abandon the faith and begin to resist it.[43] In Riga, a small castle and chapel were erected for the use of the Sword Brethren following the Order's foundation.[44]

Another important institution to be founded in this period was Livonia's first monastery, the Cistercian abbey of Mount St. Nicholas (Latvian: *Daugavgrīva*, German: *Dünamünde*). The abbey was founded north of Riga, close to the mouth of the Daugava River in 1205. The abbey was formally consecrated in 1208, and monks were translated there from the Abbey of Marienfeld in Saxony. Its first abbot was Theoderic, whom we have already met.[45]

221. An equivalent order was founded in Prussia around twenty-five years later when the Danish (backed) Bishop Christian (d. 1245), together with Konrad of Mazovien (d. 1247) took their inspiration from the Livonian order and founded the *Fratres Militiae Christi contra Prutenos*. Cf. Bysted et al., *Jerusalem in the North*, 239–41.

41 William Urban, *The Teutonic Knights: A Military History* (Barnsley: Frontline, 2011); Aleksander Pluskowski, *Environment, Colonisation, and the Baltic Crusader States: Terra Sacra I–II* (Turnhout: Brepols, 2019); Bysted et al., *Jerusalem in the North*, 269–80.

42 See the discussion in Benninghoven, *Der Orden der Schwertbrüder*, 39.

43 Bysted et al., *Jerusalem in the North*, 169–70; Fonnesberg-Schmidt, *The Popes and the Baltic Crusades 1147–1254*, 118–19 and 188; Jähnig, "Zisterzienser und Ritterorden," 79.

44 Jähnig, "Die Anfänge der Sakraltopographie von Riga," 136.

45 Lore von Poelchau, "Die Geschichte des Zisterzienserklosters Dünamünde bei Riga (1205–1305)," *Studien und Mitteilungen zur Geschichte des Benediktinerordens und seiner Zweige* 115 (2004), 72–74; Jähnig, "Die Anfänge der Sakraltopographie von Riga," 141; Tamm, "Mission and Mobility,"

Together with the other ecclesiastical institutions in Livonia, the monastery became an important participant in the ongoing missionary work.

In the first year of Albert's episcopacy, the missionary efforts concentrated on consolidating and developing the mission to the Livs who lived close to the Daugava River and in the area around Turadia. This mission also affected the Lettgallians, who lived northwest of the Livic areas. The bishop recruited people to undertake this work through his many annual preaching campaigns, in which he enlisted people for the coming year's military campaigns and for the general defence of the Livonian Church, promising indulgences as he did so. A few noblemen were enticed to come to Livonia and became the bishop's vassals, becoming permanently entrenched in the area as castellans and bailiffs. However, there is nothing in the sources to suggest that non-noble German settlers came to live in Livonia in any great numbers. This marks this area as being very different from the contemporary colonization and conquest of the Prussian lands.[46]

It appears from Henry's chronicle that the conquest and Christianization of the Livic and Lettgallian areas more or less came to an end in the period from 1206 to 1208. In the chronicle, Henry goes out of his way to tell his readers how churches were built across most of Livonia, and that the country had been divided up into parishes. He also writes that Bishop Albert formally bequeathed the whole conquered area to King Philip of Germany, who gave him the lands back as a fiefdom.[47] The bishop also decided that bailiffs should be appointed in all the conquered areas.[48] Attention among the Germans eventually shifted towards the Selonians and Semgallians living south and southwest of Livonia, and more importantly, towards the Estonian people in the north. Here, German crusaders and missionaries soon ventured into the southernmost provinces of Ugandi (German: *Ugaunien*) and Sakala (German: *Sakkala*), which were in turned followed by further forays into the northernmost provinces of Lääne (German: *Rotalien*), Harjumaa (German: *Harrien*), Järvamaa (German: *Jerwen*), Rävala (German: *Reval*), and Virumaa (German: *Wierland*), in fierce competition with the Danes who also had a strong focus on Saaremaa as an especially strong military power.[49]

19–20; Selart, "Die Eroberung Livlands," 176; Alan V. Murray, "Catholic Missionaries in the Evangelization of Livonia, 1185–1227," in *Quis est qui ligno pugnat? Missionari ed evangelizzazione nell'Europa tardoantica e medievale (secc. IV–XIII) / Quis es qui ligno pugnat? Missionaries and Evangelization in Late Antique and Medieval Europe (4th–13th Centuries)*, ed. E. Piazza (Verona: Alteritas, 2016), 356.

46 Bysted et al., *Jerusalem in the North*, 227–41 and 244–48.

47 See, e.g., HCL 10:14 and 10:17. See also Paul Johansen, "Lippstadt, Freckenhorst und Fellin in Livland: Werk und Wirkung Bernhards II, Zur Lippe im Ostseeraum," *Veröffentlichungen des Provinzialinstituts für Westfälische Landes- und Volkskunde* 1, no. 17 (1955), 109.

48 See, e.g., HCL 11:4.

49 See here Henry's own proclamation about the year 1206/07 regarding the conversion and baptism of the pagans, which followed and many battles in the country: "the whole of Livonia was converted and baptized" (*conversa et baptizata sit tota Lyvonia*): HCL 10:13. Later on in the chronicle, Henry writes that "explicit liber III de Lyvonia" (here ends the third book about Livonia) in his entry for 1208 (HCL 12:5), and furthermore, that "incipit liber quartus de Estonia" (here begins the fourth book, about Estonia), HCL 12:6. See also Selart, "Die Eroberung Livlands," 179–91.

Chapter 5

WAGING WAR IN THE WILDERNESS
WESTERN MILITARY TRADITIONS
MEET BALTIC TRADITIONS

THE MILITARY CONQUEST of both Livonia and Estonia was, by all accounts, an extremely brutal affair, characterized by a high level of violence. We have already touched upon the practices of raiding and plundering enemy lands, taking as much booty as possible while enslaving the local people. This type of warfare was carried out both by land and by sea enabling attacks deep into enemy territory and involving pretty much everybody in the region. Largescale campaigns were fought with little regard to enemy lives or properties. Often, men of fighting age were seemingly killed right away, according to contemporary sources like Henry of Livonia, whereas women and children were taken captive to be sold as slaves at one of the local slave markets or shipped off to foreign lands never to see their ancestral homes again.[1] Even fellow Christians ran the risk of becoming entrapped during these wars, especially if the enemy belonged to a different denomination as we have already seen with the German-Rus' relations between whom there were very little reverence or respect.

Neither the German nor the Danish crusaders brought warfare to a region otherwise untouched by this favoured pastime of mankind—far from it. Various forms of continual warfare with raids and larger military expeditions into enemy territory seem to have been the norm for generations among the Baltic people, predating the arrival of the Western crusaders and their novel ideas of holy wars and crusades. As such, martial cultures were strong among most of the local people. For their part, Western crusaders would have been unable to subjugate these vast territories had it not been for the direct and active support of the locals who, for one reason or the other, chose to side with the powerful newcomers in their continuous struggle against age-old local enemies, and, thereby, gain military advantage.[2] Like in so many other crusading theatres along the fringes of Christendom, it was, by no means, the crusaders who introduced the art of war among the local people. Rather, the crusaders became (new) players in already existing power struggles and age-old feuds. For centuries, the local peoples, clans, and

---

1 See for example HCL 12:6, where Henry of Livonia explicitly states that it was the custom in these lands for the armies to only spare the girls when raiding enemy villages and farms. This chapter originates in Jensen, *Med ord og ikke med slag*, 105–12, but has been much expanded. See also John Gillingham, "A Strategy of Total War? Henry of Livonia and the Conquest of Estonia, 1208–1227," *Journal of Medieval Military History* 8 (2017), 206–09; Selart, "Slavery in the Eastern Baltic."

2 That would certainly be the case with the Livic people, cf. the history about Caupo and many of his followers who became stout allied of the Germans. See also Linda Kaljundi, "Neophytes as Actors in the Livonian Crusades," in Mänd et al., *Making Livonia*, 93–94. For a highly interesting and wider perspective on these matters, see Kaljusaar, "Exploiting the Conquerors," here esp. 58 and 65.

families had fought each other and waged war on foreign intruders as part of everyday life, nurturing a dominant martial culture. Likewise, as we have already seen, some of the local people were, themselves, experienced seaborne raiders who plundered far-away shores around the Baltic Sea, bringing back booty and captives in abundance. This was especially the case with the Estonians living in the Maritime Provinces, on the larger islands of Muhu and Saaremaa and with their close cousins from Curonia. As such, the people of Livonia and Estonia were well versed and highly skilled in the art of waging war when the first crusaders arrived in these lands and immediately became embroiled in long-standing internal conflicts and local feuds, while, at the same, time seeking to pursue their own militarily, political, and ecclesiastical goals.

Livonia and Estonia constituted a region where geography and climate had a huge influence on the overall military strategies employed by the various armies as well as on specific tactics used during the fighting.[3] While roads were few and lesser tracks connected farms, villages, and markets, primarily on a local level, they also provided access to some of the important trading routes and regional markets. Huge swathes of land were generally, if not outright, impassable for large armies on the march. Dense and impenetrable forests covered large areas, creating natural boundaries between the different people living there. Lakes, rivers, streams, and impassable stretches of marshland proved to be added obstacles for armies on campaign.[4] All these environmental elements essentially formed natural barriers between the various regions and provinces, and functioned as natural buffers between the warring regions and peoples. Different seasons meant different possibilities with regard to actual military campaign, either by land or by sea. The crusaders soon learned that some natural barriers could be overcome during winter, when snow and hard frost made it far more easy to move through the landscape and cross frozen rivers and swamps, thus creating new and easier ways to move through the countryside.[5] The forests, for their part, often functioned as places of refuge for the locals who had to flee in a hurry to find safety from marauding and plundering enemy armies, attacking in the midst of winter.[6] As such, these same forests, river crossings, and frozen swamps all covered in deep snow—where armies often had to move carefully forward in long single-file columns—were also ideal places for counterattacks and ambushes, as the accounts of Henry of Livonia so often reveal. The landscapes of Livonia and Estonia became an integral part of the ongoing warfare: both the terrain and the seasons offered different military possibilities and challenges that each

---

3 Gillingham, "A Strategy of Total War," 192.

4 For a detailed study of parts of the road network in medieval Estonia, see Martti Veldi, "Roads and Hill Forts in Southern Estonia during the German Conquest in Henry's *Chronicle of Livonia*," in Valk, *Strongholds and Power Centres*, 385–416.

5 Veldi, "Roads and hill forts in southern Estonia," 393 and 398–99; Gillingham, "A Strategy of Total War," 205.

6 Henry mentions several times that Meinhard had to flee into the forest when Ikšķile was attacked by plundering Lithuanians; see HCL 1:5 (*idem predicator cum Ykescolensibus silvis committitur*). For the conduct of warfare in Livonia and Estonia, see in general Friedrich Benninghoven, "Zur Technik spätmittelalterlicher Feldzüge im Ostbaltikum," *Zeitschrift für Ostforschung* 1 (1970), 631–51.

of the warring parties had to adhere to and overcome in an effort to be able to successfully carry out military campaigns or small-scale raids.

It was not, however, only the landscape and the general geography and climate that came to play an important role in the way that the warfare unfolded in these lands. The sources also point towards a certain superiority of Western military technology compared to the local ways of fighting and available equipment.[7] A very important element introduced both by the Germans and Danes in the region was castle building in accordance with contemporary, Western traditions, with strong walls of carved stones laid in mortar. Both Livonia and Estonia did have an abundance of fortresses and strongholds, as we shall see, predating the arrival of the Westerners, but they seems to have fulfilled slightly different roles from that of the crusader castles and followed other architectural traditions.[8]

The castles were not the only powerful military implement that was introduced by Westerners. Efficient weapons, such as the powerful crossbow widely used by Western armies during this period, also came to have a deep impact on the local ways of fighting, whether they were employed during sieges or in open battle. The many telling accounts in the sources clearly demonstrate just how efficient an enemy force could be routed by (disciplined) units armed with crossbows.[9] Another crucial feature was the presence of mounted and heavily armoured knights in the Western armies, something we have already discussed in connection to the reorganization of the Danish ledung during the twelfth century. Mounted knights plays a prominent role in almost any high medieval source dealing with military matters and chroniclers like Saxo Grammaticus and Henry of Livonia have many telling descriptions of the importance of mounted knights in times of war.[10] Along similar lines, well-trained warhorses were extremely valuable and were,

---

7 Sven Ekdahl, "Horses and Crossbows: Two Important Warfare Advantages of the Teutonic Order in Prussia," in *The Military Orders, Vol. 2: Welfare and Warfare*, ed. Helen Nicholson (Aldershot: Ashgate, 1998), 119–51; Kurt Villads Jensen, "Bigger and Better: Arms Race and Change in War Technology in the Baltic in the Early Thirteenth Century," in Tamm et al., *Crusading and Chronicle Writing*, 245–64; Ain Mäesalu, "Mechanical Artillery and Warfare in the Chronicle of Henry of Livonia," in Tamm et al., *Crusading and Chronicle Writing*, 265–290; Tyerman, "Henry of Livonia and the Ideology of Crusading," 41; Gillingham, "A Strategy of Total War," 190.

8 Ain Mäesalu, "Wandlungen der Funktionen der Burgen in Südostenstland im 8.–15. Jahrhundert," in *Castella Maris Baltici II*, ed. Magnus Josephson and Mats Mogren (Nyköpking: Södermanlands museums, 1996), 103–6; Sebastian Messal, "Die mittelalterlichen Burgen des 13 und 14 Jahrhunderts im östlichen Baltikum," in *The European Frontier. Clashes and Compromises in the Middle Ages*, ed. Jörn Staecker (Stockholm: Almquist, 2004), 243–57; Evalsds Mugurevics, "Similarities and Differences among Lettigallian and German Castles in Eastern Latvia during the 9th–15th Centuries," in *Castella Maris Baltici II* (Nyköping: Södermanlands museums, 1996), 117–24.

9 The crossbow is repeatedly mentioned in Henry's chronicle. See, e.g., HCL 10:12, where he says that the Western warriors' use of the crossbow was something that distinguished them from their opponents (in this case the Rus'). In other places in the chronicle, he relates how additional warriors armed with crossbows and other Western material could make a decisive contribution to the actual fighting; see, e.g., HCL 10:9.

10 See for example Saxo 14:15.2 with regards to the benefits and disadvantages of riding a heavy

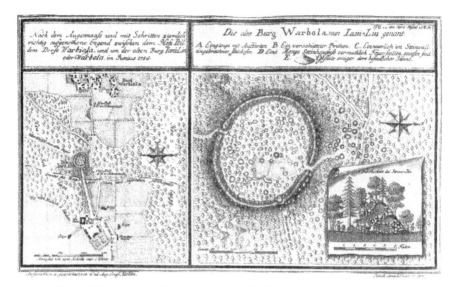

Figure 5: The important Estonian stronghold of Varbola as it appears in Count
Ludwig August Mellin's *Atlas von Liefland, oder von den beyden Gouvernementern u.
Herzogthümern Lief- und Ehstland, und der Provinz Oesel* (Berlin: 1786). Public domain.

on occasion, used as coveted gifts to appease prominent local leaders.[11] Henry also
reports how the mere sight of a knight's helmet could lead to panic among pagan warriors, making them run for their lives—even if it turned out that the helmet had actually
been taken from a German knight just killed and donned as booty by one of their own
comrades.[12] As such, there is a clear sense throughout the chronicles of the superiority
of the military technologies and specific weaponry employed by the crusaders during
the initial phase of the crusades in Livonia and Estonia, compared to the less heavily
armoured local warriors and their different modes of fighting. The texts also reveals
how rapidly the pagans (and the Rus') adopted the new types of weapons and started
using them in their own armies, thus slowly evening out the odds along the way.[13] Henry,
for example, relates at one point how some Rus' soldiers mistakenly hit some of their
own when they used a certain type of catapult for the first time. While it is true that such
stories can be of an anecdotal character, such incidents are not at all unlikely to have
happened in real life when some of the locals obtained some of the new and different

---

(Danish) horses compared the lighter Slavic horses. See also HCL 15:3.

11 See, e.g., HCL 15:3 and 10.1. With regards to the developments in military technology, see
also Jensen, "Bigger and Better," 256–58; Ekdahl, "Horses and Crossbows," 119–51; Salonen et al.,
Scandinavia in the Middle Ages, 119–22.

12 HCL 2:6: "quia videntes unam occisi Theuthonici galeam militarem" (because they saw the
helmet of a dead German). This happened in the same battle that cost Bishop Bertold his life when
he inadvertently was carried into the midst of some fleeing Liv warriors by his panicking horse.

13 HCL 10:12. See also Gillingham, "A Strategy of Total War," 190.

types of military equipment that could prove useful for themselves in the continuous fight against the Danish and German crusaders. Henry also explains that the Danes, at one point, gave various siege engines to the people at the important Estonian stronghold of Varbola.[14] Such narratives, moreover, bear witness to the speed with which new military technology was copied by the local people while, at the same time, Westerners had to adopt their preferred way of fighting to meet the local geographical challenges with regards to landscape and weather. As an example, Henry makes it apparent that the unfortunate Rus' had copied their catapults from an exempla that the Estonians on Saaremaa had constructed based on a Western model. He also relates how various local warriors would routinely capture and take away weapons from the crusaders, such as crossbows and different types of armour for their own use. He was clearly worried about this inevitable "evening-out" of the crusaders military advantages in the continuously divinely sanctioned fight between the Christians and the pagan people. Let us now have a closer look at the military organization of the Estonian societies.

"And they Worship Dragons and Animals with Wings:" Estonia and Estonian Military Organization around 1200

As already established, the Estonians were known as a powerful and very warlike people adhering to ancient old pagan beliefs—even if their actual religious practices may not have been as gruesome and colourful as imagined by some of the contemporary Christian chroniclers.[15] As already mentioned, one should not consider all Estonians as one absolute homogeneous people. Contemporary sources make clear distinctions between the Estonians who lived on the primary islands of Saaremaa, Hiiumaa, and Muhu, in the so-called Maritime Provinces of the coastal region of Läänemaa, and those

---

14 HCL 26:3. It was, however, the people of Saaremaa who had to teach the people in Varbola how to actually use various siege engines (HCL 26:4). Sometimes in the 1220s, King Valdemar II seems to have given some land to a "trebuchet master" by the name Ulrik, probably in return for his services as as a siege engine specialist. Cf. Larrea, "Kinsmen, Friends or Mercenaries," 238. With regards to the types of siege engines used at the time, see Larrea, *Polity Consolidation and Military Transformation*, 115. See also E. Tonisson, "Die Wallburg Warbola: Ein Zentrum im westlichen Estland: Aspekte zur militärischen, politischen und sozialen Funktion," in *Europeans or Not? Local Level Strategies on the Baltic Rim 1100–1400* AD, ed. N. Blomkvist and S. O. Lindquist (Oskarshamn: Gotland University College, 1999), 173–84.

15 Heiki Valk, "Das Volksreligion der Einheimischen," in Brüggemann et al., *Das Baltikum*, 354–55. For a general discussion of the paganism in the Baltic lands and the processes of conversion, see Robert Bartlett, "The Conversion of a Pagan Society in the Middle Ages," *History* 70 (1985), 185–201; Ken Dowden, *European Paganism: The Realities of Cult from Antiquity to the Middle Ages* (Abingdon: Routledge, 1999); Henrik Janson, "What Made the Pagans Pagans," in *Scandinavia and Christian Europe in the Middle Ages*, ed. Rudolf Simek and Judith Meurer (Bonn, Universität Bonn, 2003), 250–55; Henrik Janson, "*Pagani* and *Christiani*: Cultural Identity and Exclusion Around the Baltic in the Early Middle Ages," in *The Reception of Medieval Europe in the Baltic Sea Region: Papers of the XIIth Visby Symposium Held at Gotland University, Visby, Acta Visbyensia XII*, ed. Jörn Staecker (Visby: Gotland University Press, 2009), 171–92; Sylvain Gouguenheim, *Les derniers païens: Les Baltes face aux chrétiens XIIIe–XVIIIe siècle* (Paris: Passes Composes, 2022).

living further inland, separated by huge areas of dense forests, rivers, and swamps.[16] Such natural barriers separated the various Estonian people from each other and also made them react very differently to the encroachment of the German and the Danish intruders.

As previously stated, we do not know for sure if the early attempts of the 1170s to establish a Christian (Danish) mission among the Estonians bore any fruits in earnest. Some Estonians probably did convert into Christianity, and most would certainly have known of Christianity—whether it was Western Catholicism or Eastern Orthodoxy.[17] Some early Christian influence may also be detected in the changing of the burial customs among the easternmost Estonians who seem to have begun to favour ground burials instead of cremation even before the arrival of the first Western missionaries. This could point towards an early Orthodox influence predating the arrival of the German and Danish missionaries.[18] A Christian influx of ideas may also have come through various other forms of contacts like for example trading, raiding and the taking of slaves. No Christian churches have been found in Estonia that predate the massive German and Danish influx in the early thirteenth century, even if some old structures found beneath some of the Estonian churches might suggest the existence of older wooden churches.[19]

The vast majority of the Estonians, however, seem to have adhered to local forms of paganism, even if we know very little about their actual religious beliefs and specific deities. The few and rather sporadic references we have in the contemporary sources were written by Christian clerics ardently opposed to the pagan beliefs of the locals, thus having no real interest in portraying the local religious practices in any positive way. An interesting example is Adam of Bremen, who does air some strong opinions on

---

16 As one example out of many from the chronicle, see HCL 26:11, where he clearly differentiates between the Saaremaaians, the maritime people (*maritimi*), and the people of Warbole, alongside a number of other people from the various provinces of Estonia. Later national and nationalistic attempts to construct a national unity between these various peoples would have had a hard time finding any such justification in Henry's chronicle. Cf. Mägi, "Saaremaa and the Danish Kingdom," 324–25. See also Kivimäe, "Henricus the Ethnographer," 95, where the author clearly shows that the inhabitants of Saaremaa were described as *Osiliensis/Osiliani* in the chronicle, and that Henry never calls them "the Estonians of Saaremaa" or anything similar. In the chronicle, the term *Estones* is reserved for the Estonians of the mainland. See also Šnē et al., "Vor- und Frühgeschichte," 140–43.

17 See the discussion in Marika Mägi, "*Hedninger og kristne*," in Jensen et al., *Da Danskerne fik Dannebrog*, 82–89; Heiki Valk, "Christliche Religion vor den Kreuzügen," in Brüggemann et al., *Das Baltikum*, 135–36; Tiina Kala, "Die Kirche," in Brüggemann et al., *Das Baltikum*, 224–58, here esp. 224. In Livonia, some of the locals might also have been Christians even before the arrival of the first missionaries (even if their numbers were probably small) and many would certainly have known about Christianity. Cf. Linda Kaljundi, "Expanding Communities. Henry of Livonia on the Making of a Christian Colony, Early Thirteenth Century," in *Imagined Communities on the Baltic Rim, from the Eleventh to Fifteenth Centuries*, ed. Wojtek Jezierski and Lars Hermanson (Amsterdam: Amsterdam University Press, 2016), 199; Heiki Valk, "Christianisation in Estonia: A Process of Dual-Faith and Syncretism," in *The Cross Goes North: Processes of Conversion in Northern Europe, AD 30–1300*, ed. Martin Carver (York: York Medieval Press, 2003), 575.

18 Mägi, "*Hedninger og kristne*," 87.

19 Mägi, "*Hedninger og kristne*," 89.

the terrible nature of the Baltic people in his chronicle *Historia Hammaburgensis Eccle-siae*. They were people he clearly had only heard about, but never met in real life. In the chronicle, Adam states firstly that the Curonians (whom he seems to believe lived on an island) were a gruesome people worshipping pagan deities in abundance, housing soothsayers, fortune-tellers, and sorcerers in every dwelling on the island. He then describes the shocking pagan rites that thrived among the islanders of Saaremaa. They worshiped dragons, he says, as well as winged beasts to whom they would sacrifice living humans that needed to be without bodily blemish, otherwise the dragons would not accept the sacrifice.[20] Some one hundred fifty years later, and along similar lines, Henry of Livonia also suggests that human sacrifices and even cannibalism were widespread among the local people. Consequently, he often refers to the pagan religious beliefs as simple delusions installed by the devil himself. Henry also has references—directly and indirectly—to various pagan deities believed to have been part of an overall pagan pantheon.[21] Especially prominent in his chronicle is the Estonian god, Tharapita, who is said to have flown from mainland Estonia to the island of Saaremaa in a lightening bold of fire settling himself among the islanders.[22] In the later part of his chronicle, Henry is very specific about the fact that Tharapita had to be ousted before the islanders could convert into Christendom and accept baptism.[23]

One element that is strangely missing in the chronicle of Henry of Livonia, however, is specific reference to a local pagan priesthood. He refers in several places to the sacrifices of animals and humans to the pagan gods and also has several references to sacred groves, springs, and hills (not exclusively among the Estonians). Nowhere, however, does he refer to a local pagan priesthood among the Estonians (or any of the other local peoples).[24] One obvious explanation could be that the religious practices of the Estonians did not rely on a priesthood that was recognizable to the Christian newcomers. Some of the elders (male or female) and local chieftains may have had certain religious responsibilities and carried out various rites like the former Scandinavian *Gothi* without being recognizable to the missionaries as "priests" in any Christian sense.[25] Instead, they

---

20 Adam of Bremen 4:16–17.

21 See the discussion on the pagan deities in Henry of Livonia's chronicle in Jensen, *Med ord og ikke med slag*, 155–59. Narratives about cannibalism among both crusaders and their enemies were already a well-known topos during the First Crusade. See the recent discussion in Katy Mortimer, "Digesting Cannibalism: Revisiting Representations of Man-Eating Crusaders in Narrative Sources for the First Crusade," in *Chronicle, Crusade, and the Latin East: Essays in Honour of Susan B. Edgington*, ed. Andrew Buck and Thomas W. Smith (Turnhout: Brepols, 2022), 109–30.

22 In popular imagination and folkloristic tradition, the history of Tharapita's flight from the mainland to Saaremaa has been associated with the meteor crater on the island that now forms the lake of Kalii visited yearly by many tourists.

23 Jensen, *Med ord og ikke med slag*, 158.

24 Pagan priests are mentioned in the slightly older texts by Adam of Bremen, Helmold of Bossaum, and Saxo Grammaticus, for example, who refer especially to the pagan beliefs among the (primarily) pagan Slavic people of their time.

25 Only once does Henry of Livonia make a reference to an *ariolus*, suggesting perhaps a pagan priest. HCL 1:10.

would have blended in with the general population making it hard for the Germans and the Danes to single them out and/or target them as especially dangerous to the ongoing processes of Christianization and conquest.[26]

A similar situation seems to have arisen among the newcomers when they tried to identify not only the religious, but also the political power structures among the local people in an attempt to clarify with whom they had to negotiate and make agreements with both in times of war and in times of peace.[27] Henry hardly has any references to named Estonian chieftains whereas we know several Livic, Letgallian, and even Semgallian leaders by name. Instead, he simply refers to the (presumed) Estonian leaders as "the elders" (*seniors*) or "the better ones" (*meliors*).[28] Probably the political and military power in Estonia rested within a certain number of especial powerful families or clans, each having their own chieftains.[29] These structures may be somewhat blurred in the written accounts, but are recognizable in the different burial practices detected in medieval Estonia. Here we see exclusive and richly equipped stone graves that must have belonged to the members of the ruling families, whereas the common people had to do with much simpler burial forms like, for example, cremation, thereby reflecting the overall social structures of the Estonian societies.[30] The role of the women in the Estonian medieval societies is much debated with some scholars suggesting that the women did enjoy certain (political) privileges, for example, in relation to the local councils, whereas this is doubted by other scholars.[31]

Prominent in the Estonian landscape are the many strongholds and fortresses also mentioned by chroniclers like Henry of Livonia. Most of these fortresses seem to have been located close to important marketplaces, rivers, and roads guarding these important infrastructural locations while, at the same time, serving as administrative centres.[32] Contrary to the castles of the Westerners, the local strongholds and fortresses seem not to have been the permanent homes of the ruling elite or the most powerful families in Estonia. While archaeological findings suggest that there may have been smaller, permanent settlement inside the fortresses, they should mainly be seen as places of seasonal importance, housing important markets or political assemblies or

---

26 Šnē and Valk, "Vor- und Frühgeschicte," 134.

27 Marika Mägi, "Egalitære bøner eller hierarkiske slægtssamfund," in Jensen et al., *Da Danskerne fik Dannebrog*," 52–53.

28 Mägi, "Egalitære bøner eller hierarkiske slægtssamfund," 54.

29 Šnē and Valk, "Vor- und Frühgeschicte," 125, 135–38, and 141–43.

30 Šnē and Valk, "Vor- und Frühgeschicte," 125; Mägi, "Egalitære bøner eller hierarkiske slægtssamfund," 56–57.

31 Mägi, "Egalitære bøner eller hierarkiske slægtssamfund," 59 (proposing the idea of [politically] privilged women) and Šnē and Valk, "Vor- und Frühgeschicte," 141 (suggesting a more traditionally based society among the Estonians with a dominating male warrior class). For the slightly longer perspective focusing on Livonia, see Vija Stikāne, "The Legal Status of Women in Livonia, 1200–1400," in Selart, *Baltic Crusades and Societal Innovation*, 189–231.

32 Mägi, "Store estiske borge: Handels eller magtcentre?," 62–63; Kaljusaar, "Exploiting the Conquerors," 56–59.

thingsteads. Lesser wealthy families like artisans may have lived in these places on a permanent basis with their families and contingents of warriors, while the wealthy families would have lived away from the fortresses during most of the year on their farms in the surrounding areas.[33]

In times of war, the fortresses became places of refuges and strongholds from where the local people could protect themselves from enemy attack and/or endure prolonged sieges while the enemy would plunder and burn the surrounding countryside. Similarly, the local chieftains would summon all the able-bodied men in the local military hosts or warbands (often referred to by Henry of Livonia in Estonian as *Malewa*) depending on the concrete situation and the state of mobilization.[34] This system of strongholds and militarily mobilization clearly predated the arrival of the Westerners and seems to have had long historical and well-tested roots in the region. On several occasions, Henry seemingly refers to this system, when he relates how the elders of certain provinces or the Estonian lands as a whole summoned their armies and prepared themselves for war.[35] While the basic structure of the military levy in Estonia may not have differed very much from what we have seen among the people of Livonia, there are some references in the contemporary sources that point out some particular elements that seem to have put the Estonians somewhat on par with the Danes and their ledung, especially the Estonians from Saaremaa and the Maritime Provinces. We have already touched upon the fact that these people favoured strong naval forces, often operating side by side with the people from Curonia. Additionally, we are also told in the chronicle of Henry of Livonia, that the Estonian armies often contained a substantial number of light-armoured, mounted warriors. In one incident from 1210, we are told that:

> the people from Saaremaa, the people of Lääne, and the people of Rävala gathered a large and strong army (*exercitum magnum et fortem*) from all of the nearby maritime provinces. All of the elders (*omnes seniores*) of Saaremaa, Lääne, and all of Esthonia were with them and they had with them many thousands of cavalry and several thousand men who came by ship (*habentes multa milia equitum et plura milia navigio veniencium*).[36]

---

33 Mägi, "Store estiske borge: Handels eller magtcentre?," 63–64.

34 HCL 9:3 (*universae malewa*); 14:8 (*De malewa Lyvonum*); 19:9 (*quod malewa sequeretur*); 20:2 (*malewa magna*); 13:7 (*magnam paganorum malewam*). While the word itself—*malewa*—is Estonian, Henry seems to use is as a generic term for the local war hosts, whether Estonian or Livonian: Anti Selart, "Das Kriegswesen im Zeitalter der Kreuzzüge," in Brüggemann et al., *Das Baltikum*, 198–200; Kaljusaar, "Exploiting the Conquerors," 61. With regards to the concept of overlordship and local regional entities, see the discussion in Kristjan Oad, "Structures and Centres of Power in Estonia in 1200 AD: Some Alternative Interpretations," in Valk, *Strongholds and Power Centres*, 242 and 246–47.

35 See for example HCL 15:1 and 3.

36 HCL 15:3.

Such combined forces of strong naval elements operating in conjunction with equally strong cavalry forces seems to have been an Estonian specialty relying on a clear ability to strike fast and unexpected deep into enemy territory—not that dissimilar to the basic tactic of the Danish ledung. For example, the Estonian forces launched a two-way attack deep into Livonia, attacking the fortress of the Livonian Chieftain Caupo (d. 1217) located next to the Gauja River (German: Livländischer Aa). Part of the army attacked overland while the naval force in their (pirate) ships went down the coast and up the Gauja River striking several enemy inland strongholds. While the Estonians clearly favoured such rapid attacks, the same examples also reveal some of their weaker points when confronted by the combined forces of Western knights and skilled foot soldiers operating alongside their Livic and Letgallian allies. Seemingly the Estonian warriors were especially vulnerable to missile fire:

> the [crossbowmen] (*balistarii*), who had been sent from Riga to guard the fort together with the Livonians, went out to meet them in the field. The [crossbowmen] wounded many of them and killed many, since the Esthonians were unarmed, for they are not accustomed to use armour as much as other nations do (*qui non habent consuetudinem armorum in tantum, quantum alie gentes*).[37]

The Estonians then encountered another powerful Westerner weapon, namely the mounted heavy cavalry, as Henry goes on to explain how some Sword Brethren and German crusaders from Riga "donned their weapons, put the trappings on their horses (*et equos suos phalerantes*), and with their infantry, the Livonians, and their whole company they made their way to the Gauja." Upon the arrival of this relief force from Riga they "arranged the army and instructed it for the war" (*appropinquant et ordinantes exercitum eumque ad bella docents pedites*).[38] A battle then ensued between the German foot soldiers who had accompanied the mounted knights and the Estonians who also seems to have fought on foot. It was a brutal melee between the opposing forces. At some point however, the mounted knight could no longer stay out of the fight says Henry:

> the knights saw the strength of the pagans and suddenly charged through the center of the enemy. The trappings of the horses threw terror into the enemy (*equis suis phaleratis timorem eis incuciunt*). Many of them fell to the ground, the others turned to flight, and the Christians pursued those who fled. They caught them and killed them on the road and in the fields. The Livonians from the fort went out with the [crossbowmen] and met the fleeing pagans. They scattered them on the road and enveloped them. Then they slaughtered them, up to the German lines.[39]

Henry even goes on to state that the fight was so tumultuous that some of the German knights killed some of their Livic allies, seemingly mistaking them for Estonians.

---

37 HCL 15:3.

38 HCL 15:3.

39 HCL 15:3.

Probably it was some newly arrived crusaders who were still unaccustomed to the look of the locals and thus erroneously attacked and killed some of their own allies in the heat of battle.[40]

The battle, however, did not end with the routing of the Estonian land force since the those who had come by ship now withdraw down the Gauja River towards the sea. The relief force from Riga seems to have anticipated this and had stationed units of crossbowmen along the riverbanks to harass the fleeing islanders. Furthermore, an ambush had been set up a little way down the river. Accordingly, the soldiers from Riga had bridged the river at a suitable point completely blocking the escape route of the Estonians while showering them with bolts, arrows, and javelins. The Estonians became completely routed and only few escaped this military disaster says Henry.[41] He also claims that three hundred ships were taken as the booty, while two thousand Estonians had been killed and the same number of horses taken as booty also.[42]

While this was clearly a sundering defeat on behalf of the Estonians, the example from 1210 still offers some very important insight into the organization of an Estonian force with both naval and mounted elements at the time of the Danish attacks on Estonia

The Business of the Cross: The Recruitment of Crusaders

Crusaders composed an important part of Western armies fighting in Livonia and Estonia. This was especially the case in Livonia where the crusaders essentially became a more or less integrated part of the Livonian host—even if they, as we have heard, occasionally had some trouble telling friends from foes. Thus, a steady supply of crusaders was of paramount importance to the overall business of conquering and baptizing the local people through the many prolonged campaigns of preaching and fighting. The crusaders came to Livonia to fight God's war, believing firmly in the penitential character of these wars through concrete promises of indulgency. At the same time, they believed themselves to be under the guardianship of none other than the Virgin Mary.[43] It is, therefore, not surprising that chroniclers like Henry of Livonia would interpret the many wars in Livonia and Estonia as part of an overall holy history unfolding according to Gods own will. Any military action was thought to be a divine service similar to that performed by priests and monks when they celebrated masses, preached, or baptized the pagans. The Danish Archbishop Absalon had the exact same idea when he waged war against the pagan Slavs, as we heard from Saxo Grammaticus.[44]

---

40 Jensen, "Fighting in the Wilderness," forthcoming.

41 HCL 15:3.

42 HCL 15:3.

43 See, e.g., HCL 19:7, where Henry describes Livonia as the Virgin Mary's country. For the Virgin Mary as the special protector of border regions, see Angus MacKay, "Religion, Culture, and Ideology on the Late Medieval Castilian-Granadan Frontier," in *Medieval Frontier Societies*, ed. Robert Bartlett and Angus MacKay (Oxford: Clarendon Press, 1989), 230; Jensen, *Korstog ved verdens yderste rand*, 380–85.

44 Saxo 14:21.3.

In Denmark we know of preaching campaigns promoting the idea of crusading—in general, often referred to in the sources as "the business of the cross." We have already touched upon the call from Pope Alexander III in the 1170s summoning the Danes to support the planned mission among Estonians. Some ten years later came another papal call, this time from Pope Gregory VIII, urging all Christian kings, princes, and peoples to take the cross to the aid of the Holy Land where Jerusalem had just been lost to Saladin's armies, resulting once more in the preaching of a crusade.[45] During the reign of King Valdemar II, the papal involvement in the crusades intensified even more as we have seen with a young an energetic pope now occupying the seat of St. Peter. And finally, during the pontificate of Honorius III, the papal focus on the Baltic Sea region came to the fore with renewed calls and concrete preaching campaigns.[46] It is clear from the sources that the adoption of the general crusading idea among the Danes happened over time and with the help of preaching campaigns. In this respect, the many wars against the Western Slavs became a sort of proving ground amongst the Danes on how to implement the idea of crusading as a holy war against the enemies of God alongside the older traditions of missionary war and ordinary seasonal raids that had been common in the region well before the first crusades came into being. In this perspective, some of the Danish expeditions clearly had papal support and may even have been initiated by specific, or more general, papal calls for the true Christians to commend themselves to the fight against Gods enemies. Other expeditions, however, were basically (and continued to be) the result of specific royal and/or ecclesiastical plans to expand the Danish spheres of influence even further into the Baltic region. At one point, the Danes even became so accustomed to the preaching campaigns of the church urging knights and magnates to promise to go on a crusade in return for the spiritual gifts of indulgency that they saw these campaigns as opportunities to avoid paying the kings taxes. The exemption from various types of taxes had slowly become the norm as the idea of crusading had evolved in Rome. When a person vowed to take the cross and go on a crusade, he would automatically be exempted from certain (royal) taxes. This became a fiscal loophole among some European noblemen in the thirteenth century—also in Denmark: in 1238, King Valdemar II actually complained to the pope that some of the local magnates refused to serve the king and pay their taxes because they had made a vow to go on a crusade without actually fulfilling this promise.[47]

In Livonia Bishop Albert seems to have relied first and foremost on his own preaching tours, urging people to support the missions in Livonia and Estonia by setting "themselves up as a wall for the house of the Lord" (*peregrinis murum se pro domo Domini*

---

45 DD 1:3.144.

46 See the discussion in a previous chapter. The Dominicans especially rose in importance during the later preaching campaigns, see for example Marek Tamm and Anu Mänd, "Introduction: Actors and Networks in the Medieval and Early Modern Baltic Sea Region," in Mänd et al., *Making Livonia*, 9; Johnny Grandjean Gøgsig Jakobsen, "Preachers of War: Dominican Friars as Promulgators of the Crusades in the Baltic Sea Region in the Thirteenth Century," in Kotecki et al., *Christianity and War*, 101–3.

47 Jensen, "Valdemar Sejr," 36.

ponentibus).[48] This metaphor was, of course, a direct reference to the biblical stories which constantly set the narrative frame in the chronicle of Henry of Livonia. At one point, Henry concretely describes how Bishop Albert went back to Germany (probably Saxony or Westphalia) on one of his many preaching tours. Here, the bishop accordingly went "through highways and byways, through cities and forts, those who would set themselves up as a wall for the house of the Lord and take the sign of the cross (*quis crucis signum sibi affigat*) in order to go by sea to Livonia for the consolation of the few who remained there."[49] We are hardly ever informed about the exact number of crusaders that came to Livonia as a consequence of these preaching tours. In this particular case, however, we are told that Bishop Yso of Verden, Bishop Philip of Ratzeburg, and Bishop Bernard of Paderborn, together with their "knights and many other men" (*cum militibus suis et cum multis aliis*), all agreed to come to Livonia the following year.[50] Similarly, we have examples from Denmark with various magnates having made concrete promises to go on a crusade to Livonia and who needed their sworn men to come along. One such case is known from 1217, when King Valdemar's vassal, Count Albrecht II of Orlamünde vowed (once again) to go on a crusade to Livonia. It so happened, however, that his men for some reason had vowed to go on a crusade to the Holy Land. The case is known from a papal letter in which Pope Honorius III permitted the men to change their vow so that they could actually accompany their lord to Livonia instead of going to the Holy Land.[51]

In Bishop Albert's case, his entire episcopate became characterized by a nearly endless succession of recruitment campaigns in Saxony and Westphalia.[52] Wherever he went he would compel knights, and even kings, to support him. At the court of King Philip in Magdeburg, Albert even reassured the assembled magnates that the crusaders to Livonia would, of course, be covered by the same papal protection as those who headed for the Holy Land, and that they would receive a full indulgence, too.[53] It is interesting to note here, that Henry actually represents the expeditions to Livonia as real crusades, regardless of the nuances of theology or ecclesiastical politics that, in reality, may have been promoted at the time by the popes or the local magnates and ecclesiastical institutions, as we have already seen in a previous chapter. The crusades to Livonia were equivalent to the crusades to Jerusalem claimed Bishop Albert (or Henry), both

---

48 See for example HCL 6:1 and 23:1. See also the general discussion of Bishop Albert's many journeys in Tamm, "Mission and Mobility," 20–28.

49 HCL 14:4.

50 HCL 14:4.

51 DD 1:5.101. See also Jensen, "Valdemar Sejr" 23–24; Lind, "Dannebrog and the Danish Crusades to Estonia," 20–21. With regards to the close connections between the count and King Valdemar, see Kurt Villads Jensen, "King Valdemar II and Tallinn in 1219: Just Another of his Conquests or Part of a Grand Plan?" *Ajalooline Ajakiri: The Estonian Historical Journal* 180, no. 2/3 (2022), 138–39.

52 See, e.g., HCL 9:8. Tamm, "Mission and Mobility," 21.

53 HCL 3:2: "responsum vero est ea sub protectione apostolici comprehendi, qui peregrinacionem Lyvonie in plenariam peccaminum iniungens vie coequavit Ierosolimitane" (an opinion was asked for as to whether the goods of the pilgrims to Livonia were to be placed under the protection of the pope, as is the case for those who journey to Jerusalem).

in terms of the promised papal protection (which covered all crusaders) and in terms of the promised indulgence. It was clearly Henry's aim to reassure his readers that the Livonian Church as well as the crusaders had the full support of the papacy.[54]

As already mentioned, the crusaders were commonly referred to as pilgrims (*per-egrini*) in the chronicle of Henry of Livonia following in this more general trend. The first time we hear about these armed pilgrims is in connection with the description of Bishop Albert's first visit to Livonia in 1200. From that point onwards, the armed pilgrims are said to have come to Livonia more or less every year, often accompanying the bishop when he returned from one of his endless preaching tours in northern Germany.[55] Henry also explicitly describes how these pilgrims would go back to Germany having served as crusaders for a whole year—literally having "soldiered for God under the cross" (*sub cruce sua Deo militaverant*).[56] In no other place in the chronicle does Henry explicitly state that the pilgrims, as cross-signed warriors, fought under the cross (*sub cruce*). But it is clear that this is what he believed: with their crusading indulgences and the sign of the cross, they were to be understood as crusaders fighting God's war. Even though the term *peregrini* appears first in connection with Bishop Albert's first journey to Livonia, Henry does actually also mention the crusaders in the context of Bishop Bertold's conflict with the rebellious, apostate Livs in Ikšķile and Mārtiņsala in 1197–1198. Here, Bertold is said to have brought with him an army of crusaders, though without any specific references to them being pilgrims or cross-signed. He does, however, state that the pope had granted a remission of sins (the technical-theological term for indulgence) to all those who had taken the cross and followed Bishop Bertold back to Livonia to fight "the perfidious Livonians" as Henry says.[57]

While Henry of Livonia generally refers to all the crusaders who came to Livonia in the service of the Livonian Church as pilgrims, he does not use the same vocabulary about the Danish, Swedish, or Norwegian crusaders, seemingly downplaying the practical and spiritual importance of the Scandinavian forays into the region once again. He does, however, recognize their formal status when mentioning, for example, how Archbishop Anders Sunesen bestowed "the sign of the cross upon a great multitude" (*signo crucis signaverat*) for the remission of their sins before the Danish expedition to Saare-

---

54 Tyerman drily calls Albert's preaching campaigns "Bishop Albert's freelance crusade recruiting." Tyerman, "Henry of Livonia and the Ideology of Crusading," 34.

55 HCL 4:1.

56 HCL 7:5: "cum peregrinis, qui per annum illum in Lyvonia sub cruce sua Deo militaverant" (with the pilgrims, who had soldiered under the Gross for their God throughout this year in Livonia).

57 HCL 2:3: "igitur domnus papa cunctis signum crucis accipientibus et contra perfidos Lyvones se armantibus remissionem indulget peccatorum" (The lord pope, therefore, granted remission of sins to all those who should take the cross and arm themselves against the perfidious Livonians). As explained earlier, the information Henry offers about indulgences cannot immediately be taken at face value: he had clear grounds for portraying the Livonian crusades as if they were fully legitimate and supported by the papacy from the outset. See Tyerman, "Henry of Livonia and the Ideology of Crusading," 23–27 and 29–31.

maa in 1206 as we have already seen.[58] Technically, this would have left the German and the Danish on equal footing with regards to the spiritual rewards of being crusaders.

The chronicle of Henry of Livonia mentions on several occasions that the Livonian crusaders' vows included one year's service, a considerably shorter period than promised by those who planned to go to the Holy Land. In comparison, we seldom hear anything about the lengths of service among the Danish crusaders who seem, in most cases, to have signed up for relatively short expeditions and only later were required to stay in Estonia for longer periods. The crusading vows in general among crusaders setting out for the Holy Land, in most cases, seem to have entailed three years' service.[59] The reason behind the one-year vow among the German crusaders in Livonia and the likely even shorter term among the Danish crusaders, lies, above all, in the shorter distances involved between the crusaders' homelands and the lands of Livonia and Estonia. On several occasions, Henry calls the year of service among the German crusaders a "year of pilgrimage" (*annus peregrinationis*).[60] During this year, crusaders would serve as garrison troops or as part of the campaigning army, or they would be tasked with constructing and safeguarding roads, waterways, and bridges for the remission of their sins as we have already seen.[61]

By far the majority of crusaders who came to Livonia seems to have come from Germany proper, but the sources also mention for example Frisian crusaders.[62] The Germans usually embarked at Lübeck, before travelling to Riga via Visby on Gotland.[63] The voyage between the seaports of northern Germany and the Baltic lands was highly dependent on the seasons. When the winter storms became too violent and ice closed the inner part of the Baltic Sea in early December at the latest, sailing became impossible. In practice, this meant that the Westerners who lived in Livonia, and later also in Estonia, were cut off from supplies of both people and goods for the entire winter, reaching well into the spring. Around April, the waters once again became navigable, and the ships sailed to and from Livonia and Estonia.[64] Those unfortunate souls who departed

---

58 HCL 10:13.

59 Bysted et al., *Jerusalem in the North*, 177–78.

60 See, e.g., HCL 7:3 and 9:8.

61 HCL 12:2 on the construction of a bridge during a campaign. See also LEC 1:1.53. Here, Bishop Albert mentions a bridge that was constructed on his orders by named crusades for the remission of their sins and, instead, of participating in a proper military expedition. Anyone could now use the bridge without paying any taxes.

62 See, e.g., HCL 14:8; see also Arnold of Lübeck, 5:30. For Frisian crusaders more generally, see Johannes A. Mol, "Frisian Fighters and the Crusade," *Crusades* 1 (2002), 89–110.

63 Jensen, "Urban Life and the Crusades," 77; Jensen, "Valdemar Sejr," 41–42.

64 Kristin Ilves, "Sea and Seafaring in the Chronicles: The Study of the Chronicle of Henry of Livonia and the Livonian Rhymed Chronicle on Navigation on the Baltic Sea in the 12th and 13th Centuries," in *Tjop tjop! Vänbok till Christer Westerdahl med anledning av hans 70-årsdag den 13. november 2015*, ed. Staffan von Arbien (Skärhamn: Båtdokgruppen, 2015), 207; R. Simiński, "'*Qui se omnes periculis maris comittentes in Lyvoniam devenerunt*': On the History of the Sea Voyages to Livonia at the Turn of the 12th and the 13th Century as Presented in the Chronicle by Henry the Lettish," *Studia Maritima* 14, (2001), 32.

for home too late would often experience a harrying trip across the Baltic Sea. Henry describes one such incident in the year 1204. In early September some German pilgrims decided to return home from Riga to Germany (probably Lübeck) via Visby but a heavy storm blew them out of course towards the Estonian lands. Here the lonely ship—probably a cog—was attacked by no less than ten Estonian "pirate ships and twelve other ships" (*cum deem pyraticis et duodecim aliis navibus*).[65] The fight became an extremely brutal affair with many losses amongst the Estonians who could not overcome the huge cog only having their much smaller ships. Eventually, the Estonians broke off, enabling the Germans to continue their journey. Soon after, however, the Germans saw fifty ship-wrecked Christians who had been left stranded on a shore deep inside enemy territory. Mercifully, Henry says, the Germans allowed these people onboard their ship and shared what food they had with them. Seemingly, the returning pilgrims had planned for a fairly quick journey across the sea and had only taken very little provision onboard before they departed from Riga. With an additional fifty men (and women?!) onboard, the scarce supplies were soon gone. By miracle, a merchant ship came their way, offering much needed supplies of food and water to the starving Germans; some of the supplies they had to pay for, some were free. Having suffered additional storms and howling winds, the Germans finally arrived in Visby at the end of November, having spent nearly three gruelling months én route, battling both pagans and nature—normally the trip would have lasted only a few days. So advanced was the winter, that when the people continued their trip toward Denmark, the ice had become so thick that it was impossible to reach the coast. Consequently, the passengers were forced to leave the ship stuck in the ice and continue their journey towards Germany overland, through Denmark.[66] Luckily, most trips across the Baltic Sea would have been much shorter and less traumatizing.

When the first ships docked in Riga (and later also in Tallinn) in the early spring, they would unload new cohorts of crusaders and, in due course, transport the previous year's contingents back home again. The majority of these crusaders had come to take an active part in the military expeditions against the enemies of the church, and earn their share of the spiritual rewards promised them by the various church authorities. During their stay in Livonia, Henry explains that the crusaders were commanded by a man that the chronicler refers to as "leader and magistrate of the pilgrims" (*dux et advocatus peregrinorum*).[67] It was the task of this official to make sure that the crusaders fulfilled their pilgrimage in accordance with the needs of the Livonian Church whether it was actual military campaigning, or, as we shall see in a short while, other tasks that needed to be done. During the larger military campaigns, it was probably also this official who commanded the crusaders in battle as a part of the larger Livonian host. Some of the crusaders would have been veterans with several expeditions under their belts, but for others it would have been their first trip as crusaders, totally unfamiliar with these new lands. It would most certainly have been a primary task of the leader of the pilgrims to

---

65 HCL 8:3.

66 HCL 8:4.

67 HCL 28:5. The pilgrims' magistrate in question (1224) was a Saxon knight called Fredehelm.

educate the newly arrived crusaders as to who the enemy was and was not. While we do hear about military units fighting beneath their own banners, neither the chronicle of Henry of Livonia, nor the chronicle of Saxo Grammaticus indicates that the pilgrims/ crusaders had a special banner. This may be different in the somewhat younger *Livonian Rhymed Chronicle* from around 1290. During an uproar among the Semgallians in the winter of 1279–1280, the Teutonic Knights (who had by then taken over from the Sword Brethren in Livonia) summoned all available crusaders: "as soon as they received word, a brother and about a hundred men came from Cēsis to Riga to the land's defence. They came in a stately manner with a red banner decorated with strips of white fur, as was their custom."[68] A little later in the text, the brother knight is also referred to, as "their leader" and the text states that all the men "served under him willingly" (*ein brûder was ir houbtman, sie wâren im gerne undertân*).[69] It seems here that we actually have a sequence from a chronicle that might be interpreted as referring to a leader and magistrate of pilgrims performing his office during times of war (his followers are not referred to as "brothers" or brother knights, but merely as "men"). What is even more interesting is the reference to the specific design of the banner in the text said to have belonged to the castles of Cēsis in Livonia. It is described as "a red banner which was crossed by white furs, in the manner of the Wends."[70] The national flag of modern-day Latvia has taken its shape and colours precisely from this medieval text. We should, however, also remember the Danish national narrative about the appearance of Dannebrog, said to have fallen from the sky during the Battle of Lyndanise in 1219 (or perhaps as early as 1208). It is, therefore, tempting to suggest that the true (and perhaps most likely) origin of Dannebrog may, in fact, have been its service in Livonia and Estonia as a designated banner for foreign crusaders serving in these lands, substituting or even reinterpreting the white stripes from the abovementioned text as a white cross proper. Both German and Danish crusaders would have known such a banner from their time in Livonia or Estonia, and its simple heraldic layout would have made it fairly easy to copy once home again, as a commemoration of their divine service as crusaders.[71]

---

68 *Livländische Reimchronik: Mit Anmerkungen, Namenverzeichnis und Glossar*, ed. Leo Meyer (Paderborn: Olms, 1876;rept. 2013), l:9219–33: "Von Wenden was zû Rige komen zûr lantwer, als ich hân vernomen, ein brûder und wol hundert man: den wart daz mêre kunt getân. Die quamen hovedlîchen dar mit einer banier rôt gevar, daz was mit wîtze durch gesniten hûte nâch wendischen siten. Wenden ist ein burc genant, von den die banier wart bekant, und ist in Letten lant gelegen dâ die vrowen rîtens pflegen nâch den siten, als die man. Vor wâr ich ûch daz sagen kan, die banier der Letten ist." For a translation into English, see *The Livonian Rhymed Chronicle*, trans. Jerry C. Smith and William L. Urban (Madison: University of Wisconsin Press, 2001).

69 *Livländische Reimchronik*, l:9237–38.

70 The German chroniclers referred to Cēsis as Wenden, hence the reference to the "Wends."

71 For a more traditional interpretation, see Bysted et al., *Jerusalem in the North*, 205–09. See also Jensen, "Da legenden blev en national fortælling," 192–95. See also Lind, "Dannebrog and the Danish Crusades to Estonia," 7–8 and 23–26.

While the primary task of the crusaders would have been to fight the pagans and protect the Christian people of Livonia and Estonia, they could also be called upon to undertake other important work apart from just fighting. The building and maintaining of roads and bridges were considered essential tasks that could be entrusted to the crusaders—at least to those who belonged to the lower social strata! The crusaders were also set to work on the many castles in the region, like the stronghold so hastily constructed by the Danes on Saaremaa in 1206, but also the more substantial work carried out to fortify Riga with proper walls during the city's early years. Similarly, the fortification of the Danish castle on Toompea Hill following the Battle of Lyndanise would also have required the help of the crusaders in support of whatever local workers could be called upon. At one point in 1209, Henry precisely describes the walling of Riga as a work undertaken as a service to God.[72] Taking part in the construction of roads, bridges, strongholds, castles, and city walls was, therefore, also considered spiritually meritorious to the crusaders.[73]

When their year was up, the crusaders would normally return back to their respective homes having fulfilled their crusader's vow and thus earned the promised indulgences. Sometimes, however, circumstances would force the bishop of Riga to urge some crusaders to prolong their stay for another year by persuading them to take the cross with renewed promises of additional indulgences and further spiritual rewards. Some of the armed men in the military retinue seem not to have been satisfied only with spiritual gains and insisted on being paid for their military service alongside ordinary crusaders.[74] Thus, we have this interesting mix of crusaders (i.e., pilgrims) bound by their vows, and with the promise of spiritual rewards in the afterlife, fighting alongside hired soldiers fighting for pay, or in the retinues of various lords, seemingly without having made any individual vows

The Lord's Army: The Fighting Strength of the Livonian Army

Apart from the crusaders, there were other military contingents serving the Livonian Church in time of war. We have already very briefly touched upon the Sword Brethren who constituted a relative small but powerful and, above all, permanent military force amounting to approximately one hundred ten knights, twelve hundred serving brothers, and perhaps four hundred secular knights serving as the Order's vassals during the height of its power.[75] In most cases, the master of the Order was in overall command of

---

72 HCL 11:1 and 9; 13:3.

73 A similar sentiment towards such constructional work can also be found in some medieval testaments with offerings to the maintenance of roads and bridges being considered as spiritually rewarding, as the gifts to churches and monasteries, or to the poor people of the local community.

74 HCL 1:9. According to Henry in this particular case, some three hundred crusaders renewed their wows with some—perhaps some of the lesser knights and the foot soldiers needed to be hired by the bishop. See also Larrea, "Kinsmen, Friends or Mercenaries," on the use of hired troops in Scandinavia during the twelfth and thirteenth centuries.

75 Benninghoven, *Der Orden der Schwertbrüder*, 223–24 and 407–08.

the Livonian army when actually on campaign while it was the bishop of Riga's preroga-tive to summon the army in the first place.[76]

The bishop could also summon his own retinue and vassals along with the towns-people and merchants of Riga, who in some cases would also be required to fight as part of the overall army of Livonia.[77] In most cases, however, the military service of the townspeople seems to have been as a defensive militia when for example Riga itself was attacked.[78]

Foreign merchants would occasionally also be called upon to join forces with the locals when their special skills were required, and the army needed the ships for trans-portation. Of course, they would also have been engaged in protecting their own ships, warehouses, or goods in times of crises or during concrete attacks.[79] When compar-ing the Germans in Livonia with the military capability of King Valdemar one should remember that the bishops of Riga did not possesse a naval force of their own. While in reality Valdemar controlled the most powerful naval force in the entire Baltic Sea region, the situation was very different for the German bishops. The need for the mer-chants' (naval) support would become imminent when Riga was threatened by attacks from strong, seaborne raiding parties or actual enemy fleets from either Saaremaa or Curonia. Henry relates how bishop Albert of Riga, alongside the master of the Sword Brethren, realized that they had to do something about their lacking naval support. They decided, therefore, to acquire a cog that should permanently guard the lower part of the Daugava River while protecting both the waterway itself and the various harbours against sudden enemy attacks. Henry records how this particular ship was strengthened like a fort—probably with the aforementioned, so-called "castles" serving as fighting platforms at bow and stern—and manned by fifty fully armed men with crossbows.[80]

Like their Estonian counterparts, the local Livic and the Letgallian people were fully accustomed to taking part in the many wars that raged these lands and had done so well before the arrival of the first Western crusaders. Like in Estonia, local levies could be summoned in times of war by local elders who often also initiated military campaigns of their own—sometimes inviting the Germans to join them, sometimes preferring to fight

---

76 See for example HCL 13:2.

77 Jensen, "Urban Life and the Crusades," 84–93.

78 See, e.g., HCL 10:12, 14:5, and 18:6. It appears that priests and women alike were required to take part in the city's defence. See also the detailed account of the burghers' fighting obligations in Jensen, "Urban Life and the Crusades," 84–87. Henry also mentions occasions when the people of Riga were mustered by the ringing of church bells. It was a widespread practice to use church bells for this purpose. In some places, the ringing of church bells was even synonymous with rebellion, and bell-ringers risked being castrated if a city's enemies captured them. See Nicholas Wright, *Knights and Peasants: The Hundred Years War in the French Countryside* (Woodbridge: Boydell, 1998), 113–14. For merchants' participation in various engagements, see, e.g., HCL 16:2 and 19:11. Arnold of Lübeck also mentions in his chronicle that the merchants actively took part in warfare. See Arnold, 5:30 and Mark R. Munzinger, "The Profits of the Cross," 173 and 175.

79 See as examples HCL 11:5; 16:2. See also Munzinger, "The Profits of the Cross," 173 and 175–76.

80 HCL 19:11, 154–55.

on their own.[81] The occasions could be varied if, for example, local Livic or Letgallian elders felt obliged to take revenge on some of their Estonian or Rus' neighbours who had at some point raided their homelands and would suffer a similar fate through retaliatory attacks. While mounted units seem to have been an important element in the Estonians armies, the Livs and Letgallians seem mostly to have relied on warriors travelling and fighting on foot while occasionally using a few mounted troops as scouts. The local warriors of Livonia seem to have used a military equipment that probably had some strong similarities with earlier types of Scandinavian-style (round) shields, swords, axes, and spears for throwing and trusting while some would be armed also with bows. Some of the warriors probably also had lighter types of armour such as helmets, mail shirts, and perhaps other types of light body armour if they belonged to the wealthier families. In general, however, the local warriors do seem to have been lighter armed than their Christian foes.[82] As mentioned, the Livs and Letgallians at times fought on their own, but equally often formed part of the Livonian host as auxiliary troops fighting alongside the local Germans and the crusaders.[83] In an example from the winter of 1212, Bishop Albert is said to have summoned all available forces for an upcoming attack into Estonia. The size of the army is said to have been "about four thousand German infantry and knights and the same number again of Livonians and Letts."[84] When the army came together at special preselected assembly areas, often referred to by Henry as places for prayer and counsel, special masses would be said and the army prepared for battle with the Banner of the Virgin Mary marking them the Lord's Army.[85] When preparing for actual battle, each of the different units would have their special place in the battle formation, with the Germans normally deploying in the centre, with the Livs on the right wing and the Letgallians on the left wing.[86]

Fighting the Lord's Battle

As we have already seen, the Western knights clad in heavy armour, mounted on strong horses could easily defeat the local warriors normally fighting on foot with lesser armour and, thus, unable to withstand a mounted knightly charge. Additional support from well-armed infantry carrying shields, spears, and crossbow further added to the military superiority of the crusaders—at least as long as the Westerners could decide when and where to fight! The locals soon adapted to the new circumstances and learned

81 Kaljundi, "Neophytes as Actors in the Livonian Crusades," 93–94.

82 For a general view on the local military equipment, see Mati Mandel; "Eestlaste relvastus," in *Eesti aastal 1200*, ed. Marika Mägi (Tallinn: Argo, 2003), 191–204.

83 Kaljundi, "Neophytes as Actors in the Livonian Crusades," 94.

84 HCL 15:7: "et errant circiter quator milia Theuthonicorum, peditum simul et equitum, et Lyvonum et Lettorum alia totidem."

85 See for example HCL 23:9. The importance of the proper liturgy in relation to crusading (especially the act of praying) is treated in detail in M. Cecilia Gaposchkin, *Invisible Weapons: Liturgy and the Making of Crusade Ideology* (Ithaca: Cornell University Press, 2017), 41–64.

86 HCL 15:3 and 22:2.

to fight the crusaders on their own terms, favouring the tactics of lightly armed warriors fighting against heavily armoured opponents. Thus, the usual form of warfare in
the wilderness—rapid raids into enemy territories with small but highly mobile forces
attacking, looting, and burning villages, farms, and lesser fortified places coupled with
ambushes and similar types small-scale fighting, continued to be the norm in Livonia
and Estonia. These types of small-scale warfare were off-cause well-known among the
crusaders who had fought these types of wars in their homelands for generations. The
environment was different here in Livonia and Estonia, however, often not favouring
the Western style of fighting with a primary wedge on knightly attacks. Crusaders, like
locals, had to adopt each other's styles of fighting and the fine-tuning of tactics and
equipment.

During most of these raids, the attacking army often had a single assembly area, as
we have seen, close to the intended target area. Here, they would gather the army and
reorganize the various units in accordance with the chosen strategy.[87] When in enemy
country, similar bases would be established as places for the army to reassembly following the plundering and burning of neighbouring farms and villages. These locations
would also serve as places to store booty and all those who had been taken as slaves.
Finally such places could also serve as places for a defensive stance should it be necessary.[88] During some of the larger raids, the army would split up into various subunits
with each having its own base—in the case of Livonia the Livs and the Letgallians would
sometime have their own bases whereas the Germans chose a place for themselves,
reflecting the way that these armies often operated during a campaign—at least according to Henry of Livonia. That would allow parts of the Livonian army to use different
routes into the enemy territory. Sometimes however, a concrete situation would require
a more speedy approach and Henry mentions that "the Livonians and Letts and the
swifter men from the army would advance ahead of the main army" (*Lyvones et Letti
et qui errant velociores de exercitu*), probably hoping to intercept any opposing enemy
forces or simply to overwhelm the intended target areas before the locals would have
time to flee.[89] As soon as the rest of the army arrived all the settlements and outlying
farms would be plundered and then burned to the ground. As already mentioned, the
locals would either be killed (that seems often to have been the fate of the men) or taken
captive (which was normally what happened to the women and children), and any valuables and livestock taken as booty.[90]

---

87 Benninghoven, "Zur Technik spätmittelalterlicher Feldzüge im Ostbaltikum," 637–38.

88 Jensen, "Fighting in the Wilderness," forthcoming.

89 HCL 15:7. According to Henry the attack was devastating: "et domos et villas flammis tradiderunt
et multos capientes, multos interficientes spolia multa tulerunt. Et quarto die procedentes in
Gerwam diviserunt exercitum villas et multos de paganis comprehendentes occiderunt et mulieres
et parvulos captivos duxerunt et pecora multa et equos et spolia rapientes...congregationem suam
habentes omnia, que in circuitu erant, incendio vastaverunt."

90 Jensen, "Fighting in the Wilderness," forthcoming. See also Kurt Villads Jensen, "Holy War, Holy
Wrath!: Baltic Wars Between Regulated Warfare and Total Annihilation Around 1200," in *Church*

When an expedition had been successfully executed, the entire army would return home (hopefully) laden with booty and captives having dealt a severe blow to the enemy or taken revenge on a prior atrocity. Back in Livonia the army would divide the spoils and also allow the local churches to receive a part of the goods that had been taken, duly praising God for his support in this divine war against the ungodly enemies.[91]

Carrying for the Wounded and the Dead

During most expeditions—small or large—there would be a number of wounded who had survived the actual fighting but were left with injuries that needed treatment. Some of the wounded could probably be treated quite easily on the spot having suffered only minor gashes and cuts. Such wounds would need a quick clean, some herbs, and a bandage to avert inflammation and allow for quick healing. In seasoned armies, like the German and Danish armies of the time, there would most certainly have been people experienced in dressing the wounds of their companions-in-arms and there might even have been physician-like experts available in the retinues of the more important magnates. Saxo Grammaticus mentions how some warriors became skilled healers in their own right because they had cured their own wounds so many times, following this or that battle. Out of pure experience, they became experts in dressing battle wounds.[92] Based on personal experience, such men would tend to the wounded according to the medical knowledge of the time—and the social status of the wounded! A common soldier would have had access to the rather rudimentary help of his brothers-in-arms, whereas a magnate could rely on his highly paid expert physician. One particular incident is retold in the chronicle by Henry describing how a local warrior had been wounded and requested the help of the seasoned missionary Theodoric, who must have had a reputation of being able to treat various forms of illnesses and wounds that came from fighting. In return for the treatment, the Livic warrior promised to let himself be baptized by the venerable Theodoric if he was cured: "The brother [i.e., Theodoric] pounded herbs together (*herbas contundens*), therefore, and, not knowing the effects of the herbs, called upon the name of the Lord."[93] Even if this incident is not specifically tied to the aftermath of a battle—the chronicle does not state how the local warrior was wounded—the essentials of the treatment (herbs and prayers) might very well have equalled the aver-

---

and Belief in the Middle Ages: Popes, Saints, and Crusaders, ed. Kirsi Salonen and Sari Katajala Peltomaa (Amsterdam: Amsterdam University Press, 2016), 227–50.

91 Jensen, "Fighting in the Wilderness," forthcoming.

92 Saxo 7:2.2. In this particular case, Saxo is writing about a legendary hero by the name of Vitolf, who had spent most of his life as a warrior in the service of a renowned king. When his master died, Vitolf retired and became a farmer. Soon thereafter, his reputation as a healer became known and many came to ask for his help in curing their wounds. Hating their submissiveness, he offered them poison instead that would make them more ill, stating that a man should not beg for help or act submissive, but use force to take whatever he needs. Perhaps not the attitude of the ideal army physician but nevertheless a proper warrior in the eyes of Saxo. For more cases of medical treatment of wounds in the chronicle of Saxo Grammaticus, see Saxo 1:8.18, 6:8.1 and 9:4.12.

93 HCL 1:10.

age treatment available to the ordinary fighting men in a crusader army on campaign in Livonia and Estonia around 1200. In most cases, it might have been left to the accompanying priests and monks to attend the wounded and dying men at the end of battle. If they possessed any medical skills at all, like Theodoric (who seems to have been in doubt with regards to his own skills), they would most certainly have been expected to help tend to the wounded and ease their suffering. If treatment was futile, clerics would have performed the last rites to those beyond recovery and also taken care of the burial of the dead according to the Christians rites.

Both in 1206 and also in 1219, King Valdemar had the benefit of having his ships close by, making it relatively easy for the Danes to evacuate the badly wounded men onboard the ships as soon as order had been restored following the actual fighting. At the same time, however, it would be highly questionably if the more gravely wounded would have had even a small chance of surviving an exhausting and prolonged journey home across the sea without additional treatment. For those who campaigned further inland, they had to look for other means of transportation both with regards to supplies and wounded comrades.

Sometimes the expeditions took place close to rivers, enabling the armies to use riverboats. That was for example the case in the winter of 1218–1219 when the Livonian army attacked a number of Semgallian strongholds south of Livonia. Not only did a river provide the army with a supply route, but it also enabled the army to evacuate wounded from the battlefields back to Riga and the care of the various ecclesiastical institutions. In the case of the Germans, this ended in dire straits because the Semgallians managed to cut the river off, while ambushing the supply convoys going upriver.[94] In another case from Riga, the Germans were more successful in employing boats and river crafts when evacuating the wounded. During a successful attack against the rebellious Livs on the island of Mārtiņsala in 1206, the Germans had used boats to transport their attacking force. Some of the boats soon returned back towards Riga, bearing news of the successful attack but also carrying a number of wounded men who needed medical care.[95] In most cases, however, the armies in Livonia and Estonia had to rely on land transportation both with regards to supplies and the transportation of the wounded. During the larger military campaigns with relatively high numbers of armed men, a substantial number of carts and wagons would have been needed for spare weapons, food for both men and beast, siege equipment, and also booty on the way home. This becomes apparent from the many examples mentioned in the chronicle of Henry of Livonia who often refers to such baggage trains.[96] During lesser campaigns with fewer men, a low number of carts would be available or discarded all together in exchange for packhorses that could more easily traverse the rough roads of the interior of Livonia and Estonia. During

---

94 HCL 23:4.

95 HCL 10:8. See also Jensen, "Fighting in the Wilderness," forthcoming.

96 See for example HCL 30:3; 11:5. See also HCL 30:2 on the importance of supplies. In the *Livonian Rhymed Chronicle* it is also mentioned that the men themselves would be tasked with carrying supplies. Cf. *Livländische Reimchronik*, I:8980–81. See also Veldi, "Roads and Hill forts in Southern Estonia," 391.

wintertime, carts and wagons would be replaced by sleighs far more suited to the cross-country travelling in a landscape covered in deep snow.[97]

Depending on the type of campaign and the explicit target area either ships, boats, carts, wagons, spare horses, or sledges would have provided means of transportation for the more seriously wounded men following the various battles and skirmishes. Henry explicitly states how wounded (knights?) would be loaded onto horses, and even in some cases placed on stretchers hung out between two horses. Something similar is mentioned in the *Livonian Rhymed Chronicle* describing how wounded men were also transported on a stretcher between two horses.[98]

The many dead following a battle also had to be dealt with. Saxo Grammaticus has already told us how the common soldiers who died during a battle were buried pretty much where they were killed (if there were not a church or a chapel nearby), whereas the bodies of the high-ranking members of the army were treated very differently. According to Saxo, their dead bodies would be salted and taken back to their home for a proper burial.[99] Another slightly older chronicler, Helmold of Bossau, writes something similar, accounting how the body of a slain count had to be taken home to his family's preferred burial place, wherefore his body was cut into pieces, cooked, and embalmed thus enabling the bones to be transported home.[100]

When it came to the dead bodies of the slain enemies, things were completely different since the way you treated the dead had an important symbolic significance. Henry, for example, often mentions in his chronicle that dead enemies would be left unburied as a sign of contempt on behalf of the victorious part.[101] In one example, the body of a Dane by the name Hebbe, along with his companions, were left unburied for "the dogs and as food for the birds of heaven" (*canibus corrodenda...escas volatilibus celi*).[102] Along the same lines, Henry also mentions how dead Christians—this time from Riga—were thrown into the Daugava by their enemies who did not want to waste any time on a proper burial. That was left to the people of Riga once the dead bodies washed ashore not far from the city, and they were then buried according to the proper Christian traditions.[103]

According to Henry, it was equally important to the pagans that they were able to bury their dead according to their religious traditions. As an example, he mentions the

97 HCL 11:5; Veldi, "Roads and Hill Forts in Southern Estonia," 391.

98 *Livländische Reimchronik* l:9031, the term is "rossebâre."

99 Saxo 14:40.11.

100 Helmold, 2:100. Jensen, *Med ord og ikke med slag*, 235–37.

101 Jensen, *Med ord og ikke med slag*, 235.

102 Jensen, *Med ord og ikke med slag*, 166–67. The reference in HCL 26:6 is actually from the Old Testament, Jeremiah 15:3, thus inscribing the dead Dane in a biblical narrative as a testimony to the elevated status of dead Christians (even if they were in fact Danes) compared to dead pagans. For similar notions expressed by Henry, see also 15:7, 20:7, 26:5, and 26:7.

103 HCL 11:9. Not being buried properly was highly problematic according to the traditions of the church as the dead one would risk his or her salvation and consequently the eternal life. See for example Norbert Ohler, *Sterben und Tod im Mittelalter* (München: dtv, 1993), 144.

death of an Lithuanian chieftain (*princeps ac senior lettonum*) who's comrades-in-arms willingly paid a ransom for his head so that he (or rather his head) could be buried in respect to the local, pagan tradition.[104] Also among the supporters of the Livonian Church were some of the local chieftains who did not want to give up the older traditions of cremation as the proper burial form, even if it was strongly opposed by the church. One especially prominent example was that of the Livic leader Caupo, who died in 1217. He had been among the first to embrace the new religion and had been baptized as early as 1200, being a stout ally of the Germans in Riga, having at one point even made a trip to Rome to visit the pope.[105] In the chronicle, Caupo is described as the ideal pagan-becoming-Christian who eventually died as a result of wounds sustained in a battle fighting alongside the Germans. Feeling his end was near Caupo accordingly made his confessions and gave away all his worldly possessions to the local churches.[106] Following his death his body was then cremated according to the ancient local tradition after which his remains were taken back to his own lands. None of the prominent Christian people who are said to have been present at Caupo's deathbed (or Henry for that matter) seem to have reacted to this quasi-pagan burial ritual. It is possible to interpret Caupo's funeral as a pragmatic parallel to the handling of the bodies of prominent crusader who died a long way from home, who needed to be either salted, chopped up, and/ or boiled as preparation for the transport home.[107] This seems however not to be the case in this example concerning Caupo's burial, which was, essentially, a combination of the old and new ways.

At one point, Henry describes how some of the (partially) Christianized Estonians reacted to their enforced conversion by digging up their deceased family members during a rebellion, with the intention of cremating them according to their ancient traditions as a clear rejection of the Christian rites.[108] In similar way, the holy wars of the crusades in Livonia and Estonia could also be waged against the dead! Henry has several examples of (especially) pagan armies who seem to have targeted Christian churches and cemeteries during various military attacks. Both the buildings and the

---

104 HCL 17:5. Along a similar note, Henry's also mentions that warriors from Curonia cut off the head of those of their companions who were killed during an attack on Riga in 1210 before cremating the rest of their bodies: HCL 14:5. See also HCL 21:3, where Henry seems to indicate that it was only the heads of dead high class warriors that would have been removed in this way.

105 HCL 4:4. Here Caupo is mentioned for the first time as a hostage of Bishop Albert.

106 HCL 21:4. See also Jensen, *Med ord og ikke med slag*, 320. Caupo's son had been killed in battle already in 1210. He may, therefore, not have had any living male heirs. All his worldly possession was given to the churches in Livonia. See HCL 16:8.

107 Jensen, *Med ord og ikke med slag*, 171.

108 HCL 26:8: "et corpora mortuorum suorum, in cemeteriis sepulta, de sepulchris effoderunt et more paganorum pristino cremaverunt" (they disinterred the bodies of their dead, who had been buried in cemeteries, and cremated them according to their original pagan custom). It was not, however, only in terms of burial practices that the rebellious Estonians revolted against the enforced Christian traditions. Accordingly, the Estonians also took back those women whom they had been forced to let go of when the Christians (presumably) insisted that Christian men were only allowed to have one wife.

individual graves were reportedly desecrated as a particular mockery of the Christians demonstrating just how powerless the pagans considered the Christian god to be. The Christian response was to leave enemy dead unburied whenever they had the opportunity. In this way God's war encompassed both the living and the dead in this world and in the afterlife.[109]

Winter Wonderland:
The Shared Experience of Fighting During the "Great Cold"

A favoured season for waging war in the Baltics was during winter. At that time of the year, heavy frost and lots of snow would make the rivers, streams, swamps, and marchlands freeze solid, enabling raiding parties and larger armies to cross such obstacles much more easily than was the case during spring, summer or autumn. During winter, the enemy would most often stay at home in their villages, farmsteads, or strongholds, sheltering themselves against the harsh Baltic winter with its freezing temperatures and huge amounts of snow covering the entire landscape. While it was important to protect one's own family, livestock, and supplies (like crops etc.) against the harsh weather, enemy raiders also knew that a tempting booty was ripe for the taking as the local communities were caught unaware in a surprise attack. Furthermore, merchants from Germany or Scandinavia often spent the winters at some of the important markets and trading posts in either Livonia or Estonia, awaiting springtime either to return home or to continue their journeys to other regional markets. Any such rich merchant who had laid up for the winter would have been a tempting target during a winter's raid.[110] Neither the locals nor the (foreign) traders and merchants would have been unarmed as everybody knew that wintertime was the time of enemy raids. The merchants may even have hired armed escorts during their journeys enabling them to defend themselves against pirate attacks at sea or from enemy raiders or robbers on land. It is hardly a surprise that Henry of Livonia so often refers to armed merchants as partakers in various military expeditions.[111]

In a later chapter we shall return to the important visit in Livonia and Estonia by a papal legate, William of Modena, but even he preferred carry out a portion of his travels during the wintertime—probably on the advice of the locals more accustomed to the harsh climate:

after the feast of the Epiphany [January 6, 1226], when traveling is better in those cold countries on account of the snow and the ice (*cum propter nives et gelu via sit in frigidis terries illis melior ad eundum*), the [papal legate William of Modena], with clerics and servants, taking with him also Bishop Lambert of the

---

109 Jensen, *Med ord og ikke med slag*, 231–37.

110 Overwintering merchants are mentioned by Henry of Livonia on more occasions, see for example HCL 1:11. With regards to a preference for military campaigning during wintertime, see also Saxo 14:12.1–2.

111 See for example HCL 16:2.

Semgalls, John the provost of the church of Riga, citizens of Riga, some Brothers of the Militia, and many others, crossed through Livonia, came to the province of the Letts, and went from the Letts into Sakala, although he was very weak in body. He rested for two days in Viljandi and afterwards went to Jerwia.[112]

Henry of Livonia is also concerned with the many military campaigns that took place during wintertime precisely because it made marching through the landscape so much more easily due to the frozen waterways. A typical example of one such winter raid is described in the chronicle in the year of 1210 when the attempts to conquer the Estonian lands by the Germans in Livonia had begun in earnest:

> for truly, at the approach of the solemnity of the birth of the Lord, when the harshness of winter was increasing (*hyemis asperitate invalescente*), the elders of the Rigans summoned everyone from all Livonia, Lettia, and the whole area, and from all the forts of the Daugava and Gauja to come and be prepared to take vengeance on the nations of the Esthonians.[113]

Earlier that same year, the Germans and their local allies had fought some very hard battles against marauding Estonians who had first attacked and laid siege to the Sword Brethren's castle in Cēsis before fighting a series of lesser battles and skirmishes against the pursuing Germans and their Livic and Lettgallian allies. At one point during these running battles, the pursuers had suddenly become the pursued and the Estonians managed to capture some hundred Germans, Livs, and Letgallians who were tortured, as Henry of Livonia says, "in a cruel martyrdom" (*crudely martirio*). Some were roasted alive, and some were stripped naked and had crosses carved into their naked backs with swords before being killed by their captors. Even if Henry expresses the hope that all the dead would soon be accepted into the "the heavenly company of the martyrs" (*in martyrum consorcium ut speramus in celum transmiserunt*), this humiliating defeat called for revenge and led to the summoning of the Livonian army shortly before Christmas 1210 for a renewed attack against the Estonians.[114] According to Henry, some Rus' soldiers from Pskov, who at that time were at peace with the Germans in Riga, took part in the campaign. We are also told that a number of prominent local elders came along with their own retinues. The Germans seem not to have trusted the Livonians entirely at this stage, however, and demanded hostages from the elders, before commencing on the actual expedition.[115]

During the first part of the raid the army moved north along the coast in the Livonian province of Metsepole—Henry indicates that they marched day and night in an attempt to take the Estonians by surprise—before arriving in the Estonian province of Soontagana. The Estonians were well prepared having posted guards along all the important

---

112 HCL 29:7.
113 HCL 14:10.
114 HCL 14:8.
115 HCL 14:10.

roads and they soon detected the approaching enemy army.[116] The Estonians immediately left their outposts in an attempt to warn the nearby farms and villages about the approaching enemy, urging everybody to flee. The vanguard of the Livonian army consisted of some of the lighter equipped troops and scouts and managed to get ahead of the Estonians, reaching some of the villages before the locals had had time to escape, finding most people at home: "[t]hen the army spread into all the roads and villages, killed many people in every spot, and followed the remainder into the adjoining provinces, captured from them their women and boys." The raiding force then reassembled at a local fortress known to them from an earlier raid into the region.[117] The next two days the Germans, the Livonians, the Letgallians, and the Rus' soldiers continued to ravage and plunder the surrounding countryside, capturing many horses, four thousand oxen and cows, other flocks, and countless captives, says Henry. Those among the Estonians who actually managed to escape fared only a little better than their captured kin since the cold and the snow covered all of the landscape, offering very little shelter to the refugees who had just lost everything to a marauding enemy army; as Henry laconically remarks, they simply died because of the extreme cold.[118] The Livonian army then left the despoiled and now barren countryside behind and returned home laden with booty and many captives, joyfully blessing God who had provided them with a much needed vengeance against the Estonians. The booty was divided equally among those who had taken part in the raid as was common during such campaigns, and the fighters returned home to their own villages and farms.

This winter's campaign was not over and done with on the return of the Livonian army. Already in January 1211 a new army came together to attack the Estonian provinces of Sakala and Ugandi. This new campaign into Estonia proved to be a failure, however. First, the Livonian army realized that the locals had been forewarned and were nowhere to be found, having left their farms and villages with all moveable valuables. Secondly, and much worse, it also became clear to the Christians that in their absence other Estonians planned to attack their own farms and villages in Livonia. The army hurried home fully aware that they had to return to save their own families from the attacking enemy. And Henry states that "[w]hile all the people stayed in the forts, [the Estonians] burned the empty villages and churches and, with their pagan sacrifices, committed many abominations around the churches and tombs of Christians."[119] In this way, the military activities in Livonia and Estonia often turned into a deadly game of cat-and-mouse during wintertime, with the partakers never knowing for sure who was the cat and who was the mouse.

---

116 Veldi, "Roads and Hill Forts in Southern Estonia," 387.

117 HCL 14:10: "Et divisit se exercitus per omnes vias ac villas, et interfecerunt populum multum in omnibus locis et persequebantur eos in provinciis adiacentibus et ceperunt ex eis mulieres et pueros et convenerunt ad castrum."

118 HCL 14:10.

119 HCL 14:10: "Estones...et omni populo in castris existente ipsi villas vacuas et ecclesias incenderunt et nequicias multas circa ecclesias et sepulchra mortuorum christianorum immolaticiis suis exercuerunt."

A few years later, another dangerous and high-level game of cat-and-mouse materialized when the Danish King Valdemar II sailed for Estonia in the summer of 1219 with a sizable fleet intent on realizing his old plans for a permanent Danish settlement at Lyndanise that would, once and for all, demonstrate who was the stronger power in the region—namely the Danes, or so the Danish king hoped.

Chapter 6

THE DANISH EXPEDITION TO ESTONIA IN 1219 AND THE BATTLE OF LYNDANISE

ACCORDING TO HENRY of Livonia, the preparations for the Danish attack on Lyndanise had begun in the summer of 1218 when King Valdemar II summoned all important men of his realm for a meeting in Schleswig.[1] Among the participants were fifteen bishops, three dukes, and three counts, together with an unsaid number of abbots and other worthy people. The alleged primary reason for the summoning of all these important individuals was the king's wish to have his eldest son and heir, Prince Valdemar, crowned in the cathedral church of Schleswig.[2] The young prince had already been recognized as heir to the throne in 1215 and it was time to have him wear the crown like his father, thereby consolidating the order of succession. In this way, King Valdemar II followed in the footsteps of his father, King Valdemar I who was the first king of Denmark to have his son, the future King Knud VI, crowned as co-regent in 1170, while at the same having his father Knud Lavard enshrined following his recognition as a saint the previous year by the pope.[3] Now King Valdemar II followed in his father's footsteps and had his own oldest son crowned as his co-regent. The cathedral church of Schleswig must have seemed the ideal place for this important dynastic event for several reasons. It was the main town of the duchy of Southern Jylland and also conveniently located with regards to King Valdemar's involvement in the (imperial) politics of northern Germany and his many military campaigns there.

Among the high number of bishops mentioned in the sources was also probably Bishop Albert of Riga. Henry of Livonia mentions that the German bishop went to see King Valdemar, accompanied by a former German knight, Bernhard of Lippe (ca. 1140–1224), who had become abbot of the Cistercian monastery of Mount St. Nicholas (Daugavgrīva/Dünamünde) not far from Riga. Later that same year Bernhard became bishop of Semgallia and was thus closely tied to the politics of the Livonian Church.[4] Henry also mentions that "the bishop of Estonia" (*episcopus...Estiensis*) accompanied Bishop Albert to this meeting in Schleswig. It cannot have been anyone else but Bishop Theodoric who would eventually follow King Valdemar on the expedition to Estonia the following year.

---

1 HCL 22:1.

2 *Annales Ryenses* (the year 1218).

3 Jensen, "Religion and War," 192–93.

4 HCL 22:1.

In Livonia, the military situation had become increasingly critical over a number of years with almost constant wars fought along the borders of the Estonian lands and against the Rus' principalities further east. Adding to this were the constant raids by Lithuanian armies entering Livonia from the south, harrying great part of the lands. At one point, Henry dryly remarks that there was no time for rest and tranquillity among the Livonian people. A series of military expeditions from Livonia into the Estonian provinces of Lääne and Sakala had allegedly enraged many of the still free Estonians who decided to join forces in an attempt to stem the military and religious encroachment of the Germans and their Liv and Letgallian allies. Consequently, the military pressure from the Estonians became so overwhelming that Bishop Albert saw no other options than go to King Valdemar II and humbly ask him to send an army to Estonia to quell the Estonian uproar. That is, at least, what Henry of Livonia tells us in his chronicle.[5]

In Schleswig, Bishop Albert told King Valdemar that the Estonians had allied themselves with the Rus' people from the principalities of Pskov and Novgorod and together carried out a series of attacks deep into Livonia threatening even Riga itself. According to Henry, King Valdemar did, in fact, accept Bishop Albert's plea for help and promised that he would come to Estonia the following summer. Henry also stresses in his text that the expedition was to be carried out in honour of the Virgin Mary and in order for the king to atone for his sins, seemingly a clear indication that the expedition should be seen as a regular crusade, but perhaps also a hint from the side of Henry, suggesting that King Valdemar might actually need some atonement for his many sins. Bearing in mind the ongoing power struggle between the Danes and the Germans in Estonia, and to some extent also in Livonia, it is hardly surprising that Henry portrays King Valdemar as acting on a direct request for help from the side of Bishop Albert, who thus emerges as the real initiator of the Danish expedition in 1219, while the Livonian Church may, in reality, have been on the brink of collapse at this time. Considering the general Danish involvement in the region, which had spanned several decades, it is more likely that Bishop Albert sought to reach an agreement with the Danes regarding the announcement of the next year's expedition at a time when he himself was clearly under pressure from several sides. It is, therefore, more than likely that Albert, for political reasons, sought to gain influence on a campaign that the Danish king himself was already well underway in organizing. In this way, the bishop sought to prevent the Danish king and his archbishop from gaining too much power over the Livonian Church.

From a purely military perspective, it is also possible that Bishop Albert actually hoped to be able to capture the Estonians in a pincer movement through a joint campaign. In any case, Henry writes that after the meeting with the Danish king, Bishop Albert continued his journey to the northern German territories, where he sought to gather as many crusaders as possible for the defence of the Livonian Church, through the incitement of sermons and promises of indulgences for everybody who came to Livonia. Using a biblical metaphor, Henry even writes that these new crusaders were to stand up for the house of the Lord on the day of battle to protect the people and the land from the constant onslaught of the pagans. Bishop Albert thought it too late in the autumn to return to Livonia with all his newly recruited crusaders and, therefore, asked them to wait until the following year, so that he himself could return at the head of a mighty army ready to fight against God's enemies in Livonia. The new crusaders would then also have time to prepare for the upcoming campaign and sort any business at home before venturing to the lands of the pagans. Similarly, Bishop Albert would appear on more equal terms with regards to the planned Danish expedition when he arrived in Riga with a substantial number of crusaders.[6] Realizing the immediate dangers for the Livonian Church, Bishop Albert did send some seasoned knights and commanders to Livonia to prepare for an immediate defence of the Christian lands and plan the coming season's campaigns.

In February 1219, the Germans in Riga launched a major raid against the Estonians in the province of Rävala were Lyndanise is located.[7] The second part of 1218 had turned out to be as violent and desperate for the people of Livonia as expected, with several attacks by Rus' armies and their Estonian allies venturing deep into Livonia. Already in August the Livonian army had been summoned for an attack against Rävala and Harjumaa since these people "had always been rebellious and more cruel than the other [Estonians]" (*qui semper adhuc fuerant rebelles et aliis crudeliores*).[8] Bridges were built in preparation for the campaign and the Livonian army—as was its custom—came together at a place "where the army was accustomed to pray and take counsel" (*ubi locus orationis et colloquiorum*).[9] The Germans were overtaken by events as the Rus', together with Estonian warriors, suddenly attacked Livonia instead. It took some hard-fought defensive battles before the Rus' forces were finally pushed back. Alongside the Rus'-Estonian land-based attacks, seaborne warriors from Saaremaa had entered the Daugava River and had been plundering the settlements along the riverbanks as well as the smaller islands in the river itself. It was generally a well-proven strategy from the side of the Estonians and the Rus', forcing the Germans to split their forces, not know-ing when and where the primary attack would come from, either from land or sea, or perhaps even both ways as in this particular case. This time, the strategy seems to have failed as the Germans, Livs, and Letgallians successfully defeated the Rus' warriors before the people from Saaremaa became a serious threat. The most prominent casualty seems to have been a Cistercian monk living as a hermit on one of the smaller islands in the Daugava River. Since he was killed by the pagans, he was hailed as a martyr accord-ing to Henry.[10]

The Rus' offered a truce, but deciding there was no time for negotiations and not trusting the Rus', the Livonian army was summoned (once more) for the long-planned attack against the Estonians in February 1219. The rendezvous place was at the banks of the River Salis on the border between the northernmost provinces of Livonia and

---

6 HCL 22:1.

7 HCL 22:1.

8 HCL 22:2.

9 HCL 22:2.

10 HCL 22:8. See also the analysis in Jensen, "Fighting in the Wilderness," forthcoming.

Estonia proper, close to the coast. As usual, the Livonian army was commanded by the head of the Sword Brethren, Master Volquin, supported by other prominent noblemen. The knightly brethren obviously constituted an important part of the army and was supported by an unknown number of armed pilgrims fighting alongside the Livs and Letgallians, and was commanded by the "Master of Pilgrims."

What followed was a truly impressive military campaign in the middle of the winter. In the chronicle of Henry of Livonia the campaign is simply referred to as "The Cold One" (*frigada*), and we are told that the entire Livonian army went out on the frozen sea in the Gulf of Riga and began walking along the coast until they came to a stronghold deep into Estonian territory in the province of Soontagana.[11] A few years before, during another winter campaign, the Germans had raided this part of Estonia and had forced the people who were living in a local stronghold—"the castle of Soontagana" (*castrum Sontagana*)—to accept Christianity and let themselves be baptized following a long and brutal siege.[12] When the Germans arrived at the stronghold, the local Estonians were ordered to provide guides to accompany the army. It had to be local men who knew their way through the snow-covered landscape. The army then went straight north, leaving the coastal areas behind. According to Henry, the army:

> marched throughout the night to the province of Rävala. A very cold north wind met them. The cold was so rigorous that many of them lost the extremities of their limbs from the cold. Some had their noses, others their hands, and others their feet frozen. All of them, after they had returned to us at home, had the old skin drop off their faces and new skin grew in its place. Some of them, indeed, later died.[13]

The cold must have been horrific for men as well as for beasts and the injuries described by Henry are easily recognizable even today as severe frost injuries. The army however upheld its offensive capacity and on arrival in Rävala divided itself into "three lines" (*tress acies*) according to the local traditions: the Livc warriors commanded by one of their elders named Vesike formed their own battle formation and moved slightly ahead of the rest of the army keeping to the left wing. The Letgallians formed another unit on the right wing and left, as Henry says, "the middle road to the Germans, as was their usual custom" (*Theuthonicis vero viam mediam more solito dimiserunt*).[14] As mentioned previously the German knights—both the crusaders and the Sword Brethren—would normally fight on horseback whereas the Livs and Letgallians seems to have preferred to fight on foot. The Germans were also supported by their own foot-soldiers armed

11 HCL 22:9.

12 HCL 19:8.

13 HCL 22:9: "processerunt per totam noctem ad Rävalansem provinciam. Et occurrit eis ventus ab aquilone frigidissimus. Erat enim frigoris tanta asperitas, ut extremitates membrorum ipsorum in frigiditate multis perirent et aliis nasus, aliis manus aliisque pedes congelarentur et omnibus nobis domi postea redeuntibus nova cutis in facie supercresceret vetere proiecta. Quidam eciam postea mortui sunt."

14 HCL 22:9.

either with sword, spear, and shield, or with powerful crossbows much feared by their enemies.

Similar to the raids in the summer or early autumn, the smaller local villages were targeted first by the attacking army and Henry of Livonia tells us how the first village found by the Livs was burned down before dawn because the warriors wanted to warm themselves, as he laconically remarks.[15] This warned all the neighbouring villages and farms, providing the local people time to flee with whatever possessions and livestock they may have managed to collect in their obvious state of panic. The Germans who followed the Livic vanguard also became alarmed by the burning village. Believing that the Estonian guide may have let them off track, they killed him instantly. Seemingly, this first attack was not according to plan and thus caused some confusion and slight panic among the attackers themselves. When the morning came, attacks commenced and a number of other villages were also burnt. A few Estonians were killed, and some taken as slaves together with much booty, says Henry. At the end of the day, the entire army settled down in and around a village called Ladise, no more than a day's march from the coast. The next three days the Germans, Livonians, and Letgallians looted the entire area, accumulating a lot of booty, captives, and livestock before deciding to return home. They did not take the same way back to Livonia, knowing from other campaigns that a retiring army would be highly vulnerably when following its own trail back home laden with much booty: on more than one occasion, Henry describes how well-planned ambushes could annihilate a retiring enemy army forced to march more or less in single file in its own tracks due to heavy snow and cold weather.[16]

The strategy chosen by Master Volquin in this particular case was daring and highly unusual. Not only did he not want to go back the same way they had come, he simply decided (or had perhaps from the beginning of the campaign decided) that the army should return home to Livonia by way of the frozen sea. Ladise was fairly close to the coast and thus the entire army went out on the frozen sea and marched homewards along the Estonian coast, probably keeping fairly close to the shoreline but still taking advantage of the smooth surface of the frozen sea which would have made the march home comparably easier. Henry of Livonia remarks that they went out on the ice, close to the place where the Danes would soon build a castle, namely Lyndanise.[17] He goes on, stating that the army marched over the ice, halting "for ten days because of the captives and the booty, being on the lookout for the people from Saaremaa or other Esthonians, if perchance they would follow to war upon us."[18] In all likelihood, the march would have led the Livonian army down through the narrow straits between the islands of Hiiumaa, Muhu, and Saaremaa, and mainland Estonia, thus explaining Henry's worries about being caught out in the open, on the ice, by an alert enemy force. This would make

---

15 HCL 22:9.

16 See for example 25:4.

17 HCL 22:9.

18 HCL 22:9: "Et revertentes paulatim in glacie decem diebus propter captivos et predam moram fecimus, exspectantes eciam Osilienses aut alios Estones, si forte ad bellandum contra nos sequerentur." See also the discussion in Jensen, "Fighting in the Wilderness," forthcoming.

Figure 6: Archbishop Anders Sunesen, depicted during the battle of Lyndanise. Legend has it that the Danish crusaders prevailed only as long as the archbishop had the strength to lift his arms in prayer. When he tired and lowered his arms, the Estonians achieved the upper hand. In the image, clerics can be seen supporting the arms of the elderly archbishop, thereby securing the final Danish victory. The story obviously refers back to Exodus 17:11–13, in which the Israelites fought against the Amalekites while Moses held his arms high until he also tired and had to be supported by Aron and Hur. From Niels Bache, *Nordens Historie* (1881–1887). Public domain.

the Christians an easy prey, particilarly exhausted and laden with booty as they were. The ruse with the alternative route homewards seems to have taken the Estonians by surprise, averting any ambushes and retaliatory attacks. For more than two hundred kilometres did the army march on the ice before they reached Salis once again, halfway down the Gulf of Riga. Here, they halted and took time to divide the booty, captives, and livestock taken from the Estonians before each of the fighting units returned home to their respective residences in Livonia.

It is remarkable that this Livonian winter campaign targeted (to some extent) the very same lands in Estonia that were also the primary target of the Danes. This may support the idea about a (more or less) coordinated plan by the Danes and the Germans who may have agreed on a twofold strike against the northernmost and most trouble-some provinces of Estonia. Henry of Livonia certainly did have an interest in portraying the Germans as the main initiators, but some of the participants in the campaigns in Livonia in late 1218 and early 1219 seemingly point towards a more dominant Dan-ish involvement. Following Bishop Alberts visit in Schleswig, he was joined by Henry Borwin I, lord of Mecklenburg (r. 1178–1227) who was of Pomeranian decent and mar-ried to a daughter of the famous Henry the Lion, duke of Saxony and Bavaria (d. 1196). Henry Borwin had become a vassal of King Knud VI and continued his close relations to the Danes during the reign of King Valdemar II. In 1218, Henry of Borwin was one of those noblemen who went straight to Livonia to help defend the land against the Esto-nian and Rus' attack while Bishop Albert stayed behind gathering more crusaders for the next year's planned campaign. Is seems reasonable to suggest that Henry of Borwin may have joined the Livonians on the request of King Valdemar, partly to help the Ger-mans militarily in Livonia while keeping an eye on them, partly to gather information (intel in modern terms) for the Danish king's upcoming expedition in the summer of 1219. Henry fought both in the autumn campaigns and in the above-mentioned winter campaign and must have collected extremely useful information on both the enemies and the Germans.

The Battle of Lyndanise: According to Henry of Livonia

Henry of Livonia offers the earliest written account of the Battle of Lyndanise. His chron-icle was probably completed in 1227, perhaps as a sort of report meant for the papal legate, William of Modena. The legate is known to have stayed in Livonia and Estonia until the spring of 1226 while Henry made some of his last entries in the chronicle. The very final verses in the chronicle cover the early parts of 1227 which is also presumed to be the time of completion of the entire work. This leaves only eight years between the occurrence of the battle and the completion of the chronicle, making Henry's text the closest source in time regarding the historical Battle of Lyndanise.

According to Henry, one summer's day in 1219:

> the king of Denmark...rose up...with a great army. There came with him Andrew, the venerable archbishop of the church of Lund, and Bishop Nicholas,

and a third bishop, the king's chancellor. There was also with them Bishop Theodoric of the Estonians, who had once been consecrated at Riga, but had left
the Livonian church and had attached himself to the king; also the Slavic prince
Vitslav with his men. They all brought their army to the province of Rävala and
encamped at Lyndanise, which had once been a fort of the people of Rävala.[19]

This is the very brief description on the arrival of the King Valdemar and his army
in Estonia according to Henry of Livonia. Tradition has it that the Danish crusaders
arrived June 15—St. Vitus Day—also associated with the crusades against the Slavic
Wends in the twelfth century. Henry of Livonia simply states that King Valdemar had
with him "a great army" (*excrcitu magno*). Nothing more is said about the size of the
army. Instead, Henry is more preoccupied with the accompanying clerics that formed
part of the king's army, together with their retinues. Firstly, he names Archbishop
Anders Sunesen who had, a least on one occasion, participated in a crusade against
Estonia back in 1206. Of course, it did not escape Henry's attention that Bishop
Nicolas of Schleswig was among the participants, as he had also been in 1206 when
accompanying Anders Sunesen during the stay in Riga. Henry also briefly notes that
a third bishop who was the king's chancellor had also joined the king's army for this
renewed attack in 1219.[20] This third bishop was Bishop Peder Jakobsen of Roskilde
(1214–1225). The participation of the king's chancellor underlines the importance of
the campaign as the intended culmination of the Danish attempts to secure a strong
foothold in northern Estonia. What annoyed Henry the most was, without doubt, the
fact that Theodoric, appointed bishop of the Estonians, had joined King Valdemar,
thus siding with the Danes against his former masters in Riga. Bishop Theodoric was
among the first missionaries to commit himself whole-heartedly to mission amongst
the pagan Livs. Later, he was appointed abbot of the monastery of Mount St. Nicholas
(Daugavgrīva/Dünamünde) until he was consecrated bishop of the Estonians by
Bishop Albert in 1211.[21] For now, he had sided with the Danes and accompanied the
Danish king's army on the campaign into the province of Rävala.

Finally—almost as an afterthought—Henry of Livonia also briefly mentions that the
Slavic Prince Vitslav (d. 1250) "with his [men]" (*cum suis*), accompanied King Valdemar.[22] A couple of generations earlier Prince Vitslav's family probably had fought
fiercely against King Valdemar's father, King Valdemar I, during the early wars between
the Danes and the Slavic people of Rügen. Quite ironically, the people were now them-

---

19 HCL 23:2: "Surrexit eciam rex Dacie cum exercitu magno eodem tempore, et venit cum eo
Lundensis ecclesie venerabilis archiepiscopus Andreas et Nicolaus episcopus et tercius episcopus,
cancellarius regis, eratque cum eis Estiensis episcopus Theodericus, in Riga quondam consecratus,
qui relicta Lyvonensi ecclesia regi adhesit, et Wizzlaus Slavorum princeps cum suis. Qui omnes
applicuerunt exercitum suum ad Rävalansem provinciam et resederunt in Lyndanise, quod fuerat
castrum quondam Rävalansium."

20 HCL 23:2.

21 HCL 15:4.

22 HCL 23:1.

selves crusaders taking part in a Danish organized crusade against the pagan people of Estonia. Furthermore, Prince Vitslav came to play a very crucial role in the Battle of Lyndanise—at least according to Henry of Livonia, who once again gets a chance to ridicule the Danes and belittle their military capacity in his description of the battle to come.

Later in the text, Henry also makes reference to some Germans seemingly forming part of King Valdemar's army but we are not offered any details about their affiliations so we don't know whether they may have been some of the king's North German vassals or perhaps even German knights who were accompanying Bishop Theodoric. A third possibility could be that they were, in fact, a retinue sent by Bishop Albert to participate in these ventures, enabling him to sustain his claims of being independent of the Danish king and church and forming a sort of counterpart to Henry Borwin who had fought alongside the Germans while being the Danish king's vassal. It seems most likely, however, that these German knights were in fact king Valdemar's own vassals. Otherwise, one would most certainly have expected Henry to have stressed the fact that German knights loyal to the Livonian Church formed part of a Danish army that was in the process of subduing a part of Estonia that was fiercely contested by both parties.

There is little doubt that the campaign of 1219 was actually considered a proper crusade. As we have seen, papal letters had, on several occasions, admonished the Danish king to take upon himself the responsibility of a true Christian prince and protector of the (papal) church and commit himself to the defence of the newly baptized people in Livonia and Estonia and defeat the pagan armies—preferably by conquering their lands. Furthermore, it was noted that King Valdemar had promised to come to Estonia with his army "both for the honour of the Blessed Virgin and for the remission of his sins" (*ad beate Virginis honorem quam in peccatorum suorum remissionem*).[23] As such, there seem to have been little doubt that this was in fact a proper crusade organized by the Danish king in close cooperation with the archbishop of Lund as a means to strengthen the Danish interests in northern Estonia and establish a proper stronghold comparable to Riga in the south. Furthermore, the participating knights and ordinary soldiers would benefit from the promises of indulgences as concrete remissions of their sins by taking part in this particular expedition. As we have seen, already during the first phase of the German mission in Livonia, indulgences had become a powerful tool when the bishops wanted to attract armed pilgrims for the fight against the local pagans. And, the same was true for the Danes, according to Henry of Livonia.

Henry of Livonia states in his chronicle that King Valdemar brought with him a great army referring to the same army in another chapter as a "seaborne army" (*exercitum... navalem*). Apart from this, we do not have any proper indications on the actual size of the army in any of the contemporary sources. Likewise, we do not know for certain how many of the partaking Danes were actually proper crusaders with genuine vows, and how many were simply serving their lord as part of a retinue. Neither do we know how many men had been hired for this particular campaign—if any—in return for payment. It makes sense that it was the mobilized part of the ledung that constituted the main

---

23 HCL 22:2.

part of the Danish crusader fleet in 1219 with (perhaps) additional ships crewed by the personal retinues of the major Danish magnates and prelates. With that also came the contingent of Prince Vitslav and the supporting German knights.

While Annales Ryenses claimed that the king had in his fleet one thousand five hundred ships, it is by all accounts an exaggeration.[24] The reorganization of the ledung in 1168 seems to suggest that only about one hundred fifty to two hundred ships would serve as part of the actual ledung with roughly forty to forty-two men per ship, four of whom would be mounted. That would leave us with a maximum of around 7.600 ordinary fighting men and approximately eight hundred knights. A smaller number of ships would, of course, mean fewer men with perhaps only five thousand ordinary fighting men and some six hundred mounted knights, which would be very much in line with the size of contemporary crusader armies known from other theatres of operations.[25]

As stated by Henry of Livonia, King Valdemar and his army went ashore at Lyndanise, a place that has been described as the best natural anchoring place along the entire coast of northern Estonia. The massive limestone plateau of Toompea Hill was a very important sea marker for those navigating the waters between Estonia and Finland in the early thirteen century.[26] It was only here at the Gulf of Tallinn that seafarers could cross the waters without losing sight of either the Finnish or the Estonian coasts in fair weather. It made this place an ideal crossing point for merchants and other seafarers who had sailed along the southern coasts of Finland and wanted to continue westwards along the coasts of northern Estonia and further out into the Baltic Sea.[27] The importance of Lyndanise as a central location is also demonstrated through the fact that there seems to have been a Estonian stronghold and perhaps also a settlement just below Toompea Hill on which top some scholars suggest there may have been some sort of pagan holy place.[28] If so, it may have come to play a central role in the events that led to the actual battle as we shall see. According to Henry the Danes, "all brought their army to the province of Rävala and encamped at Lyndanise, which had once been a fort (*castrum*) of the people of Rävala. They destroyed the old fort and began to build another new one."[29] The Estonian fort mentioned by Henry may have been located, not on Toompea Hill itself,

---

24 *Annales Ryenses* (the year 1219).

25 See the important discussions in Powell, *Anatomy of a Crusade 1213–1221*, on the sizes of various crusader armies.

26 Literally the Estonian word "Toompea Hill" means "The Mount of the Cathedral" deriving from the German word "Domberg."

27 Mägi, "Fra fortidens havneplads til middelalderens bosættelse," 131; Markus, *Visual Culture*, 306–12.

28 Mägi, "Fra fortidens havneplads til middelalderens bosættelse," 137; Markus, *Visual Culture*, 308 and 311–12. Not everybody is convinced about the presences of an early (permanent) Estonian settlement at Lyndanise. See for example Anti Selart, "Where Was the Home of the Livonian Merchant? Early Urban Mobility in the Baltics," *Zapiski Historyczne* 84, no. 1 (2019), 47. See also the discussion in Rein Zobel, *Tallinn (Reval): Fortifications in the Middle Ages* (Tallinn: Eesti Kunstiakadeemia, 2014), 20–27.

29 HCL 23:2. Already in the previous chapter (HCL 22:9). Henry refers to this castle as constructed by the Danes; "Dani castrum suum in vinico edificaverunt."

but on a ridge called Tönismägi running from the hill itself in a southerly direction. The Estonian settlement is in turn believed to have been located below the eastern slopes of Tönismägi.[30]

In the sources, there is nothing indicating that the Danish crusaders were met with resistance when they disembarked from their ships—we have previously seen how disembarking on a hostile shore could be a perilous affair when an army would be totally disorganized and in no proper battle formation, vulnerable to a sudden enemy attack. It has been a common assumption that the Danish crusaders took the Estonians completely by surprise in 1219; the Estonians were simply unprepared for the Danish attack. It seems very unlikely that the Estonians—always on the lookout for enemy raiders—should not have detected the approaching enemy naval force well in advance of its actual arrival. Henry has many references in his chronicle to locals keeping watch along any likely enemy attack routes whether they would come by sea or by land.[31] This would most certainly have been the case also with regards to the coastal areas of northern Estonia, so often prone to enemy raids. Lookouts would have noticed the Danish fleet and sent their warnings along the coast.

Another likely explanation is that the Danes had actually made some sort of alliance with the local Estonians during the early preparations for the expedition or may even have had some "men on the ground," so to speak, that had prepared the arrival of the Danish force. Some have speculated that it could have been the intended outcome of Archbishop Anders Sunesen's expedition towards Lyndanise already in 1206 and that if it was, in reality, it could have been the actual foundation of a (small) Danish outpost at Lyndanise.[32] This is hard to prove. However, we do know of various agreements and formal alliances between the people of the Baltic Lands and the Scandinavians and the Germans when it came to securing safe passage in enemy waters, or even granting permission to make a stop in a foreign harbour as we have already seen. It has been suggested that some of the local Estonians might already have become Christians before the arrival of King Valdemar's army and would, therefore, have had a special interest in a closer alliance with the Danish king. This, however, is also mere speculation.[33] In any case, we must assume that it would have been difficult if not outright impossible for the Danes to reach Lyndanise with a relatively large fleet without being spotted from the coast by vigilant scouts or by local ships at sea. Had the Estonians thought it necessary, they could have easily prepared themselves for the arrival of the Danish fleet by assembling a huge army to counter the Danes even as they were disembarking and, thus, most vulnerable to an enemy attack. An agreement between the local Estonians and the Danes, therefore, seems to be a very probable explanation for the actual unopposed landing of the Danish crusader army.

---

30 Mägi, "Fra fortidens havneplads til middelalderens bosættelse," 133–37; Markus, *Visual Culture*, 308 and 310.

31 Generally on scouts and watchmen, see HCL 9:3; 11:5; 14:8 and 12:2.

32 See the discussions in Markus, *Visual Culture*, 261 and Markus, "Blev der grundlagt en by i Tallinn i 1206 eller 1219?," 141–53.

33 Kaljusaar, "Exploiting the Conquerors," 66–67.

Most likely, the main part of the Danish army camped east of Tõnismägi Ridge running from Toompea Hill in a south-westerly direction. The crusaders were thus not too far away from their ships and probably also had easy access to fresh drinking water from several small springs and streams in the area.[34] It is likely that the individual camps were positioned in relation to the individual lords who commanded the various ships crews or larger retinues. One should, therefore, think of the crusader camp as several smaller or larger clusters of tents in an open area below Toompea Hill without any strict or regulated plan.

According to Henry, parts of the Danish king's army chose places to camp that lay some distance away from the main camp; for example, Vitslav's men, who seem to have camped in a hollow a little away from the main force.[35] One can therefore also imagine that there were other smaller camps around the area. From other contemporary accounts, we know that armies in hostile territory could quickly construct makeshift fortifications as a defence against surprise attack, for example in the form of quickly erected earthen ramparts, fences or palisades, which would protect a camp from being overrun during a surprise attack.[36] The Danes apparently found no such precautions necessary at Lyndanise. While they had been met with no resistance at all when they landed, there seems neither to have been any substantial Estonian force close by. The old fortress was unused according to Henry, and the local inhabitants who lived in the area hardly posed any real threat to the Danes either—at least Henrik mentions nothing to that effect. Instead, he writes that the Danish crusaders immediately tore down the old fortress and began building a new one on the top of Toompea Hill. In all likelihood, this would have been a wooden castle with palisades, which were only later replaced by stone buildings and regular walls, very much like the fortress built by the Danes on Saaremaa during the raid in 1206 and immediately burned to the ground again when the Danes left the island.[37]

Henry then writes in his chronicle that the Estonians called together their elders (*seniors*) and sent them to King Valdemar to negotiate a peace treaty with him. Henry is quite clear in his description of these presumed peace talks, as he directly states that it was purely on the pretence that the Estonians wanted this peace. In reality, he says, they simply wanted more time to gather their entire military force enabling them to launch a surprise attack on the Danish crusaders' camp. In this way, Henry once again portrays the Danes—and especially King Valdemar—as a bit naive, in that they allowed themselves to be fooled by the Estonians's false words about peace. In the king's defence, however, Henry does mention that some of the Estonian elders were apparently willing to be baptized by the bishops who had accompanied the crusader army. Henry, however, also suggests that it was only to maintain the illusion of peace that they pretended to

---

34 Zobel, *Tallinn (Reval)*, 29–31. See especially the map above with the proposed attack routes of the Estonians as well as the presumed campsites of the Danes and their allies.

35 Zobel, *Tallinn (Reval)*, 30.

36 Powell, *Anatomy of a Crusade 1213–1221*, 147.

37 HCL 10:13.

embrace Christendom. Consequently, King Valdemar "gave [the Estonian elders] gifts and the bishops baptized them, sending them back joyfully" (*et dedit eis munera, et baptizaverunt eos episcopi, remittentes eos cum gaudio*).[38]

And then three days later came the surprise attack by "all the armies of the Estonians" (*cum omni exercitu suo*) during the hours of the early evening, just as the crusaders had finished eating and probably were about to make ready for the night. From Henry's account, the attack seems very well orchestrated by the Estonians, with coordinated attacks from five different sides at once: they rushed "upon the Danes in five places and fought with them without warming" (*et irruerunt super Danos in guinque locis et pugnaverunt ex improvise cum eis*).[39] Most of the crusaders seem to have panicked and were now chased through their camps by Estonian warriors killing all those who were too slow to escape the evolving massacre. Some of the crusaders probably tried to reach the ships beached nearby or simply ran along the water's edge to get away from the killings. A least one of the more prominent members of the king's army did not get away in time. Bishop Theodoric was killed immediately in his tent by the attacking Estonians as they mistook him for King Valdemar—or more likely had expected to find the king in that particular tent.[40] We will come back to this incident in a short while trying to go behind the narrative of Henry of Livonia.

Obviously the Danish crusaders were on the brink of a disaster with most of the fighting men scattered all over the area with killings still going on and sporadic defenses mounted by more or less isolated groups of crusaders trying to fend off the Estonian warriors during their furious attacks. Most likely until this time it had mostly been a foot-soldiers' battle with little or no time for the crusader knights to mount their horses since they were more busy dodging the murderous attacks by the Estonians. So, not only had the Estonian warriors managed to completely surprise the crusaders, but they had also evened out the odds even further by preventing the crusaders from employing their most powerful weapon—the mounted knights.

The turn of the tide was as unexpected as the surprise attack by the Estonians in itself. Unnoticed by the attackers, a small part of the crusader army had camped some distance away from the main camp beneath Toompea Hill. That was the aforementioned Prince Vitslav and his retinue of fierce Slavic warriors who saw the attack and the near-complete disaster befalling the rest of the army. From their camp hidden away from (or simply ignored by) the Estonians on the seaward slope of Toompea Hill, Vitslav quickly gathered his men and counterattacked the Estonians with all the force he could muster. It is not absolutely clear from the text if they were, in fact, mounted, thus enabling them to smash into the marauding Estonians, preoccupied with killing and plundering within the crusaders camps, but it seems likely. Prince Vitslav saw the approaching enemy

---

38 HCL 23:2.

39 HCL 23:2.

40 HCL 23:2. One explanation could be, that it was the same tent that the Estonians elders and the Danish king had been negotiating in the previous days.

and, according to Henry, immediately hurried towards them, together with all his men throwing themselves wildly into the fighting, eventually turning the Estonians to flight.[41]

The sudden counterattack by an unnoticed enemy force made the Estonian warriors halt their onslaught against the fleeing crusaders enabling King Valdemar to restore some order among his fleeing men: "all of the Danes gathered with the king and some Germans who were with them, and they went to meet the Estonians and fought bravely with them. The Estonians fled before them, and, after the whole multitude of them had turned to flight, the Danes, together with the Germans and Slavs, followed after them. A few men killed more than a thousand of their men and the rest fled."[42] In this way, and according to Henry of Livonia, King Valdemar and his surviving crusaders prevailed and overcame the brutal and bloody surprise attack by the Estonians. The only thing that saved the Danish crusaders was, ironically, a younger generation of Slavic princes and warriors whose fathers and grandfathers had been forced into submission and conversion by the king's older brother and his father only one or two generations earlier—now Prince Vitslav was himself a crusader saving his fellow crusaders from the pagan Estonians.

It is startling that the Danish army was so easily surprised by the Estonians, who were allegedly preparing the attack on the Danes even while they were still negotiating with King Valdemar. Added to this is the surprising timing of the attack itself, which supposedly took place at dusk, just after the Crusaders had eaten the last meal of the day. Given these considerations, and subject to Henrik's propagandistic portrayal in his chronicle of a somewhat credulous Danish king, one might wonder whether the actual course of events might not have been slightly different from what Henry claims. As argued above, it is not at all inconceivable that Valdemar had made some sort of agreement prior to his arrival with the local elders as part of the planning of that year's expedition. That may also have included the promises of some of the Estonian elders that they would in fact accept baptism if they could rely on the support of the Danish king. We saw something similar with regards to the German conquest of Livonia. Baptism was not only a formal acceptance of Christianity as a (new) religious belief, it was as much (and perhaps even more so) the acceptance of a new vassalage with the Estonians of Rävala recognizing the Danish king as their new overlord. One can very well assume that there may not have been any real need for a direct military opposition on the arrival of the Danish crusaders since it had been planned and agreed upon well in advance as part of a greater political and military scheme ignored by Henry. The local elders would have had their own retinues at hand as part of the greetings of the Danish king but nowhere near the entire military host of the northern Estonian provinces. These local Estonian warriors would most likely have been camped in the immediate vicinity of the Danish crusaders camp

---

41 HCL 23:2.

42 HCL 23:2: "Et convenerunt omnes Dani simul cum rege et Theuthonici quidam, qui erant cum eis, et occurrerunt Estonibus, dimicantes fortiter cum eis. Et fugerunt Estones coram eis. Et postquam omnis multitudo eorum conversa est in fugam, sequebantur post eos Dani cum Theuthonicis et Slavis et interfecerunt ex eis per paucos plus quam mille viros, et ceteri fugerunt."

since it was also here that the negotiations between the Danes and the Estonian elders took place. A likely scenario then, might be that there were no Estonian plans for a surprise attack on the Danes. Rather something went very wrong during the three days of negotiations. One possibility is of course that the negotiations simply broke down and turned the otherwise peaceful talks into a hostile encounter. It has recently been suggested that the sudden attack by the Estoninans may have been related to the rash construction of the new Danish castle on Toompea Hill.

As the hill may also have given room to a pagan cult site, it is conceivable that the Danes' energetic efforts to erect a new castle may have resulted in this holy place being destroyed or at least disturbed by the reckless and un-respectful behaviour of the Danish crusaders in their efforts to secure this strategically important site as quickly as possible. The destruction of the cult site—whether intentionally or not—probably would have angered some of the Estonians quite a bit, especially those who may have been less inclined to accept baptism as part of the deal with the Danes. In turn, this may have led them to refuse any further negotiations with King Valdemar and in the end provoked the "surprise" attack on the Danish camp. This may explain the tumultuous description of the fighting in the chronicle of Henry of Livonia, with Estonian warriors almost immediately being able to attack the Danes right in the middle of their camp, cutting down more or less defenceless crusaders left and right. The Estonians were in realty already among the Danes when the fight erupted because of the ongoing negotiations, and therefore could easily attack the unprepared crusaders when they learned that one of their holy places had been desecrated by the Christians!

From this point onwards the battle seems to have developed as described by Henry and the crusaders now paid dearly for their missteps. The Estonian warriors nearly overran the main camp and also stormed one of the more splendid tents, where, according to Henry of Livonia, they assumed the Danish king must be staying. The aim was clearly to kill him and thus deprive the army of its supreme leader. We do not know where the Danish king actually stayed during the negotiations. Some have speculated that he may have settled on top of Toompea Hill, where the new castle was being built. It is not unthinkable, and in any case, it was not the Danish king whom the Estonians found in the splendid looking tent. Instead, they found the German Bishop Theoderic, whom they immediately cut down. According to Henry, Bishop Theoderic thereby achieved the status of martyr as he was killed by pagans in an attempt to convert them into Christendom. It also seems plausible that the Estonians in their furry may have overlooked the encampment of Prince Vitslav who regained the initiative and forced the Estonian into a complete rout as he fought together with the remaining crusaders. Henrik also indicates that it was King Valdemar himself who managed to bring part of the fleeing crusaders to a halt, restoring discipline and organizing a proper defence together with the German knights mentioned before.[43] The unexpected counterattack by Vitslav and

---

43 At one point, the legendary appearance of Dannebrog was combined with this assumption that King Valdemar may in fact have camped on top of Toompea Hill when his army landed at Lyndanise. When he rode down the hill to rally his panicking crusaders during the Estonian attack, a cross banner carried by some of his men may have made some of the crusaders believe—so is the

his men together with King Valdemar successfully restoring discipline among the fleeing crusaders proved enough, not only to break the Estonian attack, but also force them into a headlong, wild flight. This seems also to support the assumption that the attack by the Estonians was not at all well-planned or well-coordinated as claimed by Henry. He says, however, that this counter-attack by the crusaders resulted in one thousand Estonians being killed. It seems to be a very high number of enemy casualties even if it is not completely unrealistic considering the somewhat chaotic nature of the entire fight and the cluttered nature of the battlefield. From Henry's point of view however, he may simply have wanted to stress how God himself had protected the Christians, turning an almost certain defeat into a gloriously victory—even though the victory then befell the Danes whom he still considered to be false vineyard workers unlawfully trespassing into the domains of the Livonian church. From a Danish perspective, Lyndanise became *Taani-linna*—"the Danish Castle," or more rightly: Tallinn.[44]

---

suggestion—that a divine banner was in fact descending from the sky. While this theory attempts to combine a legendary narrative with historical facts, it does not seems to be a plausible explanation. For the theory, see Heinz von zur Mühlen, "Die Schlacht bei Lyndanisse (1219) und ihre Bedeutung für die Gründung Revals," *Jahrbuch des baltischen Deutschtums 1969* (1968).

44 In many medieval texts the Danes actually referred to Tallinn as *Raeuelburgh*, meaning "Rävela Castle." Cf. Markus, *Visual Culture*, 309.

Chapter 7

CONQUERING HEARTS AND MINDS
THE AFTERMATH OF THE BATTLE

FOLLOWING THE BATTLE of Lyndanise, the Danish crusaders celebrated their
victory by praising God, thanking him for this Christian triumph over the pagans.
Thereafter, the Danes could devote themselves to the task of Christianizing the whole
region. It was time to initiate, in earnest, the important work of converting and baptizing the locals even if it required many more embittered fights in the years to come.
Consequently, the Danish stronghold on Toompea Hill became of paramount importance
for the continued work in Estonia. The wooden structures of the hastily constructed initial fortress were replaced over time with stone buildings and walls, making the castle
stronger. It was only when the Sword Brethren conquered the castle for a period, nearly
ten years later, that its first rebuild was completed.[1]

While the Danes worked on their castles and sent out missionaries, they also continued to fight the locals. Quite clearly, the people of the northernmost provinces of Estonia
had no intention of submitting freely to the power of the Danes, and also, at the same
time, had to defend themselves against the repeated German attacks from the south.
As such, the outcome of the Battle of Lyndanise was not definitive in breaking the Estonian's ability to fight back. Nor do the actual losses seem to have been as high or as
catastrophic as suggested by Henry of Livonia. Similarly, the losses or the near-defeat
suffered by the Danish crusaders did not make King Valdemar abandon his enterprise in
Estonia. Neither did it take the king long to decide that the castle—even in its unfinished
condition—was strong enough to act as the central power base of the Danish presence
in northern Estonia and the seat of a royal-appointed bailiff. When King Valdemar left
Estonia—he seems to have been back in Denmark no later than September 1219—, he
left behind a garrison in the castle. We do not know anything about the actual size of this
force. Apart from manning the castle, the main task must have been to protect the clerics who also stayed behind in Estonia, eager to commence with their missionary work.[2]
Following the death of Bishop Theoderich, the king's chaplain Wescelo was appointed
the new bishop of the Estonians.[3] His position, however, was soon challenged by Bishop
Albert's appointment of his own brother as (rivalling) bishop of the Estonians.[4] Henry
of Livonia seems to suggest that Archbishop Anders Sunesen had stayed behind when
King Valdemar returned to Denmark since we are told that the archbishop eventually

---

1 Zobel, *Tallinn (Reval)*, 35–38; Selart, "Die Eroberung Livlands," 191–92; Jensen, "Da Dannebrog
faldt ned fra himlen," 169; Markus, *Visual Culture*, 319–28.

2 HCL 23:2. Jensen, "Da Dannebrog faldt ned fra himlen," 167.

3 HCL 23:2.

4 HCL 23:11.

met with some German clerics to sort out matters with regard to who had the political and ecclesiastical sovereignty in the newly conquered Estonian provinces, the Danes or the Germans.[5]

At first, the Danes seem to have concentrated on the conquest and conversion of the provinces of Rävala and Harjumaa before turning their attention towards Järvamaa, which became the target of an invading Danish army in 1220.[6] The Germans, however, considered these lands to be their plantations and Henry argues strongly against the presence of Danish missionaries and priests among the people of Järvamaa while also claiming that Bishop Albert quickly sent missionaries to the north-western most parts of Virumaa to claim that province for the Livonian Church and accusing the Danes for reaching out for a foreign harvest.[7] In his chronicle, Henry also accuses the Danish clerics of all sorts of slyness as regards the proper pastoral behaviour among the locals in an attempt (says Henry) to enforce upon the people of Järvamaa and the people of Virumaa a Danish lordship. In this case, Henry seems to have been a very active player himself as he had been ordered by Bishop Albert to go to the provinces of Virumaa and neighbouring Järvamaa after having baptized many people in Ugandi further south. Henry went there together with another priest called Peter and they seem to have been quite successful in baptizing as many as seven hundred locals. In Henry's own words, they were successfully sowing "the seed of Christian doctrine and watered the villages lying round from the holy font of regeneration."[8] Venturing further north, Henry and Peter are said to have come upon more local villages with some of them happily accepting the baptism of the clerics. Some of the locals refused to be baptized, not because, says Henry, that they did not want to become Christians, but simply because they feared the reactions of the nearby Danes in Tallinn should they find out that they had submitted themselves to German missionaries instead of the Danish ones. For this reason, they had already called for Danish clerics to come baptize them thereby avoiding any retaliatory attacks by the Danes.[9] Henry also states in his chronicle that the fear among the locals seems to have been well-founded as a local man was hanged merely because he had accepted to be baptized by the Germans rather than the Danes, and, at the same time, had offered his son as a hostage to the Sword Brethren.[10]

Apart from the fact that German and Danish clerics came to preach and baptize in the same areas, Henry also castigates the Danes for being negligent in their pastoral work since they:

5 HCL 24:2.

6 HCL 24:2.

7 HCL 24:2.

8 HCL 24:1: "doctrine Christiane semina spargere, villas circumiacentes sacro regenerationis fonte rigabant."

9 HCL 24:5. See also Jensen, "The Lord's Vineyard," 51.

10 HCL 24:1. See also Jensen, "The Lord's Vineyard," 46–52. See also Kaljusaar, "Exploiting the Conquerors," 77–78.

desired to take over this neighbouring land for themselves and sent their priests, as it were, into a foreign harvest. They baptized some villages and sent their men to the others to which they could not come so quickly, ordering great wooden crosses to be made in all the villages. They sent [laypeople] with holy water and ordered them to baptize the women and children. They tried thereby to anticipate the Rigan priests and sought in this manner to put the land into the hands of the king of the Danes.[11]

In Henry's eyes, this was clearly not a proper way to administer the holy sacrament of baptism among the local people and it only strengthened his antipathy toward these foreign workers in the Lord's Vineyard.[12] Another incident only underlined this antipathy when some recently baptized Estonians told Henry how the men in the village had been baptized by Danish priests in a neighbouring village. Allegedly, the Danish clerics had asked them to go and "baptize" their own families,

> since we were in the village of Ialgsama when a priest of the Danes performed the sacrament of baptism there, he baptized some of our men and gave us holy water. We returned to our own villages and each of us sprinkled our families, wives and children, with that same water.[13]

Based on this experience, the Estonians did not think they needed to be baptized once more even if Henry and his companion clearly believed this practice to be illegal—or at least not properly in accordance with canon law: "[w]hen the [German] priests heard this, they smiled a bit and, shaking the dust from their feet at them, they hurried to the other villages."[14] It is important here to understand that conversion and baptism were not only a religious ritual around 1200. They also meant submission to a particular ruler who had initiated the mission and supported missionary work. To be baptized by a Danish or German cleric would either make you a subject to the Danish king or to the Livonian Church. It seems fair, therefore, to describe these pious missionary activities both as a quest for souls through new converts and, at the same time, also a quest for secular power and supremacy.[15]

---

11 HCL 24:2: "Sed Dani ipsam terram sibi vicinam preoccupare cupientes sacerdotes suos quasi in alienam messem miserunt. Qui baptizantes villas quasdam et ad alias suos mittentes, ad quas ipsi venire tarn subito non potuerunt, et cruces magnas ligneas in omnibus villis fieri precipientes et aquam benedictam per manus rusticorum mittentes et mulieres ac parvulos aspergere iubentes, sacerdotes Rigenses taliter prevenire conabantur et hoc modo totam terram ad manus regis Danorum preoccupare studebant."

12 Jensen, "The Lord's Vineyard," 48.

13 HCL 24:5: "Cum essemus in villa Iolgesim, quando sacerdos Danorum ibi baptismi sui tractavit sacramenta, baptizavit viros quosdam ex nostris et dedit nobis aquam sanctam, et reversi sumus ad proprias villas et cum eadem aqua aspersimus et baptizavimus unusquisque nostram familiam."

14 HCL 24:5: "Quo audito sacerdotes modicurn subridentes et excusso pulvere pedum in eos ad alias villas festinantes." Here Henry clearly portrays his co-worker and himself as the apostles of the New Testament. See Acts 13:51.

15 Jensen, *Med ord og ikke med slag*, 290–94; Kaljundi, "Expanding Communities," 203.

This becomes even clearer when Henry recalls how he and Peter came across a Danish priest who was busy baptizing Estonians who lived in Virumaa. He did not accept Henry's claim that this territory belonged to the Germans since "that this vineyard had been planted by the zeal of the pilgrims and the labour of the Rigans through the Blessed Virgin's banner."[16] As the Danish cleric did not back off but instead flat-out rejected the claim of the Livonian Church, all three men went to the castle of the Danes, to Tallinn, to present the case directly to the Danish Archbishop Anders Sunesen, who seems still to have been in Estonia at that time.[17] Most likely this was by no means a chance meeting between the German and Danish missionaries, since Henry explicitly states that he had been sent on this missionary trip by Bishop Albert of Riga. One can only wonder if the primary purpose of the journey really was to incite a meeting with Anders Sunesen since it seems a little out of the ordinary that two seemingly plain missionaries from the Livonian Church took upon themselves to go all the way to Tallinn to request a meeting with the Danish archbishop. It seems more likely that Henry and Peter were, in fact, acting on the direct orders of Bishop Albert who had sent them on a sort of clerical embassy rather than just to baptize the locals. In the chronicle, Henry states that:

> they went after this into the fort of the Danes with the priest and made the same statement to the venerable Archbishop Andrew of Lund. But the archbishop said that all of Estonia, whether conquered by the Rigans or not yet subjugated, belonged to the Danish king, having been made over to him by the bishops of Riga.[18]

Anders Sunesen sent the messengers back to Riga according to Henry with strict orders not "to pluck the hanging clusters of grapes, nor to send their priests to preach in the corners of Estonia." Bishop Albert had no intentions of submitting to these demands, stating instead that "the vineyard of the Esthonian church had been planted by his people for many years before the time of the Danes' arrival. It had been cultivated by the blood of many men and by the many sufferings of war and his priests had appeared, not in the corners of Estonia, but in the middle of Järvamaa and, indeed even in Virumaa and in the very face of the archbishop himself."[19]

---

16 HCL 24:2: "et vineam ipsam per vexillum beate Virginis studio peregrinorum et Rigensium labore plantatam affirmarunt."

17 HCL 24:2.

18 HCL 24:2: "Et post hoc abeuntes in castrum Danorum cum ipso sacerdote coram venerabili archiepiscopo Andrea Lundensi idem referebant. Sed archiepiscopus idem totam Estoniam, sive a Rigensibus expugnatam, sive nondum adhuc subiugatam regis Dacie esse dicebat, a Rigensibus episcopis sibi collatam."

19 HCL 24:2: "Cui rescripsit Rigensis episcopus, venerabilis Albertus, vineam ipsam Estiensis ecclesie pluribus annis ante tempora Danorum a suis iam dudum plantatam, sanguine mul-torum et bellorum incommodis multis excultam sacerdotesque suos non in angulis Estonie, sed in media Gerwa, verum eciam in Vironia et usque in faciem ipsius archiepiscopi comparuisse."

The conflict did not come to an end here, and Henry mentions that the Danes soon built churches in villages that had been baptized by the Germans.[20] According to Henry, Archbishop Anders Sunesen did invite Bishop Albert to come to Tallinn to discuss matters concerning the disputed Estonian lands. Having firmly rejected the Danish claims to all of Estonia, Bishop Albert declined the invitation—which was probably more of a command—and chose instead to travel in all haste to Rome to present his case to the pope. In reality, one gets the impression from Henry's chronicle that it was more of a flight from the side of the bishop, trying to avoid any meeting with the powerful Danes that might compromise his claim to the Estonian lands in the long run. And, perhaps even to Livonia itself should the Danish king and archbishop decide to let their claims include that part of the region as well. Bishop Albert also desperately needed papal acknowledgement of the appointment of his own brother as new bishop of Estonia, rivalling the recent Danish appointment in the same matter.

While Albert left Livonia, the Sword Brethren chose to go to the Danes at Tallinn for a meeting. Henry states that the Danish king—probably through Anders Sunesen—offered them Sakala and Unganien because these two provinces, along with some neighbouring lands, had already been conquered and baptized by the Germans.[21] The Sword Brethren, thus, seem to have used the rivalry of the Danes and the Germans in the region to their own benefit, securing for themselves a firmer position since they were by now often in conflict with Bishop Albert with regards to the sovereignty of the lands they had conquered and controlled militarily. The Danes, however, were soon to find out that the Sword Brethren were, indeed, a shrewd and unpredictably neighbour.

Archbishop Anders Sunesen rammed home the Danish claims to the disputed Estonian provinces in the absence of Bishop Albert by specifically appointing Bishop Ostrad as bishop of Virumaa and Jerwia, while also including the province of Harjumaa into the bishopric of Rävala, thus formally securing the provinces for the Danish king and church—at least for the time being.[22]

A short Swedish intermezzo in 1220 into the Estonian province of Lääne put extra pressure on the Germans, and especially on Albert's own brother, Bishop Herman, who were already hard pressed by the Danes. The Swedish King Johan Sverkersson (r. 1216–1222), together with some of his magnates and bishops, had decided on an expedition against Estonia and came with an army into Lääne.[23] According to Henry, the Swedes established themselves at Leal, which was also the episcopal seat of Bishop Herman. Immediately, the Swedes began to teach and baptize the locals while Bishop Albert strongly protested against this—in his eyes—unlawful attempt to take away a harvest that truly belonged to the Livonian Church. The Swedish mission, however, proved to be short-lived. When King Johan returned home and left a garrison to protect the Swedish missionaries, he also invited disaster! Not long after his departure, an army from

---

20 HCL 24:5.
21 HCL 24:2.
22 HCL 24:2.
23 HCL 24:3. See also Markus, *Visual Culture*, 268.

Saaremaa attacked Leal and brutally killed all the remaining Swedes, including a bishop. While Henry admits that they mourned the dead Swedes, it was left to the Danes to collect the dead bodies and burry them in a Christian manner.[24]

In the years that followed, the Estonians revolted on several occasions against the Danes, occasionally managing to force them into the defensive, which resulted in interventions by German forces from Livonia. One such incident occurred in 1222 when King Valdemar, according to Henry of Livonia, gathered a huge army (*exercitu magno*) and together with Count Albrecht II of Orlamünde, attacked Saaremaa once more.[25] Henry says the Danes began constructing a stone fortress on the island—we do not exactly know where—and became embroiled in a series of fights with the islanders.[26] Even the Germans from Riga sent reinforcements, but eventually the islanders managed to lay siege to the unfinished fortress (Henry mentions that the garrison was unable to hide inside the fortress due to the lack of houses and the unfinished state of the walls). The islanders had sought the advice of the people from Varbola to whom the Danes had given siege engines. With this new knowledge, the islanders constructed their own "throwing machines" (*patherellos et machinas*)—seventeen in all—and laid siege to the Danish stronghold, bombarding the garrison for five days. Even though the Danes (and some Germans) in the fortress fought back and wounded and killed a great many of the islanders with their crossbows, they eventually had to give up, but were allowed to leave the fortress, save for some hostages. The islanders then tore down the remainder of the castle "leaving not a stone upon a stone."[27] This Estonian victory thus paved the way for renewed attacks against the Danes on the mainland.

The situation worsened even more a few years later when, in 1223, King Valdemar II was captured by one of his German vassals, Count Henrik of Schwerin. The king remained imprisoned for two years and was only released at Christmas time in 1225. Valdemar's imprisonment had severely weakened him militarily and politically and he never regained full control of his northern German possessions, suffering a severe military defeat to his enemies at the battle of Bornhöved in Holstein in July 1227. This also came to influence the situation in Estonia.

In the spring of 1225, the papal legate Wilhelm of Modena travelled to Livonia and Estonia, eager to visit the newly planted wine yards of the Holy Church and the many new converts. The legate also visited the Danes in Tallinn, and Henry states that he was joyfully received both by the Danes and some Swedes living there.[28] While the underlying conflict between the Danes and the Germans had been slumbering for some time, the imprisonment of the Danish king had made Bishop Albert sense the dawn of better things. Renewed attempts to push back the Danes had intensified the conflict once more.

---

24 HCL 24:3.

25 HCL 24:2–4.

26 Markus, *Visual Culture*, 263–66.

27 HCL 26:4.

28 HCL 29:7.

Wilhelm of Modena was determined to create a sort of buffer zone between these two expansive and very ambitious powers in the region. The concrete plan was to let the pope take over the control of some of the most contested Estonian provinces, whereby the legate hoped to be able to minimize or even avert future conflicts between the Danes and the Germans.

In the winter of 1227, however, the Livonian Church initiated a huge military campaign against the island of Saaremaa. Bishop Albert was fully aware of the crisis that had befallen the Danes due to the imprisonment of King Valdemar and his weakened position. This was seen to be the right time for a renewed military attack against the troublesome pagans, who still refused to submit to the lordship of the Christian powers and who had, perhaps, become even bolder through the weakening of the Danes. Albert seemingly had the intention of conquering and subduing the belligerent people of Saaremaa and Muhu who were, in reality, among the main antagonists of the Danes, once and for all. The attack took place in late January, or early February, when the cold was at its strongest making rivers, swamps, lakes, and even the sea freeze solid. A huge army from Livonia, composed of Livic and Lettgallian warriors, German knights, and crusaders marched across the frozen sea towards the islands. The army was commanded by the head of the Sword Brethren, Master Volquin, accompanied by a majority of his knightly brethren and sergeants.[29]

A winter campaign required careful preparation. Bishop Albert summoned the army shortly after the feast day of the Saints Fabian and Sebastian, (January 20)[30] and Henry is very explicit about the importance of the heavy frost since he states that "snow covered the land and ice covered the waves, for the surface of the deep was solidified and the waters were as hard as stone. Ice was formed and it made a better path over both land and sea."[31] Having been summoned, the various parts of the army arrived at the designated meeting place at the river of modern-day Pärnu—in the chronicle referred to as the "Mother of Waters"(*Mater Aquarum*)—which flows into the gulf of Pärnu and and provides easy access to the sea. On several occasions, this area had been used as a meeting place for expeditions into the Estonian lands and now again served as a place of gathering for the Livonian army. Apart from the already mentioned units of fighting men, Henry also claims that some units of Estonians from the nearby provinces came to be part of the campaign directed towards the islanders of Saaremaa and Muhu.[32] German merchants from Visby also promised to take part in the campaign since they had a very real interest in eliminating the many pirate attacks coming from Saaremaa (despite the occasional peace agreements). According to Henry, the merchants had not hesitated in their preparations and required horses for the upcoming campaign, as well as weapons, before setting sail for Riga. They had arrived well before the winters frost had

---

29 HCL 30:3.

30 HCL 30:3.

31 HCL :3: "nix tegit terras et glacies undas, eo quod superficies abyssi constringitur et aque durantur ut lapides et fit glacies et est via melior super terras et super aquas."

32 HCL 30:3.

closed the sailing routes across the Baltic Sea and were among the fighting men preparing themselves for the campaign. This is also one of the very few times we have specific
references to the transportation by ship of horses to be used in a military campaign in
the Baltic if we don't include Saxo's many references to the Danish ledung. Henry and
most other chroniclers took it for granted that the knights would have brought their
mounts along when committing themselves to a crusade in Livonia or Estonia.[33] Henry
claims that the entire army comprised nearly twenty thousand men, which would have
constituted a very large army considering the available forces in Livonia, even when
adding the crusaders and German merchants from Visby.[34] We have already discussed
the size of the Order of the Sword Brethren amounting to approximately one hundred
ten knights and twelve hundred serving brothers together with some secular knights
serving as vassals.[35] The number of secular knights serving Bishop Albert is unknown,
as is the number of armed pilgrims and merchants. The only other hints on the possible
size of the Livonian army must be deducted from other examples in Henry's chronicle
describing various other military expeditions and the preparations thereof. In such
cases, he refers to armies counting between two thousand and four thousand fighting
men, with roughly half of them made up of Germans (vassals, crusaders, townspeople
from Riga, foreign merchants, Sword Brethren etc.) and the rest being local units of
Livs and Letgallians. There are also examples of larger forces consisting of between six
thousand and eight thousand men, again with roughly half of them being "Germans."[36]
Accepting the larger numbers from the chronicle, with as many as eight thousand men
mustered in 1227 with some additional Estonian warriors, we still seem to be well
below twenty thousand, and perhaps closer to ten thousand to twelve thousand fighting
men. This is, of course, still an impressively large army—probably too large, when taking into account the overall population density of the region and the presumed number
of islanders on Muhu and Saaremaa.[37] It seems safe to conclude that Henry grossly exag-
gerates the actual size of the Livonian army, implying, first of all, that it was a *very large*
army making itself ready to attack Muhu and Saaremaa!

The assembly point was fairly close to the coast, and after having celebrated the mass
in the usual manner, the army marched out onto the ice towards Muhu and Saaremaa.[38]

---

33 HCL 30:1.

34 HCL 30:3.

35 Benninghoven, *Der Orden der Schwertbrüder*, 223–24 and 407–08.

36 See the discussion in Jensen, "Fighting in the Wilderness," forthcoming. Henry of Livonia
makes references to various sizes of armies in his chronicle: referring specifically to HCL 15:7
("there were about four thousand German infantry and knights and the same number again of
Livonians and Letts"); 18:5 ("about three thousand of our men were Germans and there was an
equal number of Letts and Livonians"); 20:7 ("the bishops and the Brothers of the Militia...sent
about three thousand men to their aid"); 21:2 ("there were about three thousand chosen men in the
army"); 23:8 ("having four thousand Germans and another four thousand Livonians and Letts, they
proceeded into Holm"); 27:2 ("eight thousand of them came to the place for prayer and counsel").

37 See the general discussion in Mägi, "Saaremaa and the Danish Kingdom."

38 HCL 30:3.

Henry then describes how the army was divided into "ordered formations, each formation with its own banners" (*qui suas ordinantes acies, distincte cum vexillis propriis ambulante*).[39] Then follows a long description of the march across the ice that deserves to be rendered in full in the English translation:

> As they trod on the ice with their horses and vehicles they made a noise like a great peal of thunder, with the clashing of arms, the shaking of the vehicles, and the movement and sound of men and horses falling and getting up again here and there over the ice, which was as smooth as glass because of the south winds and the rainwater which had fallen at that time and the cold that followed. They crossed the sea with great labour until at last they joyfully came to the coast of Saaremaa.[40]

The crossing over the ice must have been an unnerving and exhausting experience for all those present, whether they were marching on foot, riding horses, or driving/guiding the baggage train. When describing the army's assembly, Henry also mentions that extra food and spare weapons were brought along for the campaign. These things were probably, for the most part, stored in carts, wagons, and sledges that followed the army out onto the ice.[41] Later in the chronicle, Henry also describes in great detail how the expedition turned into a prolonged campaign of sieges when the Livonian army reached the said islands. Essential tools and (unassembled) siege engines must have been brought along as well, stored in the wagons and on the sledges, enlarging the baggage train and the number of draft animals considerably. Did some unfortunate warriors disappear into unseen holes in the ice during the march towards Muhu and Saaremaa? This would most likely have been the case, adding to the terror of those who had to continue forward, and one can almost sense the relief through the text when Henry describes how the army finally arrived at a central fortress on Muhu after a nine-day exhausting march across the ice.

We do not know for sure the exact route used by the army, as there are several options when using the Pärnu River as a starting point and having Muhu as the first target. Ignoring the fact that Henry explicitly states that the army marched all the way on the icy surface of the sea, let us just for one second assume that the commanders may have in fact opted for the shortest possible route towards Muhu, which would then have taken the entire army across land through the province of Korbe in a north-westerly direction towards modern-day Virtsu amounting to a roughly 60 kilometres march over land. From there it would only have been some 6–8 kilometres across the ice to Muhu and a little longer to the said fortress at the centre of the island. Virtsu is, in fact, where modern travellers take the ferry from the mainland to Muhu and continue by car towards Saaremaa, crossing a narrow strait by way of a modern bridge. In the early thirteenth century, such a march over land may have been relatively short with regards

---

39 HCL 30:3.
40 HCL 30:3.
41 HCL 30:3.

to the actual number of kilometres, but we have to remember that there were very few proper roads available at that time, nor were they suitable for huge armies on the march with a heavily loaded baggage train. Therefore, a land-based route would, in all likelihood, have been close to impossible—frost or no frost. From this, it seems most likely that we should actually trust Henry in his statement that the army chose to march across the ice and that it was essentially the only realistic route for the army with so many men, horses, carts, and wagons as we have seen with other examples in the chronicle.[42]

How many kilometres did the army then have to march across the ice before reaching Muhu? Pärnu lies in the bottom of the Golf of Pärnu and, depending on how close the army stayed to the coast during the march, they would need places to rest during the night and most likely preferred these places to be on solid ground and not on the ice. They may have let themselves be guided by outlying forelands or islets as stopping points during the march. At the same time, they probably had to keep a little distance to the actual shoreline due to the risk of ice packs which would have made it difficult or even impossible for the baggage train to pass. Taking such considerations into account, we are looking at a marching distance close to a hundred kilometres almost exclusively on the ice.[43] According to Henry, the army reached the stronghold of Muhu on the ninth day suggesting an average daily distance of some 11–12 kilometres. It has been suggested that a normal distance for an army on the march during the Middle Ages would be close to 20–25 kilometres on an average.[44] Henry suggests that the army only covered half this distance during this particular expedition. Considering that it was in the middle of winter with considerably fewer hours of light each day, and an added cumbersome baggage train, it actually seems plausible that the army may have covered the distance from Pärnu to Muhu in about nine days.[45]

In the chronicle, the story of the actual attack on the fortresses on Muhu and Saaremaa is told. First, the Livonians surrounded the fortress of Muhu and began to bombard it with their siege engines as well as assault the ramparts in the hope of being able the scale the walls.[46] The islanders did have some engines of their own with which they tried to counter the bombardment by the Christians. Eventually, the besiegers managed to dig away part of the rampart undermining the palisade walls whom they dragged down one log at the time through the use of iron hooks and robes. This enabled them to access the upper rampart. Both attacker and defender called upon the divine powers to support them in this fight, says Henry, with the Christians imploring God and Jesus and the islanders hailing their own god, Tharapita.[47] A bloody fight continued on top of the rampart before the Christians eventually managed to push back the defenders, as is described in much detail in the chronicle. Henry underlines the difficulties of fighting

---

42 Jensen, "Fighting in the Wilderness," forthcoming.
43 https://www.freemaptools.com/measure-distance.htm, accessed January 10, 2024.
44 Jensen, "Fighting in the Wilderness," forthcoming.
45 Jensen, "Fighting in the Wilderness," forthcoming.
46 HCL 30:4.
47 HCL 30:4.

during winter since the hill upon which the fortress was located was very icy. The same for the stone rampart and it was almost impossible for the attackers to gain a foothold on the slopes.[48] Only when the attackers got hold of ladders and ropes did they manage to get a sufficient number of men on top of the rampart and into the fortress. Accordingly, even God had some of his angles help the Christians to overcome the walls of this pagan fortress.

While the Livic and Letgallian warriors surrounded the fortress and made sure that none of the people inside could escape, the Germans entered the fortress killing a great many of the pagans inside the stronghold. The Germans actually do seems to have taken quite a number of captives along with an abundance of booty, horses, other livestock before burning fortress and village to the ground.[49]

In Henry's description of the siege we don't hear anything about the Estonians that he claims to have been part of the army. As the Livonian army continued towards the main island of Saaremaa and the central fortress of Woldia, however, the Estonians seem to have been given the task of plundering the countryside along with the Livs and the Lettgallians and a few Germans, taking away as many horses and cattle and as much grain as possible along with other spoils of war before burning down the smaller villages and farms on the island.[50] While part of the army roamed the countryside, the rest began to lay siege to Woldia employing their siege engines. Soon, the islanders in the fortress realized just how vulnerable they were after having viewed the array of siege engines outside the fortress and being confronted with a hail of stones and bolts. Quite clearly, a huge number of non-combatants had sought refuge in the fortress when learning about the approaching enemy army, eventually realizing how impossible the situation was and pleading for peace. A peace was granted since the islanders promised to accept baptism and Henry triumphantly exclaims how "he who was once a wolf was now converted into a lamb. He who was formerly a persecutor of the Christians now became their brother, accepted peace, did not refuse to give hostages, faithfully begged for the grace of baptism, was not afraid to pay perpetual tribute."[51]

Following this major German attack on the islands of Muhu and Saaremaa that forced the inhabitants into accepting Christianity, William of Modena persevered with his plan to have some of the contested Estonian provinces on the mainland governed by a papal representative and not by the Danes or the Germans. However, the plan ditched because of two unforeseen events. Firstly, the Sword Brethren had been encouraged by the successful attack on Saaremaa and the apparent conversion of the islanders and decided to exploit the situation to their own advantage. While King Valdemar was still severely weakened by his resent imprisonment, the Sword Brethren attacked and laid siege to the Danes at Tallinn in the summer of 1227. The knightly brethren managed

---

48 HCL 30:4.

49 HCL 30:4.

50 HCL 30:5.

51 HCL 30:5: "Qui quondam lupus, modo fit agnus. Qui quondam persecutor christianorum, modo fit confrater, pacem recipiens, obsides dare non contradicens, baptismi gratiam fideliter petens, tributum perpetuum solvere non pertimescens."

to capture the castle on Toompea Hill, forcing the remaining Danish soldiers, priests, and missionaries to return to Denmark together with their bishop. It would be more than ten years before the Danes retook the castle. This happened only after the so-called Treaty of Stensby in 1238, when King Valdemar II made an agreement with the Teutonic Order concerning the possessions in Estonia. In 1236, the Order of the Sword Brethren had suffered a crushing defeat in present-day Lithuania at a place called Saule. The majority of the Order's knights, along with some crusaders, had been killed by an overwhelming Lithuanian force. The Sword Brethren had been negotiating with the Teutonic Order about a union of the two knightly orders for some time—the Teutonic Knights had established themselves firmly in Prussia in the early 1220s—, and the few surviving Sword Brethren were eventually admitted into the Teutonic Order.

The unexpected defeat of the Sword Brethren and near annihilation of the entire order paved the way for a swift and direct takeover of all its possessions in the Livonian and Estonian territories by the Teutonic Order, who became the new dominant power in the region. While the Teutonic Order agreed in 1238 to return the castle on Toompea Hill to the Danish king, the knights and the Danes also agreed to support each other and continued the fight against their pagan enemies. Danish presence in Estonia was secured for the next hundred years or so.[52]

Secondly, William of Modena's plans for a territorial buffer zone between the Danes and the Germans in Estonia was thwarted through the choosing of the wrong people to execute the plan. The papal legate had entrusted the overall control of the disputed provinces of Vironia, Jerwia, and Läänemaa to his own chaplain, Master John. The chaplain, however, seems not the have been up for the task. Henry of Livonia dryly remarks that soon the peace was broken, and Master John initiated a war with the Danes.[53] Not only did the peace not last, the local official of the papal curia became personally involved in a direct war with the Danish king's men in Estonia; surely this was not the outcome William had hoped for, whereas Bishop Albert inwardly may have been quite satisfied with the unexpected turn of events. Henry says that the Danes attacked and devastated the province of Lääne at which point Master John's "servants" (servi) pursued the Danes, killing fifty of them on the run and besieging another fifty in the stronghold of Maianpathe.[54] Following a three-day siege, the Germans and the Danes seem to have come to some sort of agreement and the later were allowed to leave the fortress. Henry says that Master John's men had mercy upon them because they were of the same religious belief and sent them away unharmed.[55] There are not many details about the fight between the Germans and the Danes apart from the fact that there seems to have been around a hundred men-at-arms in the Danish raiding party, of whom half were killed in the ensuing fight. The number seems not too unrealistic for a small-size raiding force, which was focused not on conquering new land, but simply on looting and burning as much as pos-

---

52 Jensen, "Da Dannebrog faldt ned fra himlen," 169.
53 HCL 30:2.
54 HCL 30:2.
55 HCL 30:2.

sible before retreating back home. Henry does acknowledge that the Danes had taken a large booty.[56] As for the Germans, we are only told that it was the servants of Master John who fought against the Danes. It is not possible to determine exactly who these servants were, if they simply constituted part of a local militia bolstered with some Western knight and men-at-arms, perhaps even from the retinue of William, local vassals, crusaders, or a mix of the above. If it holds true that they did in fact kill half of the Danes—we are not informed about any German losses—, they were probably a sizable force able to conduct a siege of the stronghold in which the remaining Danes took refuge.

In the chronicle of Henry of Livonia this is the last recorded incident relating to the Danish occupation of Estonia. His narrative ends the very same years with the aforementioned detailed account of the German attack on the islands of Muhu and Saaremaa. This attack, according to Henry ended opposition amongst the islanders against the Livonian Church once and for all and they accepted baptism. This, however, was a premature assessment by Henry, as the unrest and occasional rebellions among the Estonians continued well into the next century.

---

56 HCL 30:2.

Conclusion

A PENNY IN THE BOX
HOW ESTONIA CAME TO SAVE DENMARK

WHILE FOR SOME time the papacy had tried re-establish stronger bonds—perhaps even a renewed union—between the Western and Eastern churches, attempts had not been crowned with any significant success during the thirteenth century. Henry of Livonia bears great witness to the rising conflicts between the Catholic Westerners and the Orthodox Easterners during the conquest of both Livonia and Estonia.[1] Mutual tolerance was replaced by hostility and outright war between the various Rus' princes and the Germans and Danes in Livonia and Estonia; famous is the battle on Lake Peipus in 1242 with Prince Aleksandr Nevskij (1221–1263) defeating the knightly brethren of the Teutonic Order and their vassals. This was only one of many encounters throughout the hundred-year period up to 1346, when the Danish kings finally withdrew from Estonia, a region continually marked by unrest and wars.[2]

The death of King Valdemar II in 1241 meant that the Danish involvement in Estonia became somewhat weakened in the years to come. Internal conflicts concerning the succession of the dead king's sons and the various branches of the family made it difficult to pursue a consistent foreign policy in an extremely unruly region that saw the Teutonic Order strive for more power and land. Also decisive were the internal and repeated disputes between archbishops and kings in Denmark, which gained momentum under Archbishop Jakob Erlandsen (1254–1274) and reached a critical peak under Archbishop Jens Grand (1289–1302), absorbing (more or less) the full attention of the Danish rulers.[3]

Formally, of course, the Danish kings were present in Estonia even during these critical and turbulent years. There were two important Danish officials in Estonia: a bishop (in contemporary sources referred to as "the bishop of Reval," *Episcopatus Revaliensis*) and the king's bailiff. The bishopric formally belonged to the archbishopric of Lund, but ever since 1219 it had been the Danish kings who appointed the bishops of Reval/Tallinn. In addition, there was the aforementioned bailiff, who was the king's formal deputy, having his seat in the castle on Toompea Hill. Around 1282, a council was set up consisting of twelve of the king's most important vassals in the region. Together with the bailiff, this council constituted a kind of consultative

1 This final chapter is a translated and edited version of Carsten Selch Jensen, "De danske kongers herredømme i Estland frem til midten af 1300-tallet," in Jensen et al., *Da Danskerne fik Dannebrog*, 171–79. See also Selart, "Die Eroberung Livlands," 191–98.

2 Bysted et al., *Jerusalem in the North*, 269–80.

3 Bysted et al., *Jerusalem in the North*, 292–93.

assembly with influence over the internal affairs of the Estonian provinces. As
usual, the vassals were bound to the king
by an oath of allegiance, which had to be
renewed each time a new king ascended
the throne. However, there are indications that the council quickly developed
a relatively high degree of autonomy, due
to the weakened position of the kings in
Denmark, where it soon became clear
that they needed the support of the vassals more than vice versa if they were to
have any hope of maintaining their rule
over Estonia. Several of the contemporary sources notes, moreover, that the
Danish king's vassals in Estonia frequently took part in various campaigns
with the Teutonic Order, and in fact rendered their services to the Order more
often than to the Danish king.

A few years later, in 1255, King
Christoffer I (r. 1252–1259) offered
the citizens of Tallinn a wide range of
privileges along with a certain degree
of autonomy.[4] For a period of twenty
years, from 1262 to 1282, the administration of the Estonian lands was primar-
ily in the hands of Queen Margrete Sambiria (ca. 1230–1282), mother of King Erik
Klipping (r. 1259–1286). Among other things, she saw to it that Tallinn received much-
improved fortification, with extended walls.[5]

In 1286, King Erik Klipping was murdered, and the crown passed to his twelve-
year-old son, Erik Menved. As he grew up, he became consumed with the idea of
restoring his grandfather Valdemar II's Baltic empire. He became actively involved in
the ongoing political game in Estonia and Livonia, where the Teutonic Order remained
the strongest player in constant conflict with the (now) archbishops of Riga and the
citizens of the city.[6]

---

4 Tallinn/Reval had been granted the Lübeck Law in 1248. The same year we hear for the first
timer about a city council (Rat) in the town. See Ivar Leimus and Arno Mänd, "Reval (Tallinn): A City
Emerging from Maritime Trade," in *The Routledge Handbook of Maritime Trade Around Europe,
1300–1600*, ed. W. Blockmans, M. Krom, and J. Wubs-Mrozewicz (London: Routledge, 2017), 273;
Markus, *Visual Culture*, 329.

5 DD 2:2.427–31. See also Zobel, *Tallinn (Reval)*, 42–49.

6 Bysted et al., *Jerusalem in the North*, 296.

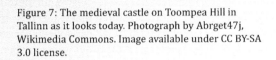

Figure 7: The medieval castle on Toompea Hill in Tallinn as it looks today. Photograph by Abrget47j, Wikimedia Commons. Image available under CC BY-SA 3.0 license.

In 1298, the king was approached by representatives of the chapter of the cathedral of Riga. They had drawn up a document on behalf of themselves and the townspeople, announcing that they would accept the Danish king as their rightful lord in return for his protection. Erik Menved accepted the request and had in turn a special letter of protection drawn up for Riga against the Teutonic Order. Formally, Erik Menved was now lord of both Tallinn and Riga and well on his way to follow in his grandfather's footsteps as overlord of the Baltic lands. Obviously, this move put him on a conflicting course with the Teutonic Knights, as well as brought him into conflict with both Swedish and Rus' actors in the region. The king was hardly blind to the key position he now occupied in relation to the lucrative trade with Novgorod and the other Rus' trading posts.[7] Through his control of Tallinn and Riga, the king had a firm hold on two of the most important trading ports in the region, and was able to control much of the trade between East and West. The Teutonic Order did not quietly accept the increased influence of the Danish king, but was hampered in the early fourteenth century by a series of papal investiga-

---

7 Bysted et al., *Jerusalem in the North*, 296–302 and 308–11.

tions due to persistent accusations that the order was obstructing the ongoing missionary work and also opposed the local (secular) churches.[8] The contemporary trial of the
Knights Templar clearly demonstrated that it was possible to break a powerful order,
and the Teutonic Order chose to tread carefully in the conflict with the pope and the
Danish king. In 1312, members of the Order were even denied entry into Riga as a result
of complaints against the Order by the cathedral chapter and the citizens. A settlement
was reached between Erik Menved and the Teutonic Order in 1314, and in the coming
years, the vassals of the Danish king in Estonia were once again seen to side with the
Order in its continued efforts to dominate Riga and the archbishop there. In 1318, King
Erik Menved even ordered the knighthood of the Estonian provinces of Harjumaa and
Vironia to assist the Order in its continued campaigns against the Lithuanians if they did
not want to lose their freedom and special privileges.[9]

When Erik Menved died in 1319, real Danish power in Estonia once again dwin-
dled to (almost) nothing. In 1321 the vassals of Estonia declared themselves ready to
pay homage to King Christoffer II (r. 1320–1326 and again 1329–1332), while he was
expected to confirm the vassals' grants and privileges. Nothing seems to have come of
these agreements, however, and on the king's death in 1332 it seems once again that the
bailiffs, councillors, and vassals were left to their own devices and had no other option
but to rely on the Teutonic Order. That the support of the Order was crucial for the
power of the Danish vassals in Estonia was clearly demonstrated during the so-called
St. George's Night Uprising from 1343 to 1346, when the Estonian rural population from
the northernmost provinces rebelled along with the people from Saaremaa against the
Germans and Danes, and were only put down with the help of the Teutonic Knights.[10]

In Denmark, an internal political crisis had accelerated dramatically under King
Christoffer II and his eldest son, Erik (d. 1331), who had been crowned as his co-ruler. By
the time of his death in 1332, Christoffer had pawned most of the kingdom to Holstein
nobles. The king's two other sons, Otto (dates unknown) and Valdemar, therefore, had to
fight hard for their inheritance rights in a more or less dissolved kingdom, where Estonia became the only "coin" remaining in the royal treasure box, so to speak! After a failed
rebellion against the Holstein nobles, Otto ended up in prison and was only released
after he had abdicated the throne and his younger brother Valdemar was crowned in
his place as King Valdemar IV (r. 1340–1375). During Otto's imprisonment in 1340,
Valdemar had offered Estonia to the Teutonic Order for no less than 13,000 marks of
silver. The Order declined on this occasion, however, and in the spring of 1343 the great

---

8 Bysted et al., *Jerusalem in the North*, 311–13.

9 Bysted et al., *Jerusalem in the North*, 317–18.

10 Juhan Kremm, "Der Aufstand in der Georgsnacht 1343," in Brüggemann et al., *Das Baltikum*,
384–85; Peeter P. Rebane, "The Jüriöö Mäss (St. George's Night Rebellion) of 1343," in *Baltic
History*, ed. Arvids Ziedonis, William L. Winter and Mardi Valgemäe (Columbus: University of
Toronto, 1974), 35–48. See also Sulev Vahtre, "Die Briefte and den Papst über den Estenaufstand
1343," in *Forschungen zur Baltischen Geschichte*, ed. Mati Laur and Karsten Brüggemann (Tartu:
Akadeemiline Ajalooselts, 2006), 45–55.

rebellion in Estonia seriously endangered Danish rule once more.[11] In 1344, King Valdemar appointed one of his trusted men, the knight Stig Andersen, as the new governor of
Estonia. It was Stig Andersen's explicit task to bring the country into as good order as
possible before Valdemar would, once again, offer the Teutonic Order the opportunity
to buy the Danish parts of Estonia—an area that the Order already controlled militarily. Somewhat remarkably, Valdemar's older brother Otto was now also part of the deal,
having been persuaded to take a vow to join the order as part of the arrangement. There
were probably both pious and pragmatic reasons for this. First, it was a meritorious act
for a relatively young nobleman to take perpetual vows to devote his life to fighting the
enemies of the church, as the custom had become established with the early crusading
movement. Secondly, Otto may well have renounced the crown in Denmark, but it must
have pleased Valdemar to be able to get rid of a possible future pretender to the throne
in this way. This time the Order accepted and even agreed to pay as much as 19,000
marks of silver for the Estonian provinces, in addition to 6,000 marks of silver that the
Order had to pay to another party in order to obtain full rights in the country, i.e., considerably more than the first offer a few years before.[12]

It is obvious to ask why the Order was willing to pay so much more for the Estonian provinces at a time when it was clear that Denmark was on its knees and could
not in reality protect its overseas possessions. In fact, one would think that the Order
must have considered whether it should simply wait and then formally take over Estonia
when Denmark (probably) completely disintegrated as a kingdom. The fact was that
King Valdemar was not just betting on one horse through his contacts with the Teutonic Order. The Swedish King Magnus (r. 1319–1364) had come forward and raised
the possibility that he would be willing to take over the Danish possessions in Estonia. Being influenced St. Birgitta of Vadstena (1303–1373) and her spiritual revelations,
the Swedish king was encouraged to prepare a crusade against the schismatic Rus' in
Novgorod. The attack would come from the Swedish possessions in Finland, and Estonia
would thus be a significant bridgehead for increased Swedish influence in the region.
The Teutonic Order was quick to realize that the Swedes could become a powerful and
dangerous new adversary if they succeeded in their endeavours, so the order decided to
pre-empt them and accept the Danish king's offer to buy Estonia, even at a considerably
higher price than in 1340.[13]

The Order could not have foreseen that King Magnus would lose everything when
his crusade resulted in a heavy defeat to the Swedes. He fled back to Sweden, where he
was subjected to a massive smear campaign from the circles around St. Birgitta, who
could not tolerate the credibility of her revelations being called into question. The king's
defeat must, therefore, have been his own fault and perhaps even an expression of his
rejection by God. King Magnus was eventually deposed in 1364 and imprisoned the following year as a result of a series of political power struggles in Sweden. The situation

---

11 Bysted et al., *Jerusalem in the North*, 320 and 325.

12 Bysted et al., *Jerusalem in the North*, 325–28.

13 Bysted et al., *Jerusalem in the North*, 329–32.

was different for King Valdemar, for whom the sale of Estonia represented a real opportunity for the recovery of his kingdom. The sale provided him with sufficient resources and support to rebuild the kingdom and consolidate his power over a number of years. For Estonia the sale meant new masters and a period of almost two hundred years under the rule of the Teutonic Order.[14]

This book has tried to describe the conquest of Estonia, especially from a Scandinavian-Danish perspective, seeing the Battle of Lyndanise1219 as one of the pivotal events in that history and a high tide in a general Danish expansion into the Baltic lands. In these endeavours the Danes were not alone. Not only did German, Swedish, and Norwegian merchants, missionaries, and crusaders become fierce rivals in the lands of Livonia and Estonia, a wide range of local people also became both fellow players and adversaries in some very complicated and delicate political, military, and religious alliances. From a distance, papal Rome made itself felt in the region through the novel ideas of missionary wars and crusades that became the ideological-religious-political backdrop for the conquest of Estonia. Onetime enemies of the Danes became close allies and saviours during the Battle of Lyndanise, when Slavic warriors that had only a generation or two before fought fiercely against a Danish expansion into their lands, actually saved King Valdemar II's crusaders from a humiliating defeat by local pagan Estonians.

At the same time, this study has hopefully also shown that the local people of the Baltic lands were far from being weak and defenceless and easily cowed by Westerners. The Baltic Crusades sprang from century-long, close relations between the Scandinavians and the Baltic people with the lands of Curonia, Livonia, and Estonia in particular being important meeting places, steppingstones, and stopovers for the Scandinavians in a thriving and prosperous network of traders and raiders that went both ways. Commercial interests went hand in hand with military expeditions turning the entire Baltic Sea region into a great political, religious, and military hotspot that came to greatly influence the histories of these various countries right up to modern times. Today, Estonia and Denmark have very close international relations, based on a shared part of history. In this respect, the Danish conquest became an important milestone in the interactions between the Danes and the Estonians. As such, the interactions of the Estonians and the Danes in the Middle Ages came to have a profound long-term cultural and political impact on both nations.

---

14 Jensen, "De danske kongers herredømme i Estland," 179.

SELECT BIBLIOGRAPHY

DD   *Diplomatarium Danicum*. Udgivet af Det Danske Sprog- og Litteraturselskab, København 1938-. Oversættelser af breve herfra gives sædvanligvis efter paralleludgaven i *Danmarks Riges Breve* (DRB).

LEC   *Liv-, Est-, und Kurländisches Urkundenbuch nebst Regesten*. Edited by F. G. Bunge, 12 Bd., Riga 1853–1910.

LUB   *Codex diplomaticus Lubecensis, Lübeckisches Urkundenbuch*, Abt. 1, Urkundenbuch der Stadt Lübeck, Teil 1–4. Edited by Friedrich Techen, 1843–73.

MGH   *Monumenta Germaniae Historica*: https://www.brepols.net/series/mgh-o, accessed May 2023.

PL   *Patrologia Latina*, vols. 1–221. Edited by J.-P. Migne, Paris 1844–55.

SRP   *Scriptores Rerum Prussicarum*, Zweiter Band, Verlag von S. Hirzel 1863.

Primary Sources

Arnold von Lübeck. *Arnoldi Chronica Slavorum*. Edited by J. M. Lappenberg. MGH SS 14. Hannover: Hahn, 1868.

The Chronicle of Henry of Livonia. Edited by James A. Brundage. New York: Columbia University Press, 1961. Reprint 2003.

Heinrich von Lettland. *Livländische Chronik: Neu übersetzt von Albert Bauer*. Darmstadt: Wissenschaftliche Buchgesellschaft, 1959.

Heinrichi Chronicon Livoniae. MGH SS 31. Edited by Leonid Arbusow and Albert Bauer. Hannover: Hahn, 1955.

Saxo Grammaticus. *Gesta Danorum, the History of the Danes*. Edited by Karsten Friis-Jensen and Peter Fischer. Oxford: Clarendon Press, 2015.

Tamm, Ditlev and Helle Vogt. *The Danish Medieval Laws: The Laws of Scania, Zealand and Jutland*. London: Routledge, 2016.

Secondary Sources

Bachrach, David S. *Religion and the Conduct of War c. 300–c. 1215*. Woodbridge: Boydell, 2003.

Bartlett, Robert. *The Making of Europe: Conquest, Colonization and Cultural Change 950–1350*. London: Penguin, 1994.

Benninghoven, Friedrich. *Der Orden der Schwertbrüder: Fratres Milicie Christi de Livonia*. Köln: Böhlau, 1965.

——. "Zur Technik spätmittelalterlicher Feldzüge im Ostbaltikum." *Zeitschrift für Ostforschung* 1 (1970): 631–51.

Brüggemann, Karsten and Ralph Tuchtenhagen. "Grundzüge." In *Das Baltikum: Geschichte einer europäischen Region*. Edited by Karsten Brüggemann, Detlef Henning, Konrad Maier, and Ralph Tuchtenhagen, 31–37. Stuttgart: Anton Hiersemann, 2018.

Brundage, James A. "Crusades, Clerics and Violence: Reflections on a Canonical Theme." In *The Experience of Crusading, Vol. 1: Western Approaches*. Edited by Marcus Bull and Norman Housley, 147–56. Cambridge: Cambridge University Press, 2003.

Bysted, Ane L., Carsten Selch Jensen, Kurt Villads Jensen, and John H. Lind, eds. *Jerusalem in the North: Denmark and the Baltic Crusades, 1100–1522*. Turnhout: Brepols, 2012.

Christiansen, Eric. *The Northern Crusades*. London: Penguin, 1997.

Dragnea, Mihai. *Christian Identity Formation Across the Elbe in the Tenth and Eleventh Centuries. Christianity and Conversion in Scandinavia and the Baltic Region, c. 800–1600*. Frankfurt am Main: Peter Lang, 2021.

——. *The Wendish Crusade, 1147: The Development of Crusading Ideology in the Twelfth Century*. London: Routledge, 2021.

Eihmane, Eva. "The Baltic Crusades: A Clash of Two Identities." In *The Clash of Cultures on the Medieval Baltic Frontier*. Edited by Alan V. Murray, 37–51. Farnham: Ashgate, 2009.

Fonnesberg-Schmidt, Iben. "Pope Honorius III and Mission and Crusades in the Baltic Region." In *The Clash of Cultures on the Medieval Baltic Frontier*. Edited by Alan V. Murray, 103–22. Farnham: Ashgate, 2009.

——. *The Popes and the Baltic Crusades, 1147–1254*. The Northern World 26. Leiden: Brill, 2007.

Gillingham, John. "A Strategy of Total War? Henry of Livonia and the Conquest of Estonia, 1208–1227." *Journal of Medieval Military History* 8 (2017): 186–213.

Heebøll-Holm, Thomas K. "Between Pagan Pirates and Glorious Sea-Warriors: The Portrayal of the Viking Pirate in Danish Twelfth-Century Latin Historiography." *Viking and Medieval Scandinavia* 8 (2012): 141–70.

Jähnig, Bernhart. "Die Anfänge der Sakraltopographie von Riga." In *Studien zu den Anfängen der Mission in Livland*. Edited by Hellmann, 123–58. Sigmaringen: Thorbecke, 1989.

Jensen, Carsten Selch. "Bishops and Abbots at War: Some Aspects of Clerical Involvement in Warfare in Twelfth and Early Thirteenth-Century Livonia and Estonia." In *Between Sword and Prayer: Warfare and Medieval Clergy in Cultural Perspective, Explorations in Medieval Culture*. Edited by Radosław Kotecki, Jacek Maciejewski, and John S. Ott, 404–34. Leiden: Brill, 2018.

——. "Clerics and War in Denmark and the Baltic: Ideals and Realities around 1200." In *Fighting for the Faith*. Edited by Kurt Villads Jensen, Janus Møller Jensen, and Carsten Selch Jensen, 187–218. Stockholm: Runica et Mediaevalia, 2018.

——. "The Early Church of Livonia, 1186–ca. 1255." In *Die Kirche im mittelalterlichen Livland*. Edited by Radosław Biskup, Johannes Götz, and Andrzej Radziminski, 79–107. Toruń: Wydawnictwo Naukowe Uniwersytetu Mikolaja Kopernika, 2019.

——. "The Lord's Vineyard: Henry of Livonia and the Danish conquest of Estonia." In *Denmark and Estonia 1219–2019*. Edited by Jens E. Olesen, 41–55. Greifswald: Panzig, 2019.

——. *Med ord og ikke med slag*. København: Gad, 2018.

——. "Religion and War in Saxo Grammaticus's *Gesta Danorum*: The Examples of Bishop Absalon and King Valdemar I." In *Christianity and War in Medieval East Central Europe and Scandinavia*. Edited by Radosław Kotecki, Carsten Selch Jensen, and Stephen Bennett, 189–206. Amsterdam: Amsterdam University Press, 2021.

——, Marika Mägi, Kersti Markus, and Janus Møller Jensen. *Da Danskerne fik Dannebrog*. Tallinn: Argo, 2019. [The book appeared simultaneously in Estonian: *Taanlaste ristisõda Eestis*. Tallinn: Argo, 2019.]

Jensen, Janus Møller. "*Sclavorum expugnator*: Conquest, Crusade, and Danish Royal Ideology in the Twelfth Century." *Crusades* 2 (2003): 55–81.

Jensen, Kurt Villads. "Holy War–Holy Wrath! Baltic Wars between Regulated Warfare and Total Annihilation Around 1200." In *Church and Belief in the Middle Ages: Popes, Saints, and Crusaders*. Edited by Kirsi Salonen and Sari Katajala Peltomaa, 227–50. Amsterdam: Amsterdam University Press, 2016.

Kaljundi, Linda. "Neophytes as Actors in the Livonian Crusades." In *Making Livonia: Actors and Networks in the Medieval and Early Modern Baltic Sea Region*. Edited by Anu Mänd and Marek Tamm, 93–112. London: Routledge, 2020.

——, with the collaboration of Kaspars Klavins. "The Chronicler and the Modern World: Henry of Livonia and the Baltic Crusades in the Enlightenment and National Traditions." In *Crusading and Chronicle Writing on the Medieval Baltic Frontier*. Edited by Marek Tamm, Linda Kaljundi, and Carsten Selch Jensen, 409–56. Farnham: Ashgate, 2011.

Kaljusaar, Kristjan. "Exploiting the Conquerors: Socio-political Strategies of Estonian Elites During the Crusades and Christianization, 1200–1300." In *Baltic Crusades and Societal Innovation in Medieval Livonia, 1200–1350*. Edited by Anti Selart, 55–88. Leiden: Brill, 2022.

——. "Martyrdom on the Field of Battle in Livonia During Thirteenth-Century Holy Wars and Christianization: Popular Belief and the Image of a Catholic Frontier." In *Christianity and War in Medieval East Central Europe and Scandinavia*. Edited by Radoslaw Kotecki, Carsten Selch Jensen, and Stephen Bennett, 245–62. Amsterdam: Amsterdam University Press, 2021.

Kersti, Markus. "From Rus' Trade to Crusade: St Olaf's Churches in the Eastern Baltic Sea Region." *Acta Historica Tallinnensia* 23 (2017): 3–25.

Kivimäe, Jüri. "Henricus the Ethnographer." In *Crusading and Chronicle Writing on the Medieval Baltic Frontier*. Edited by Marek Tamm, Linda Kaljundi, and Carsten Selch Jensen, 77–106. Farnham: Ashgate, 2011.

Larrea, Beñat Elortza. *Polity Consolidation and Military Transformation in Scandinavia from a European Perspective, c. 1035–1320*. The Northern World Series 94. Leiden: Brill, 2023.

——. "The Transformation of Naval Warfare in Scandinavia during the Twelfth Century." *Journal of Medieval Military History* 18 (2020): 81–98.

Leighton, Gregory. *Ideology and Holy Landscape in the Baltic Crusades*. Amsterdam: Arc Humanities, 2022.

Lotter, Friedrich. "The Crusading Idea and the Conquest of the Region East of the Elbe." In *Medieval Frontier Societies*. Edited by Robert Bartlett and Angus MacKay, 267–306. Oxford: Clarendon Press, 1989.

Mäesalu, Ain. "Mechanical Artillery and Warfare in the Chronicle of Henry of Livonia." In *Crusading and Chronicle Writing on the Medieval Baltic Frontier*. Edited by Marek Tamm, Linda Kaljundi, and Carsten Selch Jensen, 265–90. Aldershot: Ashgate, 2011.

Mägi, Marika, *In Austrvegr: The Role of the Eastern Baltic in Viking Age Communication across the Baltic Sea*. Leiden: Brill, 2018.

——. "Ösel and the Danish Kingdom: Revisiting Henry's Chronicle and the Archaeological Evidence." In *Crusading and Chronicle Writing on the Medieval Baltic Frontier*. Edited by Marek Tamm, Linda Kaljundi, and Carsten Selch Jensen, 317–41. Farnham: Ashgate, 2011.

Mägi, Marika. *The Viking Eastern Baltic*. Leeds: Arc Humanities, 2019.

Malmros, Rikke. *Bønder og Leding i Valdemartidens Danmark*. Aarhus: Aarhus Universitetsforlag, 2019.

Markus, Kersti. *Visual Culture and Politics in the Baltic Sea Region, 1100–1250*. Leiden: Brill, 2020.

Mühlen, Heinz v. zur. "Die Schlacht bei Lyndanisse (1219) und ihre Bedeutung für die Gründung Revals." *Jahrbuch des baltischen Deutschtums 1969* (1968): 60–66.

Munzinger, Mark R. "The Profits of the Cross: Merchant Involvement in the Baltic Crusade (c. 1180–1230)." *Journal of Medieval History* 32 (2006): 163–185.

Murray, Alan V. "Henry the Interpreter: Language, Orality and Communication in the Thirteenth-century Livonian Mission." In *Crusading and Chronicle Writing on the Medieval Baltic Frontier*. Edited by Marek Tamm, Linda Kaljundi, and Carsten Selch Jensen, 107–34. Farnham: Ashgate, 2011.

——. "The Sword Brothers at War: Observations on the Military Activity of the Knighthood of Christ in the Conquest of Livonia and Estonia (1203–1227)." *Ordines Militares* 28 (2013): 27–37.

Reynolds, Burnham W. *The Prehistory of the Crusades: Missionary War and the Baltic Crusades*. London: Bloomsbury, 2016.

Russell, Frederick H. *The Just War in the Middle Ages*. Cambridge: Cambridge University Press, 1975.

Ščavinskas, Marius, "On the Crusades and Coercive Missions in the Baltic Region in the Mid-12th Century and the Early 13th Century: The Cases of the Wends and Livonians." *Zeitschrift für Ostmitteleuropa-Forschung* 63, no. 4 (2014): 499–527.

Selart, Anti. "Die Eroberung Livlands (12. und 13. Jahrhundert)." In *Das Baltikum: Geschichte einer europäischen Region*. Edited by Karsten Brüggemann, Detlef Henning, Konrad Maier, and Ralph Tuchtenhagen, 159–209. Stuttgart: Anton Hiersemann, 2018.

——. "Das Kriegswesen im Zeitalter der Kreuzzüge." In *Das Baltikum. Geschichte einer europäischen Region*. Edited by Karsten Brüggemann, Detlef Henning, Konrad Maier, and Ralph Tuchtenhagen, 198–200. Stuttgart: Anton Hiersemann, 2018.

——. "Orthodox Responses to the Baltic Crusades." In *Christianity and War in Medieval East Central Europe and Scandinavia*. Edited by Radoslaw Kotecki, Carsten Selch Jensen, and Stephen Bennett, 262–78. Amsterdam: Arc Humanities, 2021.

——. "Slavery in the Eastern Baltic in the 12th–15th Centuries." In *Serfdom and Slavery in the European Economy 11th–18th Centuries*. Edited by Simonetta Cavaciocchi, 351–64. Firenze: Firenze University Press, 2014.

Šnē, Andris, and Heiki Valk. "Vor- und Frühgeschichte." In *Das Baltikum. Geschichte einer europäischen Region*. Edited by Karsten Brüggemann, Detlef Henning, Konrad Maier, and Ralph Tuchtenhagen, 77–143. Stuttgart: Anton Hiersemann, 2018.

Tamm, Marek. "How to Justify a Crusade? The Conquest of Livonia and New Crusade Rhetoric in the Early Thirteenth Century." *Journal of Medieval History* 39, no. 4 (2013): 431–55.

——. "Mission and Mobility: The Travels and Networking of Bishop Albert of Riga (c. 1165–1229)." In *Making Livonia: Actors and Networks in the Medieval and Early Modern Baltic Sea Region*. Edited by Anu Mänd and Marek Tamm, 17–47. London: Routledge, 2020.

Tyerman, Christopher. "Henry of Livonia and the Ideology of Crusading." In *Crusading and Chronicle Writing on the Medieval Baltic Frontier*. Edited by Marek Tamm, Linda Kaljundi, and Carsten Selch Jensen, 23–44. Farnham: Ashgate, 2011.

Valk, Heiki. "Christianisation in Estonia: A Process of Dual-Faith and Syncretism." In *The Cross Goes North: Processes of Conversion in Northern Europe, AD 30–1300*. Edited by Martin Carver, 571–79. York: York Medieval Press, 2003.

Zobel, Rein. *Tallinn (Reval): Fortifications in the Middle Ages*. Tallinn, Eesti Kunstiakadeemia, 2014.

INDEX